# Under Sail by Felix Riesenberg

On our precious globe, oceans spill their majestic waters across 70% of the Earth's surface. Over the continents, land untainted by the presence of man is becoming ever more elusive and scarce.

One area that almost retains its pristine, unspoiled look is Patagonia in South America.

This sparsely populated region is located at the southern end of South America and displays itself across the vast lands of Argentina and Chile. As a whole it comprises of the southern section of the Andes mountains as well as the deserts, pampas and grasslands east of this. Patagonia has two coasts: to the west it faces the Pacific Ocean and to the east the Atlantic Ocean.

The Colorado and Barrancas rivers, which run from the Andes to the Atlantic, are commonly considered the northern limit of Argentine Patagonia. For Chilean Patagonia it is at Reloncaví Estuary. The archipelago of Tierra del Fuego marks its abrupt southern frontier and the famed end of the world.

The name Patagonia comes from the word patagón, which was used by the Spanish explorer Magellan in 1520 to describe the native people that his expedition thought to be giants. He called them Patagons and, we think now, they were from the Tehuelche people, who tended to be taller than Europeans of the time.

Patagonia encompasses some one million square kilometers and is home to a rich and diverse landscape of plants, fauna and wildlife. It is a spectacular wilderness full of life and full of history.

Early explorers and travellers faced a sometimes difficult and uncomfortable journey to reach there. The words and pictures they brought back bear testament to a remarkable land and remarkable people.

These are their stories.

## Index of Contents
INTRODUCTION – THE SQUARE RIGGERS
CHAPTER I - OUTWARD BOUND
CHAPTER II - THE OUTWARD PASSAGE
CHAPTER III - CHRISTMAS DAY ON THE HIGH SEAS
CHAPTER IV - THE FIGHT
CHAPTER V - NEPTUNE COMES ON BOARD
CHAPTER VI - LIFE IN THE FO'C'SLE
CHAPTER VII - CAPE HORN
CHAPTER VIII - ROUNDING THE HORN
CHAPTER IX - INTO THE PACIFIC
CHAPTER X - CABIN AND FO'C'SLE
CHAPTER XI - CLEANING HOUSE AND A CELEBRATION
CHAPTER XII - MAKING PORT
CHAPTER XIII - IN HONOLULU TOWN
CHAPTER XIV - UNLOADING—WITH A BIT OF POLITICS

CHAPTER XV - HAWAIIAN HOSPITALITY
CHAPTER XVI - HONOLULU OF THE OLD DAYS
CHAPTER XVII - A DINNER ASHORE
CHAPTER XVIII - BRITISH NEIGHBORS
CHAPTER XIX - THE MATE KEEPS US BUSY
CHAPTER XX - THE LAND OF LANGUOR
CHAPTER XXI - LOADING SUGAR
CHAPTER XXII - GOOD-BYE TO HONOLULU
CHAPTER XXIII - HOMEWARD BOUND
CHAPTER XXIV - HAWAIIAN SHIPMATES
CHAPTER XXV - DRIVING SOUTHWARD
CHAPTER XXVI - CAPE HORN AGAIN
CHAPTER XXVII - MAN LOST OVERBOARD
CHAPTER XXVIII - AUSTRALIA'S STORY
CHAPTER XXIX - STORMY DAYS
CHAPTER XXX - HEADED NORTH
CHAPTER XXXI - FO'C'SLE DISCUSSIONS
CHAPTER XXXII - THROUGH THE TRADES
CHAPTER XXXIII - APPROACHING HOME
CHAPTER XXXIV - THE END OF THE VOYAGE
CHAPTER XXXV - THE LONG-LOOKED-FOR PAYDAY

## Index of Illustrations
Old Smith
Frenchy
Deck Plan of Ship A. J. Fuller
Jimmy Marshall
Fred
Joe
Skouse
Martin
Cape Horn
At Brewer's Wharf
Charlie Horse
Watching the Shore When In the Stream
Brenden Reading Letter
Jack Hitchen
Australia
Sketches of Diego Ramirez
Axel
Watching Shore at Delaware Breakwater

INTRODUCTION

THE SQUARE RIGGERS

**THE SHIP A. J. FULLER OF NEW YORK**

America is again facing forward to the sea. The ancient thrill of the wide salt spaces, of the broad horizon beyond which adventure beckons us, appeals once more to the youth of America. We are living in times when the great importance of the sea as a career comes home to us at every turn. The sea is the great bulwark of our liberty, and by the sea we must persevere or perish in the world struggle of Anglo-Saxon democracy against the powers of autocratic might.

When America returns to her own, she builds upon foundations of tradition that have their footings on the solid bed rock of the republic. One glorious era of our sea history was followed by another, and as times progressed the breed of seamen ever rose capable and triumphant to the necessities that called them forth.

The Revolutionary sailors, and those of 1812, were followed by the great commercial seamen of the clippers. The mighty fleets of the Civil War astonished the world, and in the period just previous to our seafaring decline of a score of years past, the great sailers flying the Stars and Stripes spread their white cotton canvas on every sea.

Their story has never been adequately told. They are not to be measured in terms of tonnage, or in the annals of swift passages from port to port. Their contribution to the legends of the sea remains obscure. They carried a tradition of hard driving, and were a phase of our sea life that formed and forged the link between the old and the new, between the last days of sail and the great new present of the America of steam and steel.

Men who go to sea today in our merchant marine, in positions of command, are, in many instances, graduates of the ships of these latter days of sail.

Looking back, and as time goes it is not so very far away; we can, in our mind's eye, see the great wood-built craft that lined the waterfront of South Street. These were the last of the American sailing ships, entering from, and clearing to, every sea port under heaven. They were not the famous California clippers of an earlier day, or the swift Western Ocean packet ships, or the storied tea ships of the China trade, but they were their legitimate successors. The ships of this last glorious burst of sail, under the Stars and Stripes, were larger craft, vessels built for the long voyage haul, for the grain trade, for the sugar trade, and as carriers of general cargo to the Orient and the western coast of North America.

Most of these ships were laid down in the eighties, and left the yards of Maine to find adventure and preferment in the longer routes of commerce. The Horn and the Cape of Good Hope were their turning points, and they smoked through the hum of the Roaring Forties, as they beat from the Line to Liverpool, laden with California grain, or they ran before the westerly winds, from Table Bay to Melbourne—Running Their Easting Down—black hulled, white winged ships, with New York, Boston, Baltimore, or Philadelphia standing out in golden letters on their transoms.

Only the strongest and best found ships, and the most skilful and daring seamen were fit to carry the flag across the world-long ocean courses about the storm-swept Horn, and here again America more than held her own in competition with the mariners of the old seafaring nations of Europe.

Winthrop Lippitt Marvin in his valuable work, "The American Merchant Marine,"[1] pictures this last Titanic struggle of the sea in stirring fashion—

"It was a contest of truly Olympian dignity,—of the best ships of many flags with each other and with the elements. Out through the Golden Gate there rode every year in the later seventies and the eighties, southward bound, the long lean iron models of Liverpool and Glasgow, the broader waisted, wooden New Englanders, with their fine Yankee sheer and tall, gleaming skysails, the sturdy, careful Norwegian and German ships, often launched on the Penobscot or Kennebec, and here and there a graceful Frenchman or Italian. The British were the most numerous, because the total tonnage of their merchant marine was by far the greatest. Next came the Americans. The other flags looked small by comparison. In this splendid grain trade there sailed from San Francisco for Europe in 1881-85, 761 British iron ships and 418 American wooden ships. The Americans were the largest vessels. Their average registered tonnage was 1,634 and of the fourteen ships above 2,000 tons that sailed in 1880-1, twelve flew the Stars and Stripes. The average tonnage of the British iron ships was 1,356.

[1] Chas. Scribner & Sons, N. Y.

"The wooden yards of Maine had seen their opportunity and built in quick succession many great ships and barks of from 1,400 to 2,400 tons, very strongly constructed on models happily combining carrying capacity with speed, loftily sparred, and clothed with the symmetrical, snow-white canvas for which Yankee sailmakers were famous the world around. These new vessels were not strictly clippers, though they were often called so. They were really medium clippers; that is, they were less racer-like and more capacious than the celebrated greyhounds of the decade before the Civil War. They could not compete with steam; their owners knew it. But they were launched in confident hope that they were adapted for the grain trade and for some other forms of long-voyage, bulky carrying, and that they could find a profitable occupation during their lifetime of fifteen or twenty years. They were just as fine ships in their way as the extreme clippers, and in all but speed they were more efficient. They were framed with oak, and ceiled and planked with the hard pine of the South. They were generously supplied with the new, approved devices in rig and equipment."

In the last years of the nineties there were many survivors of this noble fleet of American sailers still in the long voyage trade. Ships like the El Capitan, the Charmer, the A. J. Fuller, the Roanoke, and the

Shenandoah, were clearing from New York for deep water ports, and South Street was a thoroughfare of sailors, redolent of tar, and familiar with the wide gossip of the seas, brought to the string pieces of the street by men from the great sailing ships.

Then the crimp still throve in his repulsive power, and the Boarding Masters' Association owned the right to parcel out, fleece and ship, the deepwater seamen of the port. The Front Street House and a score of others held the humble dunnage of the fo'c'sle sailor as security, cashed his "advance" and sent him out past the Hook with nothing but a sparse kit of dog's wool and oakum slops, a sheath knife and a donkey's breakfast.

Those were the hard days of large ships and small crews. In clipper days, a flyer like the Sovereign of the Seas carried a crew of eighty seamen, and most of them were as rated—A.B. The ship A. J. Fuller, in the year 1897, left the port of New York, for the voyage around Cape Horn to Honolulu with eighteen seamen, counting the boy and the carpenter, the Fuller being a three skysail yard ship of 1,848 tons register.

It may be interesting to compare the size and crew of the Sovereign of the Seas, as given by Captain Clark in his great book, "The Clipper Ship Era,"[2] with the dimensions and crew of the ship A. J. Fuller.

| Ship | Sovereign of the Seas | | A. J. Fuller | |
|---|---|---|---|---|
| Length | 258 ft. | | 229 ft. | |
| Beam | 44 ft. | | 41.5 ft. | |
| Draft | 23.5 ft. | | 18 ft. | |
| Register Tonnage | 2,421 tons | | 1,848 tons | |
| Crew— | | | | |
| Master | 1 | | Master | 1 |
| Mates | 4 | | Mates | 2 |
| Boatswains | 2 | | Carpenters | 1 |
| Carpenters | 2 | | Able Seamen | 16 |
| Sailmakers | 2 | | Boys | 1 |
| Able Seamen | 80 | | | |
| Boys | 10 | | | |
| **TOTAL** | 101 | | **TOTAL** | 21 |

[2] G. P. Putnam and Sons.

This condition, of small crews and large ships, brought to the seven seas a reputation for relentless driving and manhandling that has clung to the minds of men as nothing else. The huge American ships were the hardest afloat, and that remarkable booklet, "The Red Record," compiled by the National Seamen's Union of America, in the middle nineties, carries a tale of cruelty and abuse on the high seas that must forever remain a blot upon the white escutcheon of sail.

These ships bred a sea officer peculiar to the time—the bucko mate of fact as well as fiction. These were hard fisted men, good sailors and excellent disciplinarians, though they lacked the polish acquired by sea officers of an earlier day when the sailer was often a passenger carrier, and intercourse with people of culture had its effect upon the men of the after guard. Also, the sea had become less attractive as a career. The boasted "high pay" of the American Merchant Marine, was $60 per month for the Chief

Mate; $30 per month for the Second Mate, and $18 per month for an A.B.—at least such were the magnificent wages paid on the A. J. Fuller of New York in the year 1897.

The mate, to earn his two dollars a day, and keep, had to be a seaman of the highest attainments. His was a knowledge won only after a long hard apprenticeship at sea. He had to have the force of character of a top-notch executive, combined with ability and initiative. Then too, he was supposed to be a navigator, a man having at least a speaking acquaintance with nautical astronomy. In addition to this he might be as rough and as foul mouthed as he saw fit, and some of them were very liberal in this respect.

Then men still signed articles, voyage after voyage, for the long drill around the Horn, or, to vary the monotony, if such it could be called, made the voyage to Australia, or to China or Japan. In the main, however, American ships clearing from New York carried cargoes to the West Coast of the United States, or to the Hawaiian Islands, where they came under the protective ruling of the coastwise shipping laws, and were not compelled to meet the stringent insurance rates of Lloyd's that barred American sailing bottoms from fair competition with the British.

The sailor men of that day were still real seamen, at least a large number of real seamen still clung to the remaining ships. They were experts, able to turn in a dead eye in wire or hemp, and could cast a lanyard knot in the stiff four-stranded stuff that was later on replaced by screws and turn buckles when metal hulls succeeded those of wood.

With the passing of the wooden ship—the wooden square rigged sailer—went the American sailor, for comparatively few steel sailing ships were built in the United States. With the sailor went the romance of bulging canvas and of storm stripped humming bolt ropes. The tragedy, and the hardships of the long voyages passed away, and with that passing is gone much of the actual physical struggle with the wind and sea that made the sailor what he was.

The square rigged breed of sailors, while not dead yet, for the old salts die hard, has, by force of circumstances, failed to rear a younger generation to take its place. But the old spirit of sea adventure is as strong as ever; the ocean rages as loud, and lies as calm, as in the days of departed glory. It is still the world route to foreign trade, and a more ample domestic prosperity. Americans are again turning toward the sea, are heeding its age old wisdom, and are building and handling the newer craft of steam, and coal, and oil, with as much skill and success as they did the sailing craft of old.

On the following pages is recorded for the seamen and landsmen of today, a personal story of one of the last voyages around Cape Horn in a wooden ship propelled by sail alone—a ship without a donkey engine, a wooden Bath-built packet at her prime in point of age and upkeep. The advance notes have been cashed by the boarding masters, who have left the crew in tow of their crimps, and, after deducting for board and slops, the last remaining dollars have been blown in on the Bowery under the watchful eyes of the runners, who see to it that the men are delivered on board.

Our ship is the A. J. Fuller of New York, Captain Charles M. Nichols, and she waits her crew, ready to cast off from her berth in the East River at the turn of the tide, at daybreak on December 5, 1897, having cleared for the port of Honolulu, capital of the Republic of Hawaii, with a general cargo consigned to the old island house of Brewer and Company.

## CHAPTER I

### OUTWARD BOUND

"Oh for a fair and gentle wind,"
I heard a fair one cry;
But give to me the roaring breeze,
And white waves beating high;
And white waves beating high, my boys,
The good ship tight and free,
The world of waters is our own,
And merry men are we.
**Jacob Faithful.**

"Cook!" bawled a deep voice from a door that burst open with a flood of yellow light under the break of the poop, "serve a round of hot cafay nore to them passengers! And Mr. Stoddard," added the mate from whom these orders issued, addressing the second officer who strode from the edge of light toward the group of men tumbling on board, "turn all hands to in five minutes! Stand by to cast off lines!"

Some of the shore crowd from the boarding houses helped to pass up the chests and bags of dunnage, and the bundles of "donkey's breakfast" as we clambered to the ice-encrusted deck of the ship A. J. Fuller, lying at her wharf near the foot of Maiden Lane. A flickering light, and the rattle of stove lids in the galley, as we passed forward to the fo'c'sle, told us that the cook was stirring, and the snorting of a tug under the starboard quarter gave notice of an early start.

It was dark when we came aboard; a cold December wind rippled the black waters of the East River, chilling to the marrow those few stragglers who walked the cobble stones of South Street at that early morning hour.

An odd lot of humanity dumped their few belongings on the fo'c'sle deck; strangers all, excepting a few who had just deserted from the British bark Falls of Ettrick, men jumbled together by strange fate, and destined to long months of close companionship, of hard knocks, and endless days and nights of unremitting labor.

No time was lost, however, in sentimental mooning; the chill morning air was charged with activity, the "after guard" was all astir and an ebb tide flowed, ready to help us on our way. Gulping down the "cafay nore" that presently was passed forward in a bucket, all hands dipping in with hook pots and pannikins, hastily dug from chest and bag, we were barely able to stow away this refreshment before a heavy fist thumped the fo'c'sle doors.

"Turn to! Turn to! This ain't a private yachting tour!" was the sarcastic invitation that sent us scrambling to the deck.

"Here! You, I mean!" yelled the mate, "come forward!" for I had headed aft, and, at this command, I found myself with some others hauling a heavy water-soaked hawser aboard the fo'c'sle head.

"All clear?" came the query from aft.

"Aye, aye! All clear!"

A long whistle sounded from our tug, as we backed slowly from the wharf; the escort of boarding house runners shivering on the string piece of the dock, gave us a dismal cheer, and the voyage around Cape Horn had fairly begun.

The first level rays of morning light began to filter over the house tops on the Brooklyn side, the misty span of the bridge loomed above the river, and a dozen bloodshot eyes among the crew forward cast their farewell glances at the Tom and Jerry signs in the saloon windows on historic South Street.

We were a lumbering lot, pushed and cuffed from station to station, our best men acting like dolts, until the exercise and crisp morning air, zipping above the river, wore off the effects of a last night spent at the Atlantic Garden. South Street, at that day still a forest of spars, with here and there a bald spot marking the advent of the coastwise steamers, slid past us, Governor's Island, the Statue, the Narrows, and the Hook, were passed unnoticed in the ceaseless hustle on our decks. The running gear, left by the shore riggers in a hopeless tangle, had to be put to rights, and the mates worked us like demons to get things in some sort of shape before we should be called upon to work the vessel under sail.

Gradually order of some sort issued from the chaos, and as the day wore on we set our fores'l, all tops'ls, main t'gan'sl, jib and stays'ls, before a stiff off-shore breeze that caused the towline to slacken, and orders were given to cast off the tug.

The new steam pilot boat New York rode the swell ahead of us, ready to take off the pilot.

"Weather main braces!" came the order; the yards were braced aback, a yawl from the New York touched our side for an instant, as we surged ahead slowly against the back push from the main, and the pilot, hanging from a Jacob's ladder, dropped into his boat.

"See you in Liverpool!" shouted the pilot, standing in the yawl and waving a final farewell to Captain Nichols.

"Brace up main yards, sir!" ordered the skipper, addressing the mate, and we swung them around with a will.

The day was well advanced by then, a low bank of cloud over the land shut in the sunset, and a spanking breeze from no'east by nor' brought our port tacks to the deck. The Fuller heeled easily beneath the force of the wind. Off to leeward, and rapidly falling astern, was the American ship Tam O'Shanter, bound for China; we heard afterward that she was lost.

Up to the first dog watch all hands had labored without a moment's rest, and at eight bells in the afternoon the courses and all plain sail to royals were drawing nicely. As soon as the gear was shipshape and coiled on the pins, all hands were mustered aft. There was a feeling of uncertainty among the crew as we filed aft to the waist, standing in an awkward group about the main fife rail, a nondescript, hard-fisted, weatherbeaten lot of men.

Above towered the vast expanse of snowy canvas, looming out of all proportion in the dark half light of the winter evening; beneath us was the rolling, palpitating sweep of deck, yielding and swaying in the constant balance 'tween the wind and sea. To windward, above the line of bulwark, a ragged mackerel sky drove across the cloud rack of scattered cirrus, touched with dull red from the high shafts of the setting sun. The black backs of the shoreward rollers swept to leeward and astern, passing us as if frightened by the lofty figure of the ship.

The watches were about to be chosen. The two mates came down into the waist, and Captain Nichols stood at the break of the poop to observe this time-honored ceremony of the sea. For better or for worse, in sunshine or in storm, we were to be parceled off to our respective task-masters for the long months of the voyage ahead. The fate of friendships was to be decided, for watchmates are far closer than mere shipmates, and a general desire to escape the clutches of the mate made all of us anxious for the ordeal to be concluded. Most of the men were in favor of the second mate, Mr. Stoddard. The mate, Mr. Zerk, was a driver, a bully, and what not, but the second mate seemed to be easier, in spite of the fact that he lost no opportunity to bawl out everyone that came across his path.

"He'll be all right when we get outside," was the remark that voiced the general opinion. Old Smith, perhaps the wisest of the real sailor-men on board, came as near to hitting the relative values of the mates as was possible. "I don't see no choice between them," he said. "One may be easier, but give me the best sailor. A good sailor aft saves work for his watch forward. See if I don't figger it right. Take it any way you like, there's no choosing between them rotten apples aft, and let it go at that."

Mr. Zerk, a man of about forty, medium in height, broad shouldered, bull necked, with close cropped yellow hair—grey eyes set in a very red, smooth-shaven face, except for a sweeping blond mustache, was a native of Nova Scotia, brought up in "blue nose" ships. He eyed us with the cold look of a surgeon about to amputate. Walking up to the group just abaft of the mainmast, he made his first choice without a moment's hesitation.

"Frenchy, come here," and Victor Mathes, of Dunkirk, went to the port watch, chosen by the mate.

"Smith," was the laconic reply of Mr. Stoddard to the first choice of the mate. Honors were even, for it was a toss up between the two men.

Brenden, a husky, well-set-up sailor, trained in the sailing ships out of Hamburg, with plenty of beef and a good head, was the next choice of the mate.

**Old Smith**

"Axel," said the second mate, scoring the first advantage in the choosing of the watches. Axel proved to be one of the best men in the crew, a big, boyish Swede, a sailor and a gentleman.

"Roth, come here," and John Roth, late of the opal mines in Australia, one of the deserters from the Falls of Ettrick, and the artist of the crew, went to port. We soon dubbed him "Australia." The mate sent "Australia" to relieve the wheel, and the second mate paused a moment weighing the merits of the remaining men.

"Tom," was his choice, and another sailor, Tom Morstad, also a deserter from the Ettrick, went to starboard.

Things were fining down, and the remaining victims in this heartless process of elimination were becoming increasingly apprehensive, while those who had been chosen grinned at us with aggravating humor. The mates were getting less and less sure of their choice as the pickings became more and more undesirable. It was getting to be a question of brains versus brawn. Husky young clodhoppers shipped as A.B. by the greedy boarding masters; young mules with nothing but their thick hides and an abundance of main strength and stupidity to recommend them, placed in the balance with such old fellows as Jimmy Marshall and Jack Hitchen. Jimmy, who claimed to be sixty-five, a wizened little old sea-horse, but a wonderful "chantey man," won the next choice and was taken by the mate.

Hitchen was called to starboard, and the honors still remained about even in the contest of wit and experience, for both mates had studied the paces of each individual with critical eyes during that eventful day.

The next choice was a painful one. There was a short pause; it seemed to us that "Charlie Horse," who had once been mate on a coaster in the oyster trade, or Dago Tony, would surely be chosen next.

"Felix, come here," said the mate, running his eye over the Dago and Charlie, and lighting on me. I stepped over to the boys lined up on the lee side, a weight lifted from my mind, as Frenchy, destined to be my chum, moved near me.

It was getting on by then. Chips went aft carrying the side lights, and Captain Nichols was stumping the poop with some impatience, as a hint to his officers to bring things to a close.

The second mate chose Charlie, and George Krug, or "Scouse" as we called him, was taken by the mate. Dago Tony went to the second mate, and Fred Erricson, a good sailor, also an Ettrick deserter, went to port.

Mike, the wood turner, went to starboard, and Joe Johnson, one time a cobbler's apprentice, and general all round husky favorite of misfortune, was taken by the mate.

The left-overs, Martin, and Peter the boy, were divided by the call of Peter to the starboard watch, and Martin fell to the mate. Peter, an American, ex-reporter on a Worcester paper, one time foreman in a corset factory, and a bright, wideawake boy of something over twenty-one, had shipped for eight dollars a month and his health. The voyage netted him his payday many times over, for he was endowed with brains and, starting out a wreck, he came back a toughhanded deepwater man.

It was close to six bells by that time. Chips had set out the running lights and was getting the big pump ready, having sounded the well and reported a foot of water.

"Starboard watch below for tucker!" ordered the mate; and then turning to the men of his watch, he ordered, "Man the pump!"

It was dark as we bent to the cranks of the big pump, and with the hum of wind and the swish of water in our ears we realized that we were truly at sea, insignificant mortals riding on the low deck of a vast fabric of wood and canvas, venturing far from land on the mighty stretches of the Western Ocean.

That first night at the pump, forerunner of many, many other nights, our little band of watch mates toiled in silence, except for a few monosyllables. Four men to each crank, two on a side, facing each other, our tired arms and backs reciprocated to the action of rotation like so many toy figures actuated by some hidden clockwork; the new labor was almost a rest after the constant pulling and hauling of the day. Finally the low, raucous wheezing of the valves told us we were sucking air, and the mate, from the darkness of the poop, called out, "Belay pump!"

It is the custom of the sea, handed down from time immemorial, that "The captain takes her out and the mate brings her back." That is, the first regular watch at sea is taken by the captain's watch on the outward passage, and the same watch is taken by the port, or mate's watch, on the start for home. Of course the second mate stands the starboard watch, except in case of emergency.

Accordingly, at four bells, we went below, and after a hasty supper we sought our bunks for a brief rest before turning out for the watch from eight to midnight. We were tired—some of us, to the point of utter exhaustion—and a few of the older men claimed that we were being cheated out of our right to the first four-hour watch below, ours having merely been a dog watch of 2 hours from 6 to 8. Anyhow, whatever we thought about that, nothing was said above a mild growling in the fo'c'sle, and as we tumbled out at eight bells, and both watches lined up in the waist to muster, the chill wind cut through us, and a moment later we were greeted by an order from aft.

"Hands aloft to overhaul the t'gallant and royal buntlines!"

Up I went on the mizzen, never caring to lag behind on an order to lay aloft, a piece of twine in my pocket. The gear was overhauled and stopped just below the blocks, so the buntlines would not chafe the sails, and at the same time the stops of cotton twine were frail enough to be easily broken. When at times they were not, some unlucky wight would clamber aloft at the critical moment of taking in sail amid the slatting of canvas and the most profuse showers of artistic abuse.

Coming down from this task, I was in time to witness a burst of profanity on the part of the mate. "Keep moving, you beach-combing —! Every lousy —! I won't have no 'lime juice' sleeping on deck this voyage. D'ye hear that?" All heard, for there was a shuffle of weary feet about the main hatch, where several of the watch had perched comfortably in the dark, and, after a moment of indecision, sprinkled with derogatory mutterings, we paired off in little groups of twos, walking the swaying deck wherever we could find places free from the back draft of the sails.

Frenchy was my first chum on the Fuller, and though for periods we drifted apart, through sheer mutual exhaustion of our interchangeable ideas, yet we always came together again. Somehow, on the very start of the voyage, when the crimps and runners bade us that sad farewell from the port of New York, we were drawn together. The night that we paired off, on our first watch at sea, it seemed natural that Frenchy and I should elect to stump the deck in company. We preempted a path from the lee main pin rail to the after end of the forward house. "It's better here than anywhere," remarked Frenchy, and I soon found he was right, as we missed the draft from the mains'l and were partly sheltered by the house on the forward leg of our walk.

**Frenchy**

Frenchy was a heavy-whiskered, ruddy specimen, sporting the square-cut beard of the French sailor. He was an ex-naval man, and one time prison guard in the penal settlement of New Caledonia. Trained to the sea since boyhood, in the fishing fleet of Dunkirk, for many years a rigger in the naval yards at Brest, a sailor man on every type of craft from the Mediterranean ybeck to a ship. Victor Mathes was one of the finest types of the Gallic seaman.

His life was a vague and many folded nebula of romance. He was full of stories of the life in New Caledonia, of the discipline on the outlying islands, of punitive expeditions, and of the intrigues and jealousies among the checkered lives that wear themselves away in those distant places.

Night after night we paced the deck during the long, cold watches, and between the calls to man this rope or that, and the horsing and rustling about that was always indulged in, we swapped information of all kinds, related all sorts of experiences, truthful and otherwise, and each man explored his mental storehouse for the amusement and benefit of his chum. For hours at a time Frenchy would talk of good things to eat; this was a hobby, in fact a sort of passion, with him and often drove me to the verge of distraction. He would go into the minutest detail of how his sister Madeleine, back in Dunkirk, prepared some particular dish, telling not only of the delightful flavor and succulent qualities, but he would go into the subject of the way things smelled, roast fowl, with all sorts of fancy stuffing. My mouth would water at these cruel recitals and I know that Frenchy suffered as much as I did at the poignant recollections of gastronomic joys long past.


CHAPTER II

THE OUTWARD PASSAGE

When well clear of the coast we roused the bower anchors up on the fo'c'sle head and lashed them. "A sure sign, sonny, that you are off soundings," said Brenden; "these wind wagons don't take no chances till they get a safe offing." The cables were unshackled, and the ends stoppered abaft the wildcats. Canvas coats were put on to them, just over the chain pipes leading to the locker. "Jackasses" were then bowsed into the hawse holes for fair, taking the "tails" to the windlass. With the ground tackle secured, the "cat" and "fish" were unrove, and this gear stowed away in the fore peak. We had entered upon the real deepwater stage of the voyage, with lee shores, and soundings, many miles away.

The Fuller[3] carried a complement of sixteen hands forward, and a "boy," not counting the "idlers"—that is, the carpenter, cook and cabin steward—a small enough crew for a vessel displacing in the neighborhood of 2,500 tons, dead weight, a craft 229 feet between perpendiculars, 41-1/2 feet beam and 23 feet depth of hold, ship rigged, with skysails, royals, single t'gans'ls, double tops'ls, and courses. Her main yard was 90 feet from tip to tip. A crojik was carried as well as a spanker. On her stays, she carried flying jib, jib tops'l, jib and fore topmast stays'l, main t'gallant stays'l, main topmast stays'l. Mizzen t'gallant stays'l and a main spencer completed her spread of canvas. When on a wind, in a whole-sail breeze, with crojik furled, and spanker set, the ship Fuller spread twenty-five kites to the wind.

[3] Data re A. J. Fuller.

Ship A. J. Fuller.
Flint and Co. The California Clipper Line, Owners.
Signal letters J.V.G.B. International Code.
Built at Bath, Maine, 1881, of wood.

| | |
|---|---|
| Gross tonnage | 1,848.76 |
| Net tonnage | 1,781.88 |
| Length | 229.3 ft. |
| Breadth | 41.5 ft. |
| Draft (mean) | 17.8 ft. |
| Depth of hold | 23.0 ft. |

Now think of the handsome way in which they manned their ships in the olden days of the tea clippers when a vessel half her size would carry forty men forward! And a vessel of equal size would carry from 80 to 90 seamen. As it was, we were hard put to it in an emergency and "all hands" was the rule on every occasion demanding quick work, in going about, or in making or taking in sail. When tacking it was "all hands, and the cook at the fore sheet." One watch could not hoist the main upper tops'l, except in the finest kind of weather, and then only by taking the halyards to the main deck capstan, and "inching" the great yard up in slow and painful fashion with much singing and "yo ho"ing.

Captain Nichols shaped a course well to the eastward, fetching almost to the Azores, before hauling his wind aft and squaring away for an easy run through the N. E. trades. Skysails and flying jib were up and down a score of times a day at this restless stage of the voyage, for every rag was kept drawing to the last moment. In squally weather, and we had plenty of it, the ship would race along, her lee scuppers boiling in white water as she heeled to the blast, hands standing by at the halyards, which were always flaked down clear for running, and every mother's son keyed to a high pitch, ready for quick work at braces, clewlines and buntlines.

To have a "wheel" or a "lookout" during the night watch was a rest, although the trick at the helm was a wideawake job, whether on a course, or "by the wind." I had a fondness for steering and often stood the wheel for Frenchy or Brenden, especially during the daytime when they were employed on sailor jobs that no one else of our watch was able to do. The mate winked at this practice, and as they often let me take their tricks at night, I was able to side step a lot of the skysail climbing that would ordinarily have fallen to me as the youngster of the watch.

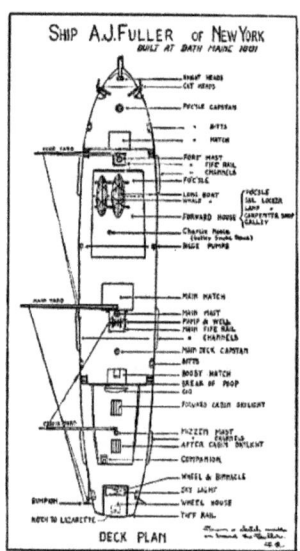

**SHIP A.J.FULLER OF NEW YORK Built at Bath Maine 1881. DECK PLAN**

My training on the old St. Mary's now stood me in good stead, and by remembering a lot of the advice given me by that prince of sailor-men, old Bos'un Dreilick of the schoolship,[4] I found myself rated with the best men in the ship, and far ahead of such fellows as Scouse, and Joe, and Martin, who were strong as bulls, but knew nothing. In between us ranged Australia and Fred, good ordinary sailors who knew the ropes, could hand, reef, and steer, but lacked that finished technique so essential to the proper able seaman. I must admit that in classing myself with men like Marshall, Frenchy, and Brenden, I am doing so at the tail end of this trio, and then only because of my skill at the helm, at heaving the "blue pigeon," and at sailing and handling boats, accomplishments that, except for steering, are rare among deep water sailors.

[4] Now Boatswain of the Schoolship Newport.

"You seem to stand the wheel a lot," the Skipper remarked one night, having noted me by the dim light of the binnacle, for I also had done a trick in the first dog watch when he happened to change the course.

The Old Man grinned, "Well, I suppose you like to be aft. Keep at it, boy, and you'll get there. But it's a lonesome life; dammit, I would rather be a farmer any day."

Captain Nichols thought this a great joke, the idea of being a farmer pleased him so he had a good laugh as he surveyed the great spread of canvas bowling along under his command. I felt sure he was joking.

Since then, I have often pondered over his remark and am now of the opinion that he was in dead earnest.

Standing lookout on the fo'c'sle head was a favorite duty that no one delegated. Finally, however, when we were well clear of the coast, the mates began to pull down the lookout whenever there was any work to be done. There always was considerable, for the mates would start something as soon as they felt the least bit sleepy and would horse their watches about even though it was absolutely unnecessary to start a single rope.

Our fare on the Fuller was of the regular deep water variety, made palatable by the fact that we were living the open air life of a lot of human gorillas. Our labors were torture, to me at least, until at last the outraged muscles adjusted themselves to the unaccustomed work. Poor Peter, he was a hundred times harder hit than I, and the four hours below were barely enough to keep him alive. One night, a few days after leaving port, when we mustered at midnight, Peter was not to be found. "Was he called?" thundered the mate, as Old Smith reported him "not present," doing so in a hesitating sort of way. "Was that — called?" again thundered the mate. "By — I'll call him!" he shouted, and strode forward, the second mate following. Peter lay half out of his bunk, one leg over the edge. He had fallen back exhausted as soon as he got his trousers on; he was dead to the cruel, hard world.

Mr. Zerk grabbed him by the leg, and, swinging him like a bag of meal, he yanked Peter clear through the fo'c'sle door, landing him on the deck with a thud, amid a shower of curses and the startled cry of the victim.

This type of brutality was calculated to "put the fear of God into us," as they say, and to strengthen discipline, and add snap and vigor to our movements. It certainly had the effect of showing us how important it was to be in the waist when the watch was mustered.

At the morning washdown the black slops that went by the name of coffee tasted like the very nectar of the gods. We dipped in with our hook pots, drinking it with relish, and the fact that it possessed mild cathartic properties, may have had something to do with the excellent state of our health. Cockroaches were not mentioned in the old scale of provisions[5] adopted by a kind Congress for the nourishment of the simple sailor-man. This was no doubt an oversight on the part of some bucolic "sailor's friend," for they might have specified that "one ounce of cockroaches may be substituted for an ounce of tea."

[5] *The following is the Scale of Provisions allowed and served out to the Crew during the voyage in addition to the daily issue of lime and lemon juice and sugar, or other antiscorbutics in any case required by law.*

|   | Bread | Beef | Pork | Flour | Peas | Rice | Barley | Tea | Coffee | Sugar | Water |
|---|---|---|---|---|---|---|---|---|---|---|---|
|   | lb. | lb. | lb. | lb. | pt. | pt. | pt. | oz. | oz. | oz. | qt. |
| Sunday | 1 | 1½ |  | ½ |  |  |  | 1/8 | ½ | 2 | 3 |
| Monday | 1 |  | 1¼ |  | 1-1/8 |  |  | 1/8 | ½ | 2 | 3 |
| Tuesday | 1 | 1½ |  | ½ |  |  |  | 1/8 | ½ | 2 | 3 |
| Wednesday | 1 |  | 1¼ |  | 1-1/8 |  |  | 1/8 | ½ | 2 | 3 |
| Thursday | 1 | 1½ |  | ½ |  |  |  | 1/8 | ½ | 2 | 3 |
| Friday | 1 |  | 1¼ |  | 1-1/8 |  |  | 1/8 | ½ | 2 | 3 |
| Saturday | 1 | 1½ |  |  |  |  |  | 1/8 | ½ | 2 | 3 |

SUBSTITUTES

One ounce of coffee or cocoa or chocolate may be substituted for one quarter ounce of tea; molasses for sugar, the quantity to be one half more; one pound of potatoes or yams; one half pound of flour or rice; one third pint of peas or one quarter pint of barley may be substituted for each other.

When fresh meat is issued, the proportion to be two pounds per man, per day, in lieu of salt meat.

Flour, rice, and peas, beef and pork, may be substituted for each other, and for potatoes onions may be substituted.

NOTE BY AUTHOR.—The above is from the fo'c'sle card of the ship A. J. Fuller, taken when I left her. This scale of provisions was greatly amplified a few years later. It was found that a shipmaster sticking close to the law in the matter of provisioning could easily starve a crew, as there was no control over quality. On the Fuller, the owners were liberal in provisioning. Such trouble as we had was due to the conditions of deep water voyages.

Our tea was never without these disgusting vermin and none of us was ever able to tell what gave it the peculiar flavor that we came to relish—the twigs and leaves floating about in the brown liquor, or the roaches lying drowned in the bottom of the can.

"They's no worse nor shrimps," philosophized Jimmy Marshall, and we tried to believe him.

The cook, an ancient Celestial named Chow, hailing from Hong Kong, had evidently put all of his gods behind him. His pigtail was gone, and with it all sense of decency, so far as preparing food for sailor-men was concerned. Those human precepts that all cooks are supposed to act upon, the ethics, if you will, of the noble profession, that Marryat tells us entitled the practitioner to wear a sword, in those good old days when the Admiralty recognized the cook, were lacking in the breast of Chow. He was a typical deepwater cook. What went aft was right, so far as looks count anyway, but the kids that left for the fo'c'sle often contained the most unsavory messes that ill-fortune can concoct. Some of the men had words with Chow about this but the result was increased carelessness and decreased portions.

"It don't do no good to scrap with the cook," was Jimmy Marshall's sage advice. "If the dirty bum wants to be dirty he can fix us all up. I knowed a cook once wot — in the soup an' bully on a English bark. The skipper, he caught him at it, an' puts him in irons. The cook had to be let out though because he was the only one wot could do the work, an' they was mighty careful aft not to rile him after they knowed wot he was. You got to leave them cooks alone."

We left Chow severely alone, and some of the crowd, Joe and Tommy especially, constituted themselves his volunteer assistants, and almost every first dog watch, one of them would be around the galley helping out. Chow rewarded them by allowing the use of the oven to make "dandy funk," a mess of broken hard tack and molasses, baked to a crisp.

When ten days had elapsed, after the final rations of fresh provisions had been issued, a tot of lime juice, that reeked suspiciously of vinegar, was served each day—by Act of Congress—to keep the sailor-man from getting scurvey. At the same time the "harness casks," beef to starboard, and pork to port, did their duty nobly and each week or so we would lift the forehatch and rouse up a slimy, wooden hooped barrel, and roll it aft to the galley door, alternating to the port and starboard harness casks.

After a month of chumming it with Frenchy, talking steadily from three to four hours a night, we were both pretty well cleaned out of experiences and ideas. Other groups had long before reached that deplorable state, and new combinations were formed in the night walks on deck. One night as we came on deck in the midwatch, Frenchy and I noticed Jimmy Marshall and Martin standing at the lee of the main hatch, in silence, after the watch had been mustered. The absence of their usual animated discussions of everything temporal and mundane attracted our attention. Soon we found ourselves at the lee of the hatch; Martin and Jimmy warmed up to us and presently Jimmy and myself were walking just aft of the forward house, and Martin and Frenchy began to pace the deck to windward.

Jimmy was a new sort of chum and the poorest listener I have ever met, which may have accounted for the peculiar one sided lay of his mind. The hard knocks of experience were alone accountable for his knowledge, varied and picturesque in the telling. He was chockful of religion and was constantly repenting the bad deeds of his youth, telling them at great length, and with such relish, that it seemed they had come to be his one unfailing source of enjoyment. A terrible drunk in his day, he had also indulged in robbery, having looted a house in Australia while tramping overland to Sydney from Port Hunter, where he had "jumped" a schooner, leaving everything behind, because of a row with the mate, in which he felled him with a handspike.

"Walked away with a piece o' change an' a whole kit o' dunnage," was the way he put it.

And also, according to his story, Jimmy had been a lightweight fighter in his youth, many, many years before. He was the best chantey-man in the crew; to hear him "sing" a rope was an inspiration to tired arms and backs.

**Jimmie Marshall**

While memory lasts, the picture of our first chantey, a few days after leaving port, will remain with me as one of the great thrills that have come my way. A heavy squall in the forenoon watch sent all of our tops'l yards to the caps, everything coming down by the run, to hang slatting in the gear. Sky sails, royals, flying jib, t'gans'ls, jib tops'l, jib, fore topmast stays'l, and then the upper tops'ls were lowered, the latter thrashing and straining against the downhauls as the ship heeled to it almost on her beam ends, gaining headway with a rush, and righting herself as we spilled the wind from the bulging canvas.

Passing as quickly as it came, the squall left us wallowing under lower tops'ls, the courses hanging in their gear.

All hands were called to make sail, and as we manned the main tops'l halyards Jimmy Marshall jumped to the pin rail, and with one leg over the top of the bulwark, he faced the line of men tailing along the deck.

"A chantey, boys!" shouted Mr. Stoddard as he took his place "beforehand" on the rope. "Come now, run her up, lads. Up! Up!" and the heavy yard commenced to creep along the mast to the sound of the creaking parral, the complaining of the blocks, and the haunting deep sea tune of "Blow the Man Down," greatest of all the two haul chanteys.

Jimmy—"Now rouse her right up boys for Liverpool town,"
Sailors—"Go way—way—blow the man down."
Jimmy—"We'll blow the man up and blow the man down,"
Sailors—"Oh, give us some time to blow the man down."
Jimmy—"We lay off the Island of Maderdegascar."
Sailors—"Hi! Ho! Blow the man down."
Jimmy—"We lowered three anchors to make her hold faster,"
Sailors—"Oh, give us some time to blow the man down."

Chorus

All hands—"Then we'll blow the man up,
And we'll blow the man down,
Go way—way—blow the man down.
We'll blow him right over to Liverpool town,
Oh, give us some time to blow the man down.
Ho! Stand by your braces,
And stand by your falls;
Hi! Ho! Blow the man down,
We'll blow him clean over to Liverpool town,
Oh, give us some time to blow the man down."

Old Marshall faced to windward, his mustache lifting in the breeze, the grey weather worn fringe of hair bending up over his battered nose. He always sang with a full quid in his cheek, and the absence of several front teeth helped to give a peculiar deep-sea quality to his voice.

"We have a man-o-war crew aboard, Mr. Zerk!" shouted the Captain from the top of the cabin, where he had come out to see the fun.

"Aye, aye, sir! Some crew!" returned the Mate, looking over us with a grim smile.

CHAPTER III

CHRISTMAS DAY ON THE HIGH SEAS

Life was not always so pleasant on board the Fuller. Hard words were the common run of things and the most frightful and artistic profanity often punctuated the working of the ship. Given a ship's company barely strong enough to handle a two thousand five hundred ton three-skysail yarder, even had they all been seasoned able seamen, our officers had to contend with a crew over half of which rated below that of the "ordinary" classification of seamanship, thick skinned clodhoppers, all thumbs on a dark night, and for many weeks after leaving port, as useless as so much living ballast. The kicking and moulding into form of this conglomerate mass of deep sea flotsam, gathered for the ship by the boarding masters, and duly signed on the ship's articles as A.B., called for all but superhuman efforts. The curse is far more potent than the gentle plea, especially when hard fists and hobnailed sea boots are backed by all of the age old authority of the sea. To work a ship of the proportions of the Fuller, with seventeen hands forward, called for man driving without thought of anything but the work required.

The latter days of the sailing ship as a carrier, before invoking the aid of steam auxiliary apparatus, in the hoisting and hauling, brought forth the brute sea officer aft, and the hardened fo'c'sle crowd, half sailor and half drudge, forward. The "bucko mate" walked her decks, and the jack tar, stripped of his pigtail, his bell mouthed canvas trousers, his varnished sailor hat, and his grog, remained in plain dungaree and cotton shirt to work the biggest sailing craft in the history of the world on the last hard stages of their storm tossed voyages.

Mixed with our real sailors were the worthless (so far as sea lore went) scrapings of the waterfront. Shipped by the boarding masters for the benefit of their three months' "advance," and furnished for sea with rotten kits of dunnage, as unreliable and unfitted for the work as the poor unfortunate dubs who were forced by an unkind fate to wear them.

On the other hand, the real sailor-men of the crew were valued accordingly, and I can hardly remember an instance where either one of the mates singled out for abuse those men who had shipped as A.B. and were so in fact. My schoolship training (St. Mary's '97) stood by me, and though barely turned eighteen, I was saved from most of the drudgery meted out to the farmers of the watch.

After washing through the heavy seas we encountered for the first few weeks of the voyage, while beating off the coast on the long reach eastward to the Azores, the long hard pine sweep of the main deck became slippery with a deposit of white salt-water slime. The sheen of this scum, in the moonlight, under a film of running water, gave the decks a ghastly "Flying Dutchman" like appearance, and the footing became so precarious that something had to be done.

"They have the 'bear' out," Scouse announced, as he trudged into the fo'c'sle carrying a "kid" of cracker hash, ditto of burgoo, a can of coffee, and a bag of hard tack, this cargo of sustenance being our regulation breakfast menu.

"The bear?" I asked, as we gathered about this appetizing spread.

"Yes, the bear," volunteered Brenden, grinning with the rest of the sailors. "The bear for Scouse, and Joe, and Martin, and Fred."

At eight bells, as we mustered aft, a subdued banter went on among the men. The starboard watch were all grinning, and as they went below four sheepish looking fellows of the other side turned the "bear" over to the farmers of our watch. "Keep that jackass baby carriage moving now. D'ye hear me?"

Keep it moving!" bellowed the mate, for there was some reluctance in taking hold, and as Scouse and Martin tailed on, opposed to Joe and Fred, the doleful scrape of the bear mingled with the general laughter at the mate's sally.

The bear consisted of a heavy box, a thick thrum mat lashed on the bottom of it, and the inside loaded with broken holy stones and charged with wet sand. Four stout rope lanyards were rigged to the corners and served to haul the thing back and forth while the sand filtered down through the mat, providing the necessary scouring agent. A day or two with the bear in constant service, both day and night, cleaned up the decks and provided us with considerable amusement, that is, those of us who were lucky enough to be kept at more dignified jobs.

Ships leaving the Atlantic Coast in the winter months bend their best suit of sails. The severe weather usually encountered in working clear of the land, and the chance of having to ratch off from a lee shore, make this precaution one of great importance. The fact that green crews are bound to be more or less slow in taking in sail during squalls may also account for the "storm suit" under which we sailed from port.

**Fred**

On our first night out, shortly before one bell in the mid watch, our crowd having just gone below, the fore topmast stays'l blew from the bolt ropes with the report of a cannon. We had already clambered into our bunks, dog tired, when this occurred, and muttered oaths, anticipating a call of "all hands," came from untold depths of weariness within the fo'c'sle. On deck there was the hurried tramping of feet, and the shouting of the second mate. We could hear the long wail of the men at brace and downhaul, the "Ah-hee-Oh-hee-ah-Ho!" with all of its variation as the slaves of the ropes launched their age-old complaint on the whipping winds. I lapsed into slumber with the dim consciousness that the second mate was handling the situation alone, and a heartfelt thanks for the warmth of the blankets in my narrow bunk; a foot above me the cold rain pattered against the roof of the fo'c'sle house, its music mingling with the swish of the water under the fore channels.

After three weeks of beating to the eastward, having fetched almost as far across as the Azores, and being in the region of the northern limit of the N. E. trades, the captain hauled his wind and squared away for the run through the trade wind belt to the doldrums and the line. Fine weather became the order of the day and life on board settled down to a more regular routine.

On a Saturday morning, the day having broken remarkably fine, a brilliant red sunset followed by a cold grey dawn, assuring us of the settled weather that the steady "glass" made more certain, all the world seemed ready to rejoice, for it was Christmas Day. Word was passed into the fo'c'sle by the other watch, as we turned out for our breakfast, "We shift sail today."

"All hands on deck for us, me boys!" piped Australia. "An' the first watch on deck tonight," chipped in Jimmy Marshall, "an' a hell of a Christmas Day!"

Jimmy lit his pipe for a morning puff; climbing into his bunk, he dangled his short legs over the frowsy head of big Scouse who sat with his dejected poll bent under the upper bunk board, a fair sample of the despondent crowd of farmers who faced a Christmas Day of labor.

"A hell of a Christmas Day, boys,
A hell of a Christmas Day,
For we are bound for the bloody Horn
Ten thousand miles away."

Jimmy rendered this little ditty of cheerfulness as Fred picked up the breakfast kids and started for the galley, while we turned out on the sun-splashed planks as the last of eight bells vibrated over the ship. She lay still in a near calm like a scene by Turner, all of her canvas hanging in picturesque festoons from the jackstays, where the starboard watch had cast off the courses and tops'ls, leaving them depending in their gear. The decks had not been washed down, in order to keep them dry, and the mate himself had turned out at four bells to start the ball rolling.

Long bundles of the fine weather canvas were stretched on the decks ready for swaying aloft. Working like demons in the forenoon, and with all hands on deck after dinner, which was dispatched in haste, we had the courses, and in turn the tops'ls and light sails, lowered to the deck, and the gantlines rigged to hoist the summer canvas; this we sent aloft in record time. These old sails, soft and mellow, veterans of a dozen voyages, patched and repatched, with whole new cloths of a lighter grade here and there streaking the dull white-weathered surface, were as smooth and pliable as a baby's bonnet.

On some of them, the fore upper tops'l especially, we found records of the many crews who had handled them before. "James Brine, Liverpool. On his last voyage," was one inscription. I hope Brine achieved his end and stayed ashore. A date under this was hardly decipherable but may have been Jan., June, or July, the day the eighth, and the year 1893.

Bending a sail calls for the nicest knowledge; the passing of the head earing must be done in a certain manner, so the head of the sail will hold well up on the yard arm; the gear, consisting of tacks, sheets, clew garnets, and buntlines, in the case of a "course," not to mention the leechlines, and bowlines, must all be rove and rigged just so. The "robands" or pieces of rope yarn, are all looped through the "head holes" ready for bending the sail to the iron jackstay on the yard, and when a sailor does the job, all goes as smooth as a wedding when the parson knows his job.

After the labors of a busy day, the ship presented the comfortable well-patched appearance of a man in the woods, free from the stiffness of new white linen, and naturally fitting into the familiar folds of old duds, unconventional but plenty good enough. The bright spars still attested to her "smartness," but we were in easy trade wind weather and dressed accordingly. The fores'l was particularly large, with extra clothes in the leeches, made to catch and hold every breath of wind blowing over the deck.

The sail locker was re-stowed with our "best suit," and between the coils of canvas we liberally spread a bundle of old newspapers brought out by the mate. "To give the rats something to chew on," he remarked, as we ran the stiff new canvas in, tier upon tier.

One thing that Frenchy called my attention to in the stowing of the locker was the fact that the storm canvas, lower tops'ls and stays'ls, were placed handy for immediate removal, the mate assuring himself of this fact by personal supervision; indeed he knew just where each particular sail was located in the locker, and could go in and lay his hand upon it in the darkest night, as he more than once demonstrated during the course of the voyage.

That night a tired lot of men sat down to supper. The cold salt beef, the hard bread and the can of tea came from the galley in their usual order. Fred, who was mess cook for that week, went back to the galley, after depositing the regulation Saturday night grub. As he left the fo'c'sle door he turned back at us with a grin on his wide good natured face, bristling with uneven outcroppings of yellow stubble. Fred reminded me of an amiable plodder hulking out in his dungaree jacket, while the watch fell to on the beef and tack.

"I guess he forgot to thank the cook for putting so many bugs in the tea," ventured Brenden.

"Maybe he's going aft to take Christmas Dinner with the captain in the cabin. They have a real plum pudding there; I saw it in the galley," said Joe.

Plum pudding! Christmas! The thoughts of loved ones far away, and of those distant homes that perhaps were remembering some of us out on the broad bosom of the deep waters, came as a pang. All of us, I believe, felt this. For a moment or two silence ensued, then Fred burst through the fo'c'sle door with the big surprise.

"Pie, boys! Pie!" he shouted, depositing three tin plates on the fo'c'sle deck, for we dined with the deck as a table, sitting about the kids on low benches. The precious pie was cut with the greatest regard for equality by no less an expert hand than that of Frenchy, assisted by Australia, who showed us how to cut a pie into three parts by measuring across the diameter with a knife, adding a little to this, and then this length went three times into the circumference.

Jimmy Marshall failed to agree with this theory, but was fairly beaten in the result, for Australia was right. The pie certainly was cut into three very equal parts.

"An engineer in the mines showed me this," said Australia. "He says, 'Pie times across the pie, is all the way around.' Mathematics is wot he calls this." Australia was nearly right at that, and the marks he made on the crust of the confections baked by Chow served as a reliable guide for Frenchy, also bolstering him immensely in the eyes of the more humble members of the port watch. That Australia chap certainly knew a thing or two, even if he was not the best sailor in the world.

But Jimmy Marshall's comment was simply, "Rats!"

After supper, when pipes were glowing, and most of us sought our bunks for the hour or so that remained to us in the last dog watch, a discussion arose as to what kind of pie it was. Frenchy, the great gastronomic authority, claimed it was English currant pie. "They taste so bitter, that's why I know," he added with an air of finality.

Others differed with him. Scouse said it was red crabapple pie. Martin claimed it was nothing but plum pie. I thought it tasted like cranberry, but was not sure. At last, to settle the matter, and at the earnest request of the crabbed Jimmy, Fred trudged aft to the galley to consult Chow and wind up the argument. He returned in triumph with a large tin can done up in a gaudy red label marked "Pie Fruit."

Shortly after entering the N. E. trades we encountered the region of tropic rains, of daily thunder storms, and of abundant drinking and washing water. We rigged an old sail over the gallows frame in the main deck to catch the rain, which was teemed through a canvas pipe to the main tank, a large upright iron cylinder standing on the keelson blocks in the main hold just abaft of the main mast. Our allowance of three quarts a day, per man, was anything but satisfying in the tropic atmosphere of the torrid zone. At least half of this "whack" of water went to the galley for use in the preparation of food and the rest was divided between the scuttle butt and the water barrel, from which it was drawn sparingly for washing purposes; usually a mere rinse to clean off the salt of a sea water scrub.

In the extreme heat, during the frequent periods of calm, our suffering through the lack of water became intense. The Fuller, like many other ships sailing from New York, put to sea with her water tank barely a quarter full, relying on the tropic rains to replenish the supply. When the rains did finally come we fairly reveled in the luxury of abundant fresh water, drinking, washing clothes, bathing, and just plain wasteful wallowing in the refreshing element. With the first douse of rain all hands turned out on deck to fill their pannikins under the spouting drains from the forward house.

The conduct of a deep water sailing voyage in the old days of wooden ships called for what today would be considered the highest type of scientific management. In the maintenance of the vessel, each part of the complicated fabric received its due attention at some particular point in the voyage where the weather was favorable for that certain operation. So in the entry to the rainy belt, that uncertain region of the doldrums where almost constant precipitation takes turn about with calm or light baffling winds, we were turned loose on the job of scrubbing paintwork. The work was started aft and each watch did its own side of the ship, there being much rivalry as to who was doing the most work. Everybody took a hand in this and Brenden and Marshall would curse unmercifully at the job when well out of earshot of the after guard. Our hands became wrinkled with the constant wet, the calloused flesh getting soft and cheesy, while our oilskins, in which we worked during the worst downpours, became soaked and clammy through constant use.

We were not allowed the bucket of classic "sewgee" of the steam ship sailor, a mixture of caustic soda, soft soap and water, but were provided with nothing but a small tin of brick dust and a rag of burlap; a rope handled deck bucket and a small swab completed the outfit. Add to this formula an abundance of "elbow grease," and slithers of tropic rain, and you get paintwork polished smooth and white as ivory. A week or so, with all hands on the paintwork, whenever the working of the ship would permit, transformed her into a model of neatness. Woe to the luckless wretch who by any chance marred the deck or paintwork with a drop of grease or tar.

About this time we made our acquaintance with the flying fish, these swift travellers often shooting over our deck at night and being caught in the belly of one of the courses or the spanker. A flying fish for breakfast is not bad, and many were caught by the men on deck keeping a sharp lookout for them. The mates were also watching for the bag of flying fish and whenever one landed on the poop or in the waist, one or the other of the mates would call out and have a hand bring the fish aft.

One night a fish landed somewhere in the waist. We could hear the wet splatter of the flying fins, as it was calm and the deck quiet. Mr. Zerk, who was leaning against the weather swifter of the mizzen shrouds, roused himself and called out for someone to bring the fish aft.

Several of the watch started to search for the visitor, for we also had heard him land, but without success.

"How about that fish?" shouted the mate, after a decent interval, while the search was going on.

"Can't find it, sir," Joe piped up.

"The hell you can't!" thundered the mate. "There he is," and again we heard a faint "splash, splash" of the wings.

"Get a light, you damn fools," was the order, for it was mighty dark. "Come now quick. Pronto!" and as Scouse banged on the door of the deck room occupied by Chips, in order to get him to open the lamp locker, we thought we heard the "splash, splash" again.

**Joe**

With the aid of a lantern and all of the watch the entire deck was searched. Finally, Jimmy Marshall let out a whoop, "Here he was! Here he was!" Some water on the deck, near the coils of rope hanging from the main pin rail, looked as though Jimmy was close to the flying fish.

"Here he was!" again shouted the excited Jimmy, grabbing the lantern from the hand of Scouse.

"Here he what?" demanded the mate, coming down into the waist. The mate bent over the wet spot and exploded in a string of oaths. "No flying fish ever made that! Here, you!" and he grabbed Jimmy. "This is some of your damn monkey shines, you old dried up bundle of sea tripe! — your gray hairs, I'll flying fish you! Lay aloft to the main skysail yard and watch the stars! I'll call you down on deck whenever we need you!"

For several nights after that Jimmy spent his time climbing up and down the main rigging, for no sooner would he get up than the mate would think of something to do that required his presence on deck.

The flying fish episode furnished us with something to talk about in the fo'c'sle, and while Jimmy always tried to leave the impression that the joke was on the mate and the rest of us, we felt that his over zeal in discovering the puddle of water in which his clever hand had simulated the nervous flapping of the fins of a flying fish had turned the tables. My idea was that Jimmy, after seeing how well the thing was taking, could not resist the temptation to get the credit.

We also harpooned our first bonita, a very active, virile fish, shaped like a short double ended spindle buoy, and striped lengthwise. These fish are exceedingly lively and jump about with terrific energy when brought on deck. Before taking this fish to the galley, Old Smith of the other watch, and Frenchy, and of course Jimmy Marshall, tested the meat with a silver coin, to see if it was of the poison variety.

"If the silver turns black the fish is poison," explained Frenchy. In this case the bonita was pronounced "good to eat," and a great feast was on that night; however, I never cared much for fish anyway and did not touch it. Chow had certainly made an ill looking mess of it, garnished with broken tack, and basted with pork fat.

"You'll wisht you had a bit of this tucker afore we get to Honolulu," was the comment of Joe, who proceeded to help himself liberally.

CHAPTER IV

THE FIGHT

An undercurrent of trouble had been running for some time, finding expression in much subdued comment and criticism, at odd moments, when small groups of the watch would foregather about the fo'c'sle during the dog watch below. These dog watch hours were, during fine weather, given over largely to yarning, smoking, reading, or playing cards, or checkers, and to the performance of such odd jobs as sailors do during their few leisure moments. Big George, or Scouse, as we called him, had become something of a bully, and Joe, the most independent of his subjects, had on several occasions taken pains to let Scouse understand that he resented the way in which the big fellow carried on among the farmers of the watch. Of course Scouse never dared open his mouth to any of the real sailors, but he had gradually set himself up as a sort of autocrat among the pushers of the "bear."

The development of this condition was so long in process of evolution, that several times Frenchy and Brenden threatened to clean things up and put an end to the stumbling block that threatened our fo'c'sle democracy. Always, however, Jimmy Marshall intervened. "Leave 'em alone. Things will break, see if they don't, an' 'e'll get it good, 'e will."

Following our siege of paint-scrubbing, we started to tar down the standing rigging, work that devolved largely upon Scouse and his gang of understrappers, making them the bright particular stars in the firmament of wrath whenever, by any chance, they happened to drop so much as a pin point of tar on the immaculate paintwork or deck.

The mate on these occasions outdid himself, and by the fluency of his language and the surprising richness of his imagery he afforded a certain amusement to those of us who were the listeners. The targets of these profane outbursts had no redress, and, if they lost none of their self respect, it was simply because none of that useless commodity was left clinging to their devoted hides. Scouse, Fred and Martin had received recent broadsides, and with half an eye we could see that Mr. Zerk was watching Joe with a view to exercising a few new epithets.

It was our afternoon watch on deck; we turned out at seven bells to get our dinner, and Joe, who was mess carrier for that week, turned out lively to get the "kids" of cracker hash from the galley. A gentle sea was rolling in on our quarter and Joe entered the fo'c'sle door, the kid of cracker hash under his arm, the bread bag full of hard tack in one hand, and a large can of steaming hot tea in the other, the Fuller gave one of her corkscrew twists, and Joe stumbled over the sill, dousing Scouse with about half of the hot tea.

Scouse was furious, and at the same time half of our whack of tea was running in the scuppers.

Little things assume monstrous proportions after a group of men have been in close quarters for a long time. This is particularly so when they have to live in such intimate and trying proximity as that in the fo'c'sle of a sailing ship. On a deepwaterman, months at sea without even a smell of land, let alone a sight of it, the community life is bound to wear thin the edges of daily intercourse. Every small incident is magnified far beyond its worth, and only a trifle is needed to start a racket of some kind. Brenden and Frenchy cursed the luckless Joe for a clumsy lout. Jimmy called him a "bloody rum cat," a favorite expression of the little sailor, and Scouse, foaming with rage, was only restrained by the rest of us from sailing right into Joe, regardless of the cracker hash, the remaining tea, or anything else. Joe was equally furious. He refused to touch the tea, saying he had spilled his whack, and the rest of us might shut up our talk about it.

At this Australia and Fred insisted that Joe have his tea, sharing with the rest. Talk became loud, and in the midst of the whole affair eight bells struck and we tumbled on deck, our dinner half finished. Scouse and Joe went to their work in the main rigging; some were to leeward of the deckhouse stitching sails, while I passed a ball of marline for Frenchy, who was serving the wire bolt rope of the foot of an old lower tops'l that we were repairing.

He was facing aft toward the main shrouds, when suddenly he started, his eyes seemed to bulge from his head, and he dropped his serving mallet, while at the same time there was a bump behind me on the deck, and Frenchy gasped, "Ma foi! Look, Felix!"

I turned quickly and there on the white deck below the main rigging was a big black greasy splotch of tar, and Joe's tar pot rolling into the scupper.

The silence that followed was painful. Mr. Zerk came forward from the weather quarterbitt where he was smoking his after dinner pipe, and Joe dropped down the Jacob's ladder to the deck under a fire of insulting profanity from the mate. Whipping off his dungaree jacket, he started to swab up the defiling tar before it could soak well into the deck planks.

Scouse, whom Frenchy saw unhitch the lanyard of the pot as he worked above Joe, went on with his tarring without batting an eye. Trouble was on foot, however, in the port watch.

We went below at eight bells, four o'clock in the afternoon, but Joe remained on deck to remove the last vestiges of tar, and Scouse entered the fo'c'sle, speaking to no one. The trick played on Joe was so contemptible that, so far as the common feeling went, Scouse had placed himself beyond the pale, and no man cared to break the ice by addressing him. That big Scouse felt this was certain, and the fact that it hurt at least attested a few remaining embers of decent feeling.

The first dog watch that day was unusually quiet, all hands mending and reading and wondering what the outcome would be when Joe got the tar cleaned up on deck. At five bells Joe returned to the fo'c'sle with the supper, a kid of salt pork and cabbage. Martin, who had busied himself in the galley, brought in a pan of "dandy funk," a baked mass of hard tack and molasses, a great delicacy with us and only possible at rare intervals when Chow would permit us to take up the space in his galley range. However, the dandy funk went begging. Joe was sullen and refused to touch it. Scouse ignored it, and so did everyone else with the exception of Martin, who for once enjoyed a complete meal of our favorite dessert. Conversation during supper was strained to the breaking point, and we were all glad to be away as soon as possible and get out on deck.

Skouse

The second dog watch went by without incident, as we were rushed about the braces, sweating up for the night, trimming yards, and laboring at the bilge pumps. It was clear, but with no moon, and at eight bells we went forward to the square under the fo'c'sle head. The starboard watch were called aft by the second mate, to some task of horsing up this yard or that, and everything was propitious for the coming battle. Blood alone could wipe out the feud between Scouse and Joe.

"And I hope he gets a damn good lickin'," confided Martin to me as we went forward, referring to Scouse.

"Too heavy, Mart," was my opinion.

"But Australia says as how Joe can handle his self. That boy ain't no slouch, and he's mad. You bet he's mad," insisted Martin.

That Joe was mad, fighting mad, went without saying. He had the stinging insults from the mate still ringing in his ears, and the vile tactics of Scouse, culminating in the tar pot trick, had steeled Joe to the point of desperation. Scouse, on the other hand, faced the question of fighting for his right to exist in the fo'c'sle. For a man to be ostracized by the crowd forward is a living hell, as has been proven on other voyages.

Aggravated as the situation was by the hedging discipline of the ship, the preparations for the battle were as secret as though we were an illegal boxing club operating in some blue-stocking community.

Jimmy Marshall decided all the details, jumping around as busy as a field louse at harvest time. He elected himself referee and told off Australia and Brenden to look after Scouse, while Martin and myself were detailed to take care of Joe.

Our men stripped to the waist, bare knuckles and bare feet, with the "ring" bounded by the fore pinrail to leeward, the fife rail, the knight heads, and the fore side of the fo'c'sle, all dimly lighted by the fo'c'sle lamp, moved to the doorway by Jimmy, and shedding a faint yellow gleam over the space on deck.

Aft, the watch under the second mate were going through the first half hour of trimming yards, and the general shake up of things with which the officers usually "woke up" their crowd. No time had been lost by Jimmy, for he know just what to do, and Joe was facing Scouse with blood in his eyes, a very few minutes after eight bells.

"Not much room, but good enough for a fight, if it's fight you want," said Jimmy, buzzing around the men to see that all was in order. Two buckets were filled with water from over side, hand swabs were got from the deck chest, and our men lined up for work.

Scouse weighed about two hundred pounds, topping Joe by twenty pounds, but for all that they were well matched, as Joe had the advantage of agility and the better chance to dodge the hard knocks of the very substantial deck fixtures all about.

Jimmy brought out a big silver watch and announced that the rounds would be three minutes, "An' no punchin' in a clinch, an' no noise. These is the Mark o' Queensberry rules," said Jimmy with great emphasis.

The fo'c'sle lookout of the other watch came aft to the break of the fo'c'sle head and stood by the mast, ready to warn us of a surprise from aft. It was to be a silent fight, a desperate, uncompromising battle for the freedom of the fo'c'sle slaves, and the general edification of all hands, long wearied by the bickering between Joe and the red head.

The men backed off in the gloom.

"Go to it!" cried Jimmy.

They clashed with the hard thuds of calloused fists. Both men were in the prime of condition. Both were crazy to fight. Big Scouse swung at Joe, landing a fraction before Joe connected with the big fellow's wind. The blow brought blood spurting from Joe's nose and cut his lip. "Play for his wind, Joe! The bread basket, Joe! Bat 'im in the eye! Kill him!" The side lines, hid in the shadow of the fo'c'sle, were with Joe.

For a minute or two there was a rapid exchange of blows without thought of guard or parry. To get in as many and as strong a lot of blows as possible was the simple system.

Jimmy cried out "time," but no account of time or rounds was contemplated in the scheme of things. Fight was the business, and to a finish.

"Biff!" They slammed against the side of the deck house; a splotch of blood, dimly visible in the night, smeared the white paint. Once again they swung back, when the ship gave a sudden roll, as a blow from Joe's right landed on Scouse's nose, toppling him backward against the fife rail. An iron pin, the one used to belay the chain sheets of the lower tops'l, caught Scouse behind the ear and, with a grunt, he was "out."

Fortunately, nothing but rumors of the fight got aft. Scouse was well beaten, and came to in his bunk, after Australia and Brenden had doused him with salt water. Joe was badly battered up, and both men carried "shiners." As Jimmy Marshall said, "Honors is even, but it was a wery wery ragged fight."

The mate next morning greeted the watch with a broad grin, and the story of the mill, told to the starboard watch by their lookout Tommy, lost nothing in the telling. As for the port watch, we were glad it was over and once again the atmosphere below returned to normal. A few nights later Joe and Scouse chummed together, and from that day to the night in Honolulu, when Joe deserted and went out on the barkentine Irmgard to Frisco, he and Scouse were inseparable.

CHAPTER V

NEPTUNE COMES ON BOARD

We were then in about five degrees of North Latitude, the trades had failed us, and the doldrums claimed their share of bracing and hauling, giving us little time for any other work. Every ripple on the brazen sea called for a different angle of the yards, and in dead calm we lay with our head yards braced sharp up and the after yards square, the courses guyed out from the masts by slap lines and bowlines. During the day a vertical sun beat down on our bare deck in unmerciful fashion, lifting the scorching pitch from the seams and all but addling our senses with the heat. The mates became more and more exacting, every job palled, and the stuffy, unpalatable food of the fo'c'sle stuck in our throats. The vessel was a chip of hell floating on the unforgiving ocean; riveted for days, that stretched to weeks, amid the patches of rusty sea weed, a thousand feet across, that tangled about the rudder post, great sun-scorched fragments of the dead Sargasso Sea.

And all of this time we knew that the Southern branch of the Equatorial Current was sending us back to the W. N. W. at the rate of several miles a day!

In watch below, choking with the heat, we lay tossing sleeplessly in our bunks while the sickly smell of the bilges came up from the fore peak through the wind sails let down to ventilate the hold. Cockroaches throve in added millions, and we were treated to our first rations of weevily tack. The little white worms seemed to be everywhere. The cracker hash was riddled with them as Chow selected the rottenest bread for this purpose. Most of us developed boils, and the dark brown taste, left by the vile food, resulted in a general loss of appetite. The heat even forced the rats from the hold and on a dark night we could hear them scampering about under the fo'c'sle head. The healthy sea tan of the temperate zone left our faces, and we became peevish and morose.

Some of us tried to forget our misery by reading the books sent aboard by the Seamen's Friend Society, others whiled away the hot watches below, when sleep was impossible, by making wonderful models of ships in bottles, almost a lost art nowadays, and revived on board the Fuller by Frenchy. Most of these works of art found resting places behind the bars of waterfront saloons in Honolulu.

One blessing that came to us in this hell afloat was the fact that the mates winked at the snatching of a few hours' sleep during the night watches on deck, otherwise there is no telling how some of us would have survived.

Our fo'c'sle scuttle butt soured, and Old Smith of the starboard watch emptied it one Sunday morning and charred the inside with a bundle of rope yarns to which he set fire. He told us how water gets bad in the tropics, and then how its own impurities destroy themselves. "The bugs scoff each other and die," and, went on Smithy, "they drops to the bottom of the butt, like white skeletons, and the water is as clean and good as ever."

About this time considerable activity went on forward among the old sailors in both watches. One dog watch, men from both sides of the fo'c'sle went aft and interviewed the captain.

"We are near the line," said Frenchy to me shortly afterward. "Don't make any fuss about what goes on, and you'll get off easy," he cautioned.

There were quite a few of us who had never crossed the equator, and the preparations in the dog watches augured ill for those who chose to resist the just tribute demanded by Father Neptune of all green sailors who, in those days, ventured across the magic bounds.

A fair slant of wind had helped us along for a few days, when the Old Man called Jimmy aft and imparted important information.

At eight bells in the afternoon watch, as all hands were mustering in the waist, a hoarse hail from forward greeted us.

"Ship Ahoy! Ship Ahoy!" came the deep bass summons from a point beneath the bow.

"Forward, there! Who hails us?" answered the captain, who stood out on the poop, replying to the voice from forward.

"Father Neptune hails us, Captain," answered Hitchen, returning from the bow. "He asks if there are any of his children on board who would receive his blessing on their heads."

"Aye, bring him on board," ordered the skipper, a broad grin lighting his features, and the two mates reflected the feeling aft by joining in the smiles.

A noise of trudging along the deck followed, the King of the Sea, his own whiskers hidden behind a broad beard of rope yarns, a bright red harpoon in his right hand serving as a trident, and a large razor, made of hoop iron, stuck in his belt, walked aft. He was draped in the folds of an old boat sail, and for all of his regal trimmings we recognized the famous Jimmy. A retinue followed, rigged out in true deepwater style, and carrying a tub between them, which was deposited on deck just aft of the mainmast.

"Captain," said Neptune, "I am told as 'ow you 'ave green 'ands on board who 'ave to be shaved."

"Yes, Your Majesty, we have some with the hayseed still in their whiskers," answered the skipper.

"Bring 'em forth!" thundered the King, unlimbering his razor and passing the trident to the safe keeping of his wife, Amphitrite, in the person of Axel, who towered two feet above the head of the King.

However, what Jimmy lacked in stature he made up in efficiency, and in the imperious glance of scorn with which he greeted eight of us who were lined up for his inspection.

Old Smith grabbed me by the neck; I was seated on the bottom of an upturned bucket at the feet of the King.

"Your name?" demanded His Majesty, and as I was about to answer a filthy swab of soapsuds and grease was thrust in my mouth and smeared over my face and the shaving began, ending by a back somersault into the tub of water behind.

"Next!" called Neptune in true barber shop style, and so, in turn, each of the green hands went through the ordeal; the least willing getting the most attention. Scouse and Joe were among the lubbers, and were accorded special rites to the vast amusement of all hands. Australia wound up the entertainment by handing Scouse and Joe pieces of gunny sack, smeared with black paint, with which to wipe their faces.

"All right now!" called the mate, after the skipper had left the deck. "Turn to and clean up," and we were back again to the rigid discipline of the sea, relaxed for a brief hour to let King Neptune hold his sway.

After crossing the line we picked up the first whisperings of the S. E. trades, that soon began to blow steadily and ushered in another busy stage of the voyage. The refreshing wind and falling temperature brought renewed vigor to our jaded crew. Although we had commenced to feel the lack of fresh provisions, scurvy did not bother us, possibly owing to the regular issue of lime juice, but the constant repetition of salt pork and salt beef, the weevily hard tack, and the abominable slumgullion, a stew made from canned mutton, made us crave for something decent to eat.

Frenchy often drove us to the verge of distraction with his stories of the cooks at home in Dunkirk, until we finally had to put the ban on that sort of discourse. Again, we landed several bonitas teeming with energy, and, after the silver coin test, all hands fell to with a will, myself included. We also hooked a shark and hauled him on board by a "handy billy" snatched to the fore rigging.

The regular routine of setting up shrouds and stays preparatory to entering the heavy weather off the Horn, now began in earnest. We had left New York with a full set of new hemp lanyards in our lower rigging. The lanyard knots were turned in in a slovenly manner, with a lubberly disregard for appearances, that proved an eyesore to Captain Nichols. We cast new knots in these, and set up all standing rigging anew; a long, interesting job that initiated us into the mysteries of "rackings" and the "Spanish windlass," and the practical workings of the various "purchases" and "burtons"; the "luff tackles," and the "gun tackles."

The mate was the leading spirit in these proceedings, staying on deck practically all day to supervise the work. As we would set up one pair of shrouds to port and another to starboard, bringing them to a "full due," the mate was always there to say when to clap on the racking and "come up" on the rigging luffs.

How the mate stood it often amazed me, for he was very lively at night, but toward the end of this work the second mate would stand his last dog watch for him, giving our first officer a six hour spell of sleep every other day. What this means on a watch and watch racket, sailors who have traveled the long voyage route will know.

The real sailors came to the fore during this time in both watches, and Frenchy, Brenden, and Marshall, of our side, with Smith, Axel, and Hitchen of the starboard watch, proved their rightful claim to the full rating of A. B. Mr. Stoddard, who was a bit weak on his marline spike seamanship, though a good watch officer, made up for things by the way he bawled about and hurried and scurried his watch during the time the mate was on deck. His men hated him thoroughly and we were glad that he had very little to do with us.

Aboard a real shipshape and Bristol fashion deepwaterman of the old school, if there be any such left today, everything is done according to the custom of the sea. From the main truck to the keel, from the outermost end of the flying jibboom to the last band on the spanker, the ancient art of seamanship has decreed the exact way in which certain things shall be done. The deadeyes carry their knots inboard, forward to starboard, and aft to port. The lanyard lengths are justly proportioned to the length of the stay they extend, so the required "give" will be right, and the shroud pairs, stays, and backstays, are passed over the mast heads and rest upon the trestle trees, in due and proper form; the same in all ships worthy of the name.

Nations differ in their customs, and likewise in their rigs. No Italian ship can sail the sea with a straight martingale, and no other ship would venture forth with one that was anything but true.

For weeks at a time, after our entry into the southern trades, it was hardly necessary to touch a brace except for the sweating up each night in the last dog watch, when a swig or two on the ropes would bring back any slack that had worked around the pins. The job of setting up standing rigging completed, we turned our attention to the running gear. We rove off new whips on all the braces, using an eye splice that was a favorite with the mate, being tucked after the manner of a sailmaker's splice, that is, the continuity of the strands of the rope was preserved, the appearance of the whips being very trim.

The tops'l downhauls were rove off with new rope, and the gear of all the lower stays'ls, lower tops'ls and courses was overhauled and replaced where needed.

As we began to lift the Southern Cross and the trades left us, we again shifted sail, an all day job that this time fell on a Sunday, and when completed found us under our best suit of canvas ready for that storm corner of the voyage, Cape Horn. We overhauled the rudder tackles, reeving new purchases "with the sun," as indeed all purchases are rove. Oil bags were made, shaped like beech nuts, bound with ratline stuff, and fitted with a stout becket. By filling these with heavy non-freezing animal or vegetable oil and puncturing them with a sail needle, they afforded the best means for spreading oil on the waters in time of storm.

One sail in particular that we bent at this time made a great impression on me; this was a heavy storm spencer made of dark hemp canvas, soft and pliable even when wet, unlike the stiff white American cotton stuff that rips out your finger nails when fighting the bellying folds, tough as sheet iron, as it slams out from a bucking yard. The main spencer was evidently an acquisition from some Asiatic or European voyage. It bent to an iron jackstay, and furled in to the mast with a set of brails, being cut "leg-o'-mutton," the sheet hauling aft to big eyebolts on either side of the waist.

Double lashings were passed on all of the lifeboat gripes. Rolling and jumper tackles were got ready for the lower and tops'l yards, to relieve the stress on yards and parrals, and straps and whips were prepared, and laid aside, for use as preventer braces should the necessity arise. In these preparations on the Fuller we had a foresight of what to expect when off the dreaded Cape; at the same time we were certain that no vessel was ever better or more intelligently groomed for heavy weather.

These preparations carried us well down to the latitude of the River Plate; here we were warned by the wise ones to expect some weather, which was not long in coming.

Our watch had just gone below at midnight, when a sou'wester zipped in from the distant land, a live whole gale, sweetened with the breath of the Patagonian prairies that stretched for leagues beneath its origin. The starboard watch started to shorten sail, but by four bells in the midwatch things were getting so far ahead of them that all hands were called, and we tumbled out in the midst of a Bedlam of thrashing gear and general confusion.

Most of the port watch were ordered aloft to take in the fore upper tops'l, thrashing in its gear, while the ship plunged ahead under lower tops'ls, reefed fore course and stays'ls. The starboard watch were completing the job of furling the main tops'l, and with two of our men to help, were about to tackle the mains'l.

I was on the fore upper tops'l yard, with Frenchy at the lee yardarm, and Scouse in between me and the mast. We were just passing the last of the sea gaskets, when the lower tops'l yard seemed to lift up in the air with a sudden jump for we were standing on it, instead of on the footropes of the upper tops'l. A great smashing below us, and the loud impact of something big and hard banging against the yard under our feet, sent us clambering to the upper stick for our lives.

"Lee fore sheet's adrift!" someone shouted. There was a rush in to the mast to escape the heavy spectacle iron, and the cluster of flying clew garnet blocks, and the next thing we knew we were ordered to lay out on the fore yard and secure the sail.

"Lay down and secure fores'l!" came the order from the mate, who stood on the fo'c'sle head, back to the gale, bellowing up his instructions.

Six of us slid down to the top and out on the jumping foreyard. The buntlines and leechlines were finally hauled home, and we got our gaskets about the flying iron. A weird morning light was then breaking in the east and as our watch below was gone, all hands remained on deck for morning coffee after we hove her to under lower tops'ls, fore and main storm stays'ls, and trys'l.

The Pampero gave us a taste of real weather, and came as an actual relief after the long monotonous passage through the trades and doldrums.

CHAPTER VI

LIFE IN THE FO'C'SLE

With livelier weather of the Southern latitudes we were often exercised in tacking and wearing ship, and soon became a very well drilled company, sending the big three-sticker about in record time. The Fuller was lively in stays and with our small crew required the smartest kind of work in handling.

With all hands, including the "idlers," that is, the carpenter, cook and cabin steward, we mustered twenty men forward, hardly a man-o'-war complement, but enough, when driven and directed by superior seamanship, to send the long braces clicking through the sheaves of the patent blocks with a merry chatter.

"Hands about ship!" meant all hands, and the cook at the fore sheet, a time honored station filled by the Celestial with all the importance in the world. It was all the work that Chow ever did on deck and the heathenish glee with which he would "let go" at the proper time, added a certain zest to our movements, particularly as we always hoped to have a sea come over and douse him, which often happened.

At the order, "Ready! Ready!" the gear of the main and cro'jik was thrown down from the pins, clear for running. The command "Ease down the helm!" and the order "Spanker boom amidships!" would quickly follow, the vessel running rapidly into the eye of the wind with everything shaking, and then flat aback.

"Rise tacks and sheets!" and the hands at the clew garnets would sway up on the courses, lifting them clear of the bulwarks. Then all hands would jump like monkeys to the main and cro'jik braces, at the order, "Weather main, lee cro'jik braces!" the second mate, and Chips, standing by to cast off on the other sides. By then, the wind being a point on the weather bow, would come the hearty warning, "Haul taut!" and "Now, boys, mainsail haul!" and the after yards, aback, with the wind on their weather leeches, would spin about, the gear running through the blocks like snakes afire, and the men on deck pawing it in at the pins with feverish haste, belaying as the yards slammed back against the lee swifters on the other tack.

By that time the ship would be practically about, with head yards and head sails aiding in the evolution. As soon as the wind was on the bow, all hands would spring to the lee fore braces. "Haul taut—let go and haul!" thundered the order from aft. Chow would let out a wild yell as he unhitched the fore sheet, and around would go the head yards. Then with jib sheets shifted over, and the spanker eased off, as the tacks were boarded, and the sheets hauled aft, we would pause to get our breath amid the tangle of gear on deck.

"Steady out the bowlines—go below, watch below!" and as the watch below would leave the deck, the order "Lay up the gear clear for running," was the signal for the crowd on deck to get busy while the good ship raced away on the new tack with the wind six points on the bow, a bone in her teeth, and a half point of leeway showing in the wake.

"I hope she holds this tack for a month," was a wish often expressed after one of these frantic evolutions; but such hopes were vain with the variable nature of the strong winds between the Plate and Staten Land, that often sent us about a half dozen times a day, insuring us plenty of healthful exercise and a minimum amount of sleep.

On a wind was the Fuller's best point of sailing, so far as handling was concerned, and she was as easy with the helm as a catboat.

"Keep the weather cloth of the mizzen skys'l shaking," was the order for "full and by," and, under all plain sail, a spoke of the wheel would hold her for hours, with a quarter turn of weather helm.

While our port watch crowd had at first thought themselves the losers in the choice of officers, we soon realized that we were being favored in many ways, mainly because of the superior ability of the mate. He cursed unmercifully and made no bones about cuffing some of the crew in a playful sort of fashion, accompanied with some ribald jest that was meant to carry off the sting of a heavy blow, yet he managed to give us the advantage in most operations requiring all hands. He never hesitated to rouse out the starboard watch an hour ahead of time when a sudden shortening of sail demanded all hands. On these occasions we would work like fury and get below with the loss of a half hour's less sleep than the other watch.

Ill feeling among the men of the second mate's watch became more and more apparent as these tactics continued, and the talk in the fo'c'sle had it that the second mate was afraid to stand up for his rights. He was accordingly blamed for every trouble forward, so far as his own watch was concerned. Things culminated in the wake of a squall that struck us soon after passing the River Plate. The tops'l yards having been lowered to the caps, we were called out near the end of the afternoon watch to man tops'l halyards.

Tony, of the starboard watch, was "beforehand" with Axel and the second mate, on the main tops'l halyards. The rest of the ship's company tailed along the deck from the lead block bending their "beef" on the rope to the refrain of "Ranzo, boys, Ranzo." The deck was slippery with the wet, and a high sea, in which the Fuller wallowed without sail enough to steady her, made footing precarious.

At the order "Belay!" given by the mate, and the sharp "Come up behind" of the second officer, Tony failed to hold on to the rope, and the consequence was a slight loss as the man next the lead block hitched the halyard over the pin.

"You lazy dago —! Why did you let go that rope?" shouted Mr. Stoddard, at the same time making a lunge for Tony and smashing him on the side of the face with his fist. The Dago blocked as best he could, and the second mate drove home a second blow on the Dago's nose. Tony clinched, the blood spurted right and left as they went to the deck, rolling over and over, first one on top and then the other.

"What's this?" shouted the mate. "You dirty bum, — you!" he exploded, jumping into the scramble, while all hands lined up in a threatening attitude, determined to see some sort of fair play.

The mate grabbed Tony by the shirt, as he was on top, and yanked him over. The fact that the Dago had Mr. Stoddard down seemed to rile the mate beyond all reason. He ripped off the shirt of the Dago, and as he threw him across the deck a knife flashed and the mate kicked it into the scuppers, at the same time digging his heavy sea boots into the side of the Italian. The second mate staggered to his feet, a jagged streak of blood on his face where Tony had landed, and his jacket covered with gore.

This scene, common enough perhaps in the annals of the sea, made a deep impression on us. His watchmates carried the Italian forward, and Mr. Stoddard went to his room under the starboard side of the poop. Bad as the feeling had been toward our officers, up to this time it had mingled with it a certain element of respect. Artistic and fluent profanity never hurt anybody, and was almost always justified by some bungling piece of work on the part of the lubbers who "gummed up" their action whenever the least chance was afforded them. But in the attack of the second mate on Tony there was something that looked like deliberate planning, and in the mixup a number of us saw the mate jerk the knife from the Dago's belt.

As Mr. Zerk went aft he picked up the knife from the scuppers. "Irons for you!" he hissed at the Dago as they took him to the fo'c'sle.

But we heard nothing more of it. The captain had come out on deck in the height of the excitement, following the fight, and called the mate to his side; he was wise in his day, and knew a thing or two about the tactics of his officers.

Soon we were tailing again to the halyard, tautening out the leeches of the tops'l, an embittered crowd who but a few moments before were singing at the ropes. Peter, in the meantime, was swabbing up the bloody deck.

One who has never been there can hardly realize the absolute subjugation under which a crew may be placed by their officers, especially if they are on a deep-sea voyage under sail. None of us is perfect, and the humble sailor-man as well as the rest of the human race is prone to take things as easy as the law of the craft on which he sails will allow. This fact, coupled with the hard circumstances under which a small crew is compelled to work a very large ship, may, in a measure, condone the tactics which have for their object the putting the "fear of God" into a crew.

Young officers at times are inclined to be a bit "easy" with men, thinking it will result in more willingness. The more seasoned members of the cloth, men who have sailed as merchant officers for many years, realize that the maintenance of discipline aboard ship is only possible under a rule of autocratic severity, demanding instant obedience to orders and quick punishment for the first departure from the iron bonds. This is as necessary as life itself. The least hesitation, the slightest possibility of argument, when ordering men to places of danger or extreme difficulty, would soon result in disaster.

At sea we have the sharp distinction of caste—the wonderful potency of Mister So and So. He is an officer, if not always a gentleman. To forget the "sir" when addressing one of our mates would have been a dangerous thing to do. In fact only one man ever did it, but he was a Kanaka and signs on later in the story.

In many ships, captain and mates never fail to use their "handles" in addressing each other, and this was so on the Fuller, in fact there was as little familiarity aft, in the personal relations of our officers, as one might expect to find between the representatives of two armies meeting to arrange a truce. And the wonderful part of it was that they left the ship at the end of the voyage as coldly distant as the day they stepped aboard; that is all but the second mate, which is again running me ahead of the lawful progress of this yarn.

However, to get back to the deck and to the lives of our particular little sea community, plowing their painful way over the cruel surface of the many wrinkled ocean, we resented the underhanded flavor of the affair between the mates and Tony. With all the excuses for hazing granted and allowed for, there is nothing to be said in favor of lying about a fight. The imputation of the knife, held as evidence by the mate, and the whole character of the mixup left a bad taste in our mouths for many weeks.

From that time on we entered upon a stage of the voyage notable for its hardship. The officers were drivers from the time we dropped the Navesink Highlands, but for a long time after the incident off the

River Plate, nothing but harsh words found any place in their vocabulary. Weather conditions became more unsettled and severe and one blow followed close on the heels of another. We were in oilskins for weeks at a time, soaked to the skin through the worn out "slickers." Most of us developed salt water boils and one formed on my left wrist, through the constant chafing, and has left a scar to this day, as I had the habit of stopping the sleeves of my coat with a few turns of marline to keep the water out. It was impossible to dry things in the brief four hours below, and the "slop chest" was soon depleted of its stock of new oil clothing. It would be hard to picture a more depressing period than that through which we passed just before entering the real weather off Cape Horn.

In one of our brief periods below some of us were patching the tears in our oilskin coats and pants, resulting from a tussle with the fore upper tops'l, the downhauls having carried away, and left the sail a bellying fighting mess of canvas that four of us were ordered to subdue. Sewing oiled cloth is a poor job, and a loosened finger nail on my right thumb, added nothing to the cheerfulness of the sewing party.

"I'll bet few lads would go to sea if they could look in here for a half hour," I remarked, following a turn of thought that revolved more or less about my own folly.

"An' I don't think you would stay in 'ere or out on deck or anywhere else in this leaky old bucket if you knowed what is afore us," chipped in Jimmy. "You 'aven't never gone round the Horn yet, so God 'elp you, is wot I says."

"Yes, Gott help all of us," said Scouse with a heartfelt grunt from the sea chest at the forward end of the fo'c'sle where he and Joe were playing checkers on a new "heavy weather" board just made by the resourceful Joseph. This board was covered with a piece of canvas, the squares being marked off with pencil. The checkers (and here is where Joe prided himself) were made by sawing pieces from an old broom handle, and Joe had driven a sharp brad through each one of them so they would cling to the canvas on the checker board.

On deck chanties had ceased to enliven us, and we went through the hard watches in a dogged spirit of endurance. We felt like martyrs, a state of mind not altogether without its compensations. In the watch below, in a steaming atmosphere of gloom, lighted by a single oil lamp set into a hole in the partition bulkhead between the two sides of the fo'c'sle, we slept as much as possible, which was not half enough, ate our rude meals, and had our dreams of happier days to come. Each man respected the rights of his neighbors and each bunk was a sort of damp narrow castle. Here in the smelly air, in the dim light, cold, tired, and often hungry, we lived, or rather, existed.

CHAPTER VII

CAPE HORN

On a clear Monday morning, the seventh of February, 1898, to be exact, the captain, after working up his A. M. sight, came on deck and announced a good observation. It was the first time the sun had been visible in some days, and by working a Sumner he found we were on a line cutting close past Cape St. John, on Staten Land, having sailed the ship down between the Falkland Islands and Cape Virgins by dead reckoning. We were coiling down the gear after the morning washdown, and I was busy at the monkey rail when he came on deck with his results, and imparted the above information to the mate in my hearing.

"Better send a hand to the main skys'l yard, Mr. Zerk," said the captain, in conclusion.

I was handy, and at a nod from the mate sprang up the Jacob's ladder and onto the ratlines, going up like a monkey, out over the futtock shrouds, up the topmast rigging, narrowing to the topmast crosstrees, in through the horns of the crosstrees, and on farther up the t'gallant and royal rigging, on the slight rope ladders abaft the mast. Coming to the skysail mast, hardly larger round than the stick of a fair catboat, I shinned up with the help of the halyards, and swung myself astride of the yard, my arm about the aerie pinnacle of the main truck. From my vantage point the sea was truly an inspiring sight; clear as crystal, the limpid air stretched free to the distant horizon without a mist or cloud to mar the panorama of vast blue ocean. I felt as though I had suddenly been elevated to a heaven far above the strife and trouble of the decks below.

For the moment I forgot the object of my climb in the contemplation of the sparkling scene stretching as far as eye could reach. I glanced down to the narrow deck far beneath, white in the sun, the black top of the bulwarks outlining the plan of the ship against the deep blue waters; my eye followed the easy curves of the squared canvas on the main, the great breadth of the yards extending to port and starboard, and I wondered that so small a ship could support such an avalanche of sail as bowled along under my feet. Aft, a foamy wake stretched for a mile or two, for we were sailing at a fairish speed with the wind from the north, a point on the port quarter.

I saw the men flaking down the fore tops'l halyards, clear for running, on the top of the forward house, and I saw the mate watching me from the weather fore pinrail, his head thrown back as he gazed aloft; something told me to get busy, and I looked far ahead to the south.

A faint blue streak on the horizon held my eyes. Accustomed to the sight of land from out at sea, through my voyages in the schoolship; still I hesitated to name it land. We were sixty-two days out, and land looked strange. Again I brought my sight to bear upon the distant skyline ahead; there was no mistaking the dim outline of land rising from the sea at a point immediately to the south of us and reaching westward.

"Land ho!" I hailed the deck.

"Where away?" came the voice of Captain Nichols.

"A point on the lee bow, sir!"

"All right! Lay down!" shouted the mate, evidently not intending that I should further enjoy my lofty perch on the skysail yard.

We raised the land rapidly, the breeze increasing slightly as the day advanced. At noon Staten Land was visible from the deck, and by eight bells in the afternoon watch we were sailing past the bold shores, some ten miles distant, and drawing the land well abeam. Running south for a good offing, and taking in our light sails with the coming of darkness, we hauled our wind to the starboard quarter at the end of the last dog watch and headed bravely for old "Cape Stiff."

Captain Nichols might have ventured through the Strait of Le Maire, with the weather we were having, though at the best it is taking chances to keep the land too close aboard when in the troubled latitudes of Terra Del Fuego. Countless ships, with the fine Duchesse de Berry among the last of them, have ground their ribs against the pitiless rocks that gird those coasts. However, we were enjoying the rarest of Cape Horn weather—sunshine, fair wind, and a moderate sea.

For the first time in many weary days we livened things up with a chantey as we swigged away on the braces and tautened every stitch of canvas with well stretched sheets and halyards.

Jimmy Marshall had just started "Whiskey for my Johnnie," and the captain came forward on the break of the poop and joined in the chorus in a funny, squeaky voice—but none of us dared laugh at him. He was so delighted with the progress we were making and the chance that we might slip by the "corner" in record time, that nothing was too good for us. The mate came down from his high horse and with Mr. Stoddard and Chips, who had just finished their supper and were stepping out on deck, to join them, the full after guard took up the refrain—and the words rose in a great volume of deep sea song.

"Oh, whiskey—my Johnnie;
Yes, whiskey made me sell my coat
Whiskey, my Johnnie.
Oh, whiskey's what keeps me afloat,
Oh whiskey for my Johnnie."

When we pumped her out that night at the main pump, for the ship was almost on an even keel, we noted the skipper had begun to stump the quarter deck in a very excited way, constantly ducking up and down the companion, and scanning the horizon with an anxious eye. Cape pigeons were circling close to the ship with an endless chatter, and far above us swung a huge, dun-colored fulmar gull, its white belly clean against the grey sky.

"There is something doing with the glass," remarked Frenchy, eyeing the skipper. "We'll have some weather to look out for before long," and all of us watched the gull with fascinated eyes. Jimmy and Brenden agreed with Frenchy that we were in for heavy weather.

But in spite of these dire predictions, and in spite of a "red dawn," the day broke and continued fair, and we were again regaled with a glimpse of land, jagged somber peaks, jutting into the sky to the north like the cruel teeth of a ragged saw, grey blue above the far horizon.

I was aft flaking down the mizzen tops'l halyards on the morning following the landfall when Captain Nichols stumped past me from the break of the poop to the companion. He had been up all night, and the continuation of fine weather evidently pleased and surprised him. He had a pair of binoculars in his hand, and, in passing, he stopped and offered the glasses to me, pointing to the southernmost promontory, a cold blue knob rising from the sea.

"That's Cape Horn over there, Felix. Take a good look at it. You may never see it again, if you were born lucky."

Almost staggered by this sudden good fortune, I brought the captain's glasses in focus on the dreaded cape, my whole being thrilled with the pleasure of looking through those excellent binoculars at that distant point of rock, the outpost of the New World, jutting far into the southern ocean. I doubt if the gallant old Dutchman, Schouten, who first "doubled" it, experienced half the exhilaration that I did on first beholding that storied headland. At four bells in the morning watch I went to the wheel, and while the watch swabbed down the decks after the morning washdown, I was privileged to look at the Cape out of the corner of my eye, between times; keeping the "lubber's line" of the compass bowl on sou'west by sou', for the skipper had shaped a course a point or so further off shore, as the currents had evidently set us in toward the land during the night and he wished to keep his safe offing.

**Martin**

The wind in the meantime had veered round to west-nor'-west, blowing directly off the land and with increasing force. The light sails were taken in again, and by eight bells we were under t'gans'ls, upper and lower tops'ls, reefed fores'l, reefed mains'l, spanker, jib and topmast stays'ls.

As I left the wheel and went forward, I determined to attempt a pencil sketch of Cape Horn, the weather being too dull for a photograph, even if the land were not too distant. The result, after some trials, and the loss of my breakfast, which was nothing, resulted in a fair representation of what we saw of the Cape, and I turned into my bunk with a feeling of satisfaction. After all, it was worth a good deal to have actually set eyes upon the Horn.

When we turned out at one bell, for dinner, we found the wind had veered farther to the west, we were sailing by the wind with the starboard tacks aboard, the cold spray from a rising sea, breaking over the fo'c'sle head, and spattering against the fo'c'sle door.

Jimmy sat up and rubbed his eyes as the watch was called and swore gently under his breath. Brenden went out on deck to take a look at the weather. "Hell, we got it now. I have seen this before. D'you feel the ice?" he asked.

Indeed we all felt the drop in temperature, and the short snappy jerk of the ship, as she met the new direction of the sea, was anything but pleasant.

Coffee was served out to us that noon instead of lime juice, and the warmth was welcome; it helped wash down the last cooked meal that Chow was able to prepare for ten days.

Mustering on deck at eight bells, we found we were driving south under a leaden sky. Cape Horn, still dimly visible, was soon shut off, vanishing in a cloud cap over the land astern. We were sailing due south, the wind having headed us, and at four bells, the wind rapidly increasing in violence, the starboard watch turned out to help in shortening down. We at once took in the t'gans'ls, mains'l, and jib, and these were followed in quick succession by other canvas until at eight bells we had the Fuller stripped to her lower tops'ls, close reefed main upper tops'l, and storm stays'ls. The sea rose to mammoth proportions, fetching as it did from the very edge of the Antarctic ice barrier.

The canvas aloft soon became stiff with ice and all gear on the ship was coated with frozen rain, as we were swept by a succession of rain and hail storms. At nightfall we were hove to, on the starboard tack under goose winged main lower tops'l, reefed main trys'l, and storm stays'l. The oil tank forward was dripping its contents on the sea, and two oil bags were slung from the fore and main weather channels.

The storm, for the wind had now increased to fully sixty miles an hour, held steady from the west until midnight. Then it suddenly went to nor'west, and in the squalls, when the wind rose to hurricane force, the Fuller lay over on her beam ends. A vicious cross sea added its danger to the situation. All hands were then on deck, remaining aft near the mizzen rigging. The fo'c'sle, galley, and forward cabin were awash. Four men braced themselves at the spokes of the wheel, under the eye of the second mate, and relieving tackles were hooked to ease the "kick" of the tiller. Preventer braces and rolling tackles, got up earlier in the day, were hove taut to steady the heavy spars aloft. All loose gear was streaming to leeward, washing in the sea, through the open scuppers and freeing ports. A fierce boiling of white phosphorescent wave caps lit the sea as it broke over the ship, intensifying the black pandemonium overhead. The sleet-laden spume shot over the prostrate vessel in a continuous roar, drowning all attempts at shouting of orders.

It was during the wild but fascinating hours of this night that I realized the high quality of seamanship that had prepared us for an ordeal such as we were going through. The consummate skill with which the great wooden craft was being handled came home to me with a force that could not be denied. How easily a bungling lubber might have omitted some precaution, or carried sail improperly, or have done, or not done, the thousand things that would have spelled disaster!

The captain and mate stood at the lee of the mizzen mast, each with a turn of the tops'l sheets about him, and hitched over the monkey rail. The rest of us, crouching at the lee of the cabin trunk, knee deep in the water when she went over in the heavier squalls, held our places wondering what turn things would take next. Looking through one of the after cabin ports, on my way to the wheel, I saw Chow and Komoto, the cabin boy, packing a box by the light of the small lamp swinging in its gimbals. They were evidently getting ready to leave—where to—themselves and their gods alone knew.

All things have an end, and the Stygian blackness of the night gave way to gray streaks of dawn that broke upon us, revealing a scene of utmost desolation. A note of order was given to the wild confusion of the gale-wracked fabric, when Chips, his lanky figure skimming along the life line, and his sounding rod sheltered under his long oil coat, ventured to the main fife rail to sound the well. As for the crew, we were soaked with salt water and frozen to the marrow. The main lower tops'l had blown from the bolt ropes during the night; we never missed it until morning. Twenty feet of the lee bulwark—the port side—was gone, and a flapping rag of canvas at the main hatch told us that the tarpaulin was torn. Looking forward through the whistle of wind and spume that cut across the sharply tilted rigging, the scene was one of terrific strife, as though some demon ruler of the sea had massed his forces, and was making a desperate drive for the destruction of the wooden handiwork of man upon which he dared to venture over those forbidden wastes.

## CHAPTER VIII

### ROUNDING THE HORN

No matter how miserable one may be, action of some kind always comes as a relief. Our hard lot on the Fuller was positively made more bearable by the added hardships of the storm, and when the night was past we were glad to force our chilled limbs and hungry bellies to some sort of effort. Anything was better than to hang to the mizzen rigging and slowly freeze to death. The torn hatch tarpaulin was a serious matter. The merchant service holds no higher duty, where passengers are not carried, than the duty toward cargo. This is often forgotten by men who lack the true traditions of the sea. But our officers were well alive to the importance, not only of bringing our ship around the Horn, but of bringing her cargo through in good condition.

The mate, followed by Axel, Brenden, Frenchy, and Mike, a husky, well-set-up sailor of the starboard watch, went into the waist and worked their way along the deck at great peril. After much trouble they managed to wedge down the flapping canvas, which was under a constant deluge of blue water, whole seas coming aboard in quick succession.

By noon the weather abated somewhat, and we got the ship under fore and mizzen lower tops'ls, and close reefed main upper tops'l. Before nightfall we had sent down what remained of the main lower tops'l, and bent a new sail. That afternoon we experienced an adventure fraught with much excitement to us of the port watch. The jib having worked loose from the gaskets, by constant dipping into the sea, as the ragged crests of blue water buried the bowsprit and jibboom, six of us were ordered out to secure the sail by passing a three-inch manila line around the sail and boom.

Brenden, Scouse, Frenchy and I were on the weather side, and Joe and Martin went out on the boom to leeward. The job was almost finished, two seas had already drenched us, and we were chilled with the dip in the cold water, when the ship rose to a heavy roller, her bow lifted high into the eye of the wind, and then plunged down into the deep trough between two seas. The momentum was so great that she failed to rise quickly enough, and her jibboom stabbed right into the heart of the onrushing wall of cold blue water, regardless of the half dozen luckless wretches clinging to the furled canvas with all their might. The great sea went on over us, thundering down on the fo'c'sle head, and rushing aft along the deck in a noisy white cataract of foam. When she shook free we were left clinging to the jibboom like drowned rats, that is, all of us but Joe.

Aft on the poop, the mate heard our cries, and, springing to the lee rail, he yanked a bight of line from a pin and hove it overboard, catching Joe just in time as he rose close along side. When she heeled to leeward, ready hands hauled the half-drowned Joe on board. Captain Nichols had come up on the first cry, and taking Joe into the cabin, he poured out a liberal hooker of whiskey from the medicine chest. The funny part of the whole thing was that Joe was more thankful for the drink than for his escape from certain death, for we never could have lowered a boat in that sea.

We got a watch below that night, and the cook managed to heat some coffee, but cold salt beef and hard tack were all that the kids contained when we went below for supper. Wrapped in our damp clothes we managed to peg in a few hours of necessary sleep. Life, for a week afterward, was not worth living, unless one held some latent strain of the old berserker flowing through his veins. It was a fight, and the elements charged us and flanked us in midnight fury, increasingly cold as we edged farther to the south in our attempt to round the meridian of Cape Horn.

In latitude 56° 29' S. and longitude 68° 42' W. from Greenwich, about sixty sea miles S. W. by W. from Cape Horn, lies the island of Diego Ramirez, a weather-worn rock jutting from the black waters of the sub-antarctic. Ten days after fetching away from the Cape, we beat south and sighted this grim sentinel, the outpost of the tempest and the gale—ten days of such seagoing as seldom falls to the men who nowadays go down to the sea in steamers.

Under conditions of the kind we experienced, every man was put to the test, and his worth as a member of the crew clearly established. Fortunately for us, and for the races representative in our small company—of which we boasted quite a few—no strain of yellow fear developed during the days and nights when the work aloft called for the performance of duty dangerous in the extreme. Not one of us but had been shipmates with men lost overboard, or maimed for life in accidents to sail or spars. Never was there a moment's hesitation to lay aloft, or out on a swaying bucking yard in the black cover of night, to grapple with canvas hard and unruly. No work was too trying, and no hours of labor too long. We thought nothing of the eternal injustice of a fate that sent us out to sea to fight for our very lives on a ship far too big for so small a crew to handle safely, if indeed any crew of mere men could ever safely handle so large a ship.

Never was there a suspicion of holding back, and through it all, the discipline of the disgruntled warmer latitudes was dropped and orders were quickly obeyed as a matter of course; yes, as a matter of self-preservation. The disgusting profanity of warmer climes was laid in the discard for a while, and we were men doing men's work.

Wet and hunger were the rule; to be chilled with the cold was normal, and our salvation was the constant struggle with the working of the ship. Accidents occurred, and old Jimmy lay in his bunk with his right arm in a bandage from a dislocation due to a fall on the slippery deck. This was roughly set by the captain with the help of the mate and the carpenter. The galley fire had hardly been lighted an hour at a time as the seas flooded everything forward. Cold salt junk—from the harness casks to the kids—comprised the mainstay of our ration, not to mention the daily whack of mouldy, weevily hard tack. Had it not been for an occasional steaming hot can of slops called tea and coffee, we should have surely perished.

Our oilskins were in shreds, boots leaked, and every stitch of clothing in the ship was damp, except when dried by the heat of our bodies. Had I been told of this before starting out—well, I suppose I would not have believed it—and, when I say that during it all we had a fairly good time and managed to crack jokes and act like a lot of irresponsible asses, it goes to prove that man was born to be kicked; be he on a sailing ship around the Horn, on the hard edge of the Arctic littoral, or in the bloody trenches; fate is always there to step in and deliver the necessary bumping.

When south of Diego Ramirez, we passed the American ship Shenandoah, Captain "Shotgun" Murphy, bound from 'Frisco to Liverpool, with a cargo of grain. She was racing two English four-masted barks, and we were told that she dropped her hook in the Mersey a month ahead of them.

When sighting the Shenandoah we were close to the wind on the starboard tack, standing about due west; the Shenandoah was running free, with the wind two points abaft her port beam, carrying everything to t'gans'ls, stays'ls, and jigger, a truly magnificent sight and the first sail we had seen close aboard since leaving the Tam O'Shanter off Sandy Hook.

When abeam we exchanged the courtesies of the sea, dipping our ensign from the monkey gaff, and running aloft our "number," the gay string of lively colored flags, pennant, and burgee—J. V. G. B. of the International Code—the universal language of the sea.

The Shenandoah also ran up her number, a spot of color in the beautiful spread of white cotton canvas on her yards. The sky was dull, but the clear air set her off with cameo like distinctness against the grey background of the horizon. The deep blue of the sea smothered white under her bow and, as she rolled gracefully, the yellow gleam of her copper flashed along under her sleek black side, or else we caught a glimpse of her white decks over the line of her bulwarks, as she dipped to leeward.

We had sighted the sail ahead, and, having our starboard tacks aboard, were accorded the right of way. Hitchen, of the other watch, gathered with a group of us on the fo'c'sle head to watch the stranger drive past us. Being somewhat of a scholar, the little Englishman delivered himself of the following verse:

"If close hauled on the starboard tack,
No other ship can cross your track;
If on the port tack you appear,
Ships going free must all keep clear;
While you must yield when going free,
To sail close hauled or on your lee.
And, if you have the wind right aft,
Keep clear of every sailing craft."

In obedience to this Law of the Sea, the four-masted ship Shenandoah starboarded a point, passing the Fuller well to windward, and some five miles south of the Island of Diego Ramirez.

CHAPTER IX

INTO THE PACIFIC

After close to two and a half months at sea we had reached the turning point on the long course to Honolulu. The Atlantic with its trials lay behind us, and just in our wake the sullen waters of the Horn lashed themselves against the coast of Terra Del Fuego. Ahead stretched the broad Pacific, greatest of oceans, and fraught with every angle of adventure that comes to the men who sail. Indeed the sailing of a great ship like the Fuller is the rarest kind of sport from the standpoint of seamanship, where every stitch of canvas is made to draw to its full capacity in every wind that blows. From the cold latitudes of the Cape up to abreast of Valparaiso, we had good lively sailing. Great rollers followed us, for the winds were mostly fair, and, as the seas overtook us and expended themselves to the north, we drove onward, cutting down the latitude in record time; the cape pigeons were left behind, but several albatross formed a convoy almost to the edge of Capricorn.

During these weeks of strenuous weather a favored few of us were told off to lay up sennet for use in making chafing mats, and as "service" on the backstays, where subject to the wear of gear. We would perch ourselves on the coils of rope stowed on the fore hatch tarpaulin under the fo'c'sle head, where we were sheltered from the weather and at the same time within easy call from aft.

Frenchy was the leading sailor in these arts and taught us to lay up round, flat, and French sennet. The less skilled men busied themselves in making nettles and foxes, using the primitive "spinning jinney," and rubbing down the small stuff with canvas to "smooth" it before balling. Here, too, we were initiated into the fine points of marling spike work, Frenchy, Brenden, and Jimmy Marshall showing the less knowing ones how to turn in many a splice and knot. Turk's heads of three, five, and seven strands were made, and the more difficult series of four, six and eight strands were mastered by some of us. Jimmy worked a wonderful set of manropes for the after companion, crosspointing them in red, white and blue, and topping them with rose knots.

I was delighted to pick up a vast amount of interesting and useful knowledge about the different knots and hitches used at sea. How many sailors today can properly cast a carrick bend, turn in a mariner's splice, or a Flemish eye, or work a cringle into a Bolt rope? Hitchen, of the starboard watch, taught us how to make the English bag knot, an intricate and beautiful formation cast in the bight of a line.

Our work under the fo'c'sle head got all hands started, and during many a dismal wet dog watch we practiced the forming of every knot from the bowline down; Peter, the boy, and myself trying to outdo each other in the variety of our achievements. Frenchy taught us a new way to form that "king of knots," the bowline, in which the loop is passed through the gooseneck twice, forming a double loop, a most useful knot employed in the French Navy. When a man is to be lowered over side, he sits in one of the loops and the other is passed under his arm pits, the gooseneck coming against his chest. His weight tautens the part under the arms, and it is impossible for a man to drop out of this bowline, even though he becomes unconscious.

In this manner much of the unrecorded lore of the sea was passed on to us in the Fuller as the same things have been handed down through the ages since the Phoenicians, the Norsemen, and the more ancient sailors of Cathay first rigged their barks, fashioning their bends and hitches in the same manner as the sailors of today. Where the marvelous knots originated, no one can tell. Who invented them, no one knows; but we do know that the rope craft of the sea is standard and defies improvement. It takes time to learn the knots, bends, hitches, and splices; how much longer it must have taken to discover them can only be imagined.

In time, much of this will be entirely superseded by wire and steel, as indeed all lower standing rigging is already of wire. But turnbuckles and riveted plates are part of the metal ships, unyielding and stiff, that buckle the hollow steel masts, or sheer the channel plates clean from the hull, when wrenched by the resistless power of the sea.

In the days of wood, of tough live oak, and tarred hemp lanyards, with their "give" and "spring," the old style rigging knots and splices endured for thousands of years. Can steel and steam resist the hands of time as well?

On the Fuller we were taught that everything had to be done just so to be "shipshape and Bristol fashion," as the old sea phrase has it. It was always:

Worm and parcel with the lay,
Then turn and serve the other way.

And the humblest tools have had their form decreed since the art of seamanship began. The serving board and the serving mallet used by Noah; the fid, the marling spike, the sewing palm, and the caulking iron, are the ultimate tools of the most ancient handicraft; the art of building and rigging ships. We used all of these implements with industry as the blustery weather sent us up from the Horn to Honolulu. We saw how able sailors fit a cringle to the tough four-stranded hempen bolt ropes on the storm canvas; we learned the proper way to strop a block, with the splice where it belongs, as every sailor knows, and the throat seizing frapped and hitched in sailor fashion.

The hours spent under the fo'c'sle head during those days of the voyage were not so tedious. The Horn was behind us and the prospect of fine weather ahead. Yarning was always going on, and often we spent the dog watches in making fancy plaitings and knottings for sea chest covers and the like. I realized that such men as Marshall, Old Smith, Hitchen, Axel, Brenden, and Frenchy were of a dwindling breed, soon to be as rare as the makers of stone axes, or the seamen of the Roman galleys.

One other sailor of the ship's company asked odds of no one in the range of his knowledge of the sea. Whatever else we may have thought of him, we were forced to acknowledge Mr. Zerk a seaman of the most accomplished sort. Versed in the art of wire splicing and up to every dodge in sailmaking and rigging, he combined the ability of the marling spike man with the gift of the larger seamanship involved in the handling of a vessel under all conditions. If his eye ever lights on this, and I hope it will, I herewith accord to him the full measure of my admiration, for the combination of these two types of sailor is rare; as rare as the few remaining ships of the school that brought him forth.

The Fuller was a wooden vessel, Bath built, and coppered, not with the beautiful "red copper" we read about in Clark Russell, but with a composition resembling brass, tough, yellow, and antifouling; a less expensive sheathing than the pure copper, and, to my mind, every bit as good a color, the bright yellow, between the deep blue sea and the black hull, striking a pleasing line that glints like gold when the sun just hits it at the proper angle.

Our ship was a full-bodied model, really a medium clipper, surprisingly sharp, and with a clean run aft that gave her a handy pair of heels in any kind of a favorable wind. Like most ships "of a certain age," the old girl was troubled with her timbers and joints. These had an uncomfortable way of sliding over each other and complaining in a truly agonizing manner.

"She has lots of 'give' to her," one of the men remarked on our running into the first sea after leaving port.

The working of the vessel's timbers kept her bilge "sweet" by admitting a liberal quantity of nice cool sea water seeping in all the way from the garboard strake to the channels, a circumstance that necessitated constant pumping, back breaking labor that in heavy weather continued during the whole of the twenty-four hours, with two hands bending over the lee bilge pump. The wheel, the lookout at night, and the bilge pump, were taken in rotation by all hands. For back breaking, soul destroying labor, nominate the bilge pump. I had a standing offer in the fo'c'sle to stand two wheels for one bilge pump, Scouse and Fred and Martin being my best customers until I was dated up so far in advance on the steering that I had to take this on as well as the pumping, which came along oftener as it called for two men.

In the matter of small trading we did a thriving business in the fo'c'sle, some of us even branching out into foreign trade with the starboard watch. I was the one to introduce this practice on board the Fuller, a relic of my schoolship days, when pools were formed in the different messes and five and ten rations of cold corned beef traded off for potatoes, or potatoes and butter paid out as rental for the use of the precious frying pans of which there were a few on board. When I worked out a system of credits for different kinds of grub on the Fuller it was found to be a source of diversion and made possible some adjustment along the lines of personal taste, in the matter of our meals. We had stock fish every once in a while, no doubt as a concession to the Scandinavian contingent, to be found in every ship that sails the seas. I invariably passed off my share of this delicacy to Fred or Martin and would be credited with their rations of apple jack, a stew of musty dried apples; or I would contract for half of their whack of lime juice and vinegar.

Mr. Zerk, with whom I always was a favorite, that is until we got to Honolulu, occasionally gave me a jar of preserves, of which he had a large store. These were home-made pickles and jams, and when brought into the fo'c'sle caused quite a commotion.

"Rats with 'im and 'is rotten marmerlade," declared Jimmy in great dudgeon when I brought forward the first fruits of my "stand in."

"Eat it yerself but don't ast no self-respectin' man to touch it," was the sarcastic way in which the haughty Marshall voiced his sentiments. "Wot do you say?" he demanded, glaring about the fo'c'sle to see if anyone dared dispute him.

"Righto," piped up Joe. "That rotten skunk aft has poisoned the stuff, I'll bet."

"No, it's good," I declared, dipping in with the tip of my sheath knife. It was a jar of very red cherry jam. It also had a very pleasant aroma as well as a pleasing taste. I purposely took a second very large helping and could see that the temptation to fall was great.

"Here, Frenchy, don't eat any, now. Just taste it, perhaps it does taste a little funny." Frenchy tasted. "I don't know. It does taste funny," he said.

"Here, gimme a piece o' tack," and Joe was sampling the jam very liberally.

In a moment all hands, including Jimmy, were tasting it, and all declared it tasted funny. As a matter of fact it did taste very funny if we accepted apple jack as a standard.

As the last smear of jam was cleaned from the jar the hypercritical Jimmy had the nerve to remark, "That was the rottenest marmerlade I ever tasted."

However, after that no questions were raised when I brought a donation forward, though to tell the truth these treats were scarce, as the mate's private stock ran out long before we got to Honolulu.

CHAPTER X

CABIN AND FO'C'SLE

Captain Nichols was a good deal of a mystery to us forward. He seldom came on deck except for a few moments of a fine morning, when he would bob up, "take a sight" and stump deliberately down the companion to the chronometer, counting the seconds out loud on his way. At noon he "took the sun" alone in solitary scientific grandeur; only once do I remember seeing the mate take an observation. One noon, I was at the wheel at the time, our first officer came aft shortly before eight bells, carrying an ancient "hog yoke." His sleeves were rolled up, and a greasy shine on the arc of his instrument told of efforts at polishing. Somehow he could not get the sun to behave, for the curious relic seemed sadly in need of adjustment. He retired in disgust when the captain "made eight bells," and stumped forward without answering, when the skipper asked him what he had for altitude.

Tipping me the shadow of a wink, the captain went below to work up the position.

The captain on the other hand was quite regular in his methods of navigation. He watched the course closely, having a particularly fine tell-tale compass swung beneath the skylight in his private cabin, as every one of us had evidence by the uncanny way in which he would pop up out of the companion at the most unheard of hours of the night and walk quickly to the binnacle, and seldom except when the helmsman was off his course.

I met the captain a number of years afterward in Philadelphia. He was then in command of a fine steamer and I was second mate of another vessel of the same line. In the course of a pleasant visit talking over old times on the Fuller, I asked him how he managed to keep such close watch on the navigation of his ship without any particular assistance from his officers.

"By staying awake nights, sir," was his laconic reply.

At any rate, whatever his method, Captain Nichols knew pretty well where we were at all times.

On the old ships, and the Fuller was a very good example of her class, the master was housed in truly palatial style. On our ship the captain's quarters were spacious, taking up two-thirds of the cabin and running the whole width of the vessel, and fore and aft from the mizzen mast to the lazarette. The captain's stateroom was most commodious; he enjoyed the comfort of slumber in a large mahogany bunk built after the lines of a Dutch galiot, as broad as it was long. This room took up the space of three ordinary staterooms on the starboard quarter. At the foot of the companion was a cozy after cabin luxuriously paneled in mahogany between fluted columns of the same wood picked out with gold leaf at base and capital. Other rare woods of a lighter shade were inlaid on the center panels, and the whole furnishing of cushioned lockers, round table, and skylight, with its tell-tale compass, book and chart cases, gave it the air of a costly yacht cabin.

His bathroom, connected with a large salt-water tank, filled each morning by the deck washers, was on the port side, and two spare staterooms opened into the after cabin from port. A bulkhead divided these private quarters from the forward or mess cabin, off which were the pantry, storeroom, steward's room and slop chest. The mates were berthed in two staterooms on either side of the after cabin, but their doors opened into a sort of thwart ship vestibule running the width of the after cabin just below the break of the poop. The mizzen mast came down through the after end of the mess cabin, and a large brass lamp swung in gimbals just below the long skylight.

A repeating rifle in a rack above the captain's bunk, and two revolvers on each side of the chart table, composed the offensive battery. A long brass telescope reposed in a rack in the companion, and at the foot of this was slung a very good mercurial barometer. Typical of the best traditions of the sea, such were the quarters of the after guard.

Forward we were not done so well. The fo'c'sle took up the forward part of the deck house and was sheltered from the force of the sea and wind by the high break of the fo'c'sle head. These quarters were divided by a bulkhead running fore and aft, to separate the watches, and plain unpainted bunks lined the sides. Light was afforded by a poor lamp set in a hole in the wall between the two sides, a cheap expedient thought of, no doubt, by some thrifty soul who knew that this was far better than the traditional whale oil, or slush dip, of the hoary days when sailor men were shoved below decks in reeking quarters just over the fore peak.

However, the fo'c'sle was home to us. We lived there and had our being amid an atmosphere not altogether bad; what we lacked in conveniences we made up for in ingenuity. Above a few of the bunks were rough calendars marked on the woodwork, some of them from previous voyages. Brenden kept track of our position by notching each day on the scantling overhead. Under these marks he had signs that stood for the N. E. trades, the Line, the S. E. trades, etc. All sorts of little shelves were rigged up to hold tobacco, matches, ditty bags, well thumbed books, old newspapers, and what not. Lines of marline were stretched above the bunks for drying clothes.

The scheme of society within the sacred walls of our castle was a sort of despotic democracy. The ruling class, the able seamen of the watch, Marshall, Frenchy, Brenden, were the arbiters of all matters temporal and mundane. This was by mutual consent and should be so. In addition to this, Jimmy was the autocrat of the crowd and ruled us with an iron hand, though there was not a man forward but could have hove him overboard.

Scouse, after the balance of power had been reestablished in the conflict with Joe, became one of the common folks again, and was glad of it. The bunks were arranged in order of desirability, the able seamen taking the best bunks on the upper tier and near the two ports or the lamp. Australia and I were about on a par as far as social standing went, and when it came to talking about the mines or discussing matters other than those relating to the sea, we often took the center of the stage.

Martin, who had been a wood turner in his youth, and Fred, who was a good average sailor with a discharge from the Revenue Cutter Service, generally acted as spear carriers in our little fo'c'sle comedy. They were excellent eaters, both of them, standing well up in the forefront with Scouse and Joe; the rottenest cracker hash or the most greasy salt pork never phased them. To the mate these men were a constant inspiration in his flights of blasphemy, and hardly a day passed but that he vented his wrath on one of them.

Never once during the entire voyage did any member of the crew miss a single bit of personal property. Add to this the fact that the general moral tone of conversation among us was far above the average of men who would consider themselves superior, and we have to at least respect the crew of the Fuller as they respected themselves.

Chips, a melancholy Norwegian, a long, lanky, cadaverous knight of the caulking iron and the carpenter's bench, berthed in a little room next to the lamp locker. He was kept busy sounding the well, and making the constant repairs that a well groomed wooden ship requires. In the intervals of this duty he looked after the hatch tarpaulins sheltering the precious cargo, tended the running lights, served out the daily whack of water, oiled the tiller tackles, and sat down to dinner with the second mate. Poor Chips! A gentleman of the lower caste, eating aft and living forward. He was a good fellow, but far too gloomy for us, who were of the "people," light hearted ourselves and ready to crack a joke at the least opportunity.

Chips had one other duty which he performed twice on our voyage round the Horn. On these occasions he was called upon to "salt the masts." A small plug was taken out of the lower mast heads, and salt filled into the hollow core of these great "sticks." The fore and main masts were "built up," that is, made up of four quadrantal pieces, scarfed full length, and banded by stout iron hoops. At the outside juncture of the built-up pieces they were beveled, forming the "chapels" of the mast, the latter being painted white and giving the lower masts on the fore and main a checkerboard appearance.

Each morning of the voyage, and particularly during the fair weather part of it, we were exercised at the washdown. This is more than a mere part of the work at sea; it is an established institution, a sacred rite that is carried on through all conditions of wind and weather. In the tropics the washdown is a pleasure, and also a necessity, as it alone keeps the decks tight and the ship sanitary.

A "water spar" would be rigged over the side to leeward at a point in the waist abreast of the main hatch. A clump block and a single whip with a canvas water bucket, the rim weighted with a ring of lead, was used to haul aboard the water which was dumped into a deck barrel. Coir brooms, wooden buckets, and much slopping about in bare feet would usher in the day, no part of the deck being neglected.

The routine was: At four o'clock in the morning, "Get your gear on the pins," everything being laid up clear of the deck. "Rig water spar," and then old Chow would run out of the galley with a bag of hard bread and a big can of slops, while the Japanese steward would hurry along the deck with a cup and saucer; coffee—cabin style, for the refreshment of the mate, who would sing out: "Get your coffee," and for a few minutes we would all sit on the main hatch, in fine weather, or crowd in the lee of the forward house if it was stormy, and dip into the steaming chicory.

Then—"Get out your washdeck gear! Wash down!" and the day's work would begin.

CHAPTER XI

CLEANING HOUSE AND A CELEBRATION

The rough passage around the Horn—seagoing with the bark on—worked the discontent out of our systems, and with the return of fine weather, all hands cheered up and life became more and more worth living. The dog watches were lively, with hotly contested arguments on all topics under heaven.

The less the debaters knew about a subject, the more they would have to say about it; resembling in this regard large numbers of more sophisticated folk ashore. Some of the discussions would last for days, being carried on as a serial story, from dog watch to dog watch, with overflow sessions on deck at night. As none of the contenders would ever budge an inch from their positions, the points at issue always remained undecided except in the fish argument, which was settled by the mate.

For a long time Martin, Joe and Scouse indulged in heated discussion as to whether fish was meat, or whether it was something else. Joe contended for the negative, that fish was not meat, while Martin and Scouse insisted that fish and meat were the same thing.

Joe had two against him, but being quicker with his tongue he was able to hold Scouse and Martin pretty well in check.

"If fish ain't meat, wot is it?" demanded Martin. "Is it wegetables, or wot?"

This always stumped Joe, but he stuck to his guns and came back stronger each time: "It's fish, that's wot it is, F-I-S-H—FISH!" his voice rising above everything else in the heat of argument.

The debate finally closed in a particularly violent session that continued as our side went aft to muster in the second dog watch.

"Fish you say!" shouted the mate at the unheard of disrespect on the part of Joe, who was frothing at the mouth in the defense of his contention. "I'll fish you, you thick-headed ass," and as Joe woke up to the fact that a new champion had come into the field, the whole watch broke into a laugh at the sequel. "Fish, is it? Well, I'll fish you good and proper. Get a pot of slush and rub down the mizzen topmast. Drop a spot, and you stay on deck tomorrow forenoon, you fisherman!" The last with biting sarcasm.

Joe lay aloft with his slush pot, and as a bright moon gave him plenty of light at his work, it also enabled the mate to watch him closely. However, this ended the argument, much to the satisfaction of all of us, for it was a bit wearing.

Jimmy Marshall had a large dog-eared Bible in his possession; a red stamp on the title page read as follows: "Property of Seamen's Bethel, Sydney. Do not take from chapel." While lying up with his arm in a sling, having been tossed between the spare main yard and the after bitts, by a sea, he delved industriously into the lore of the good book; and when he was back on deck again Jimmy refused to chantey to the tune of "Whiskey," and his verses, when singing a rope to "Molly Brown," were painfully proper.

Each night in the dog watch he insisted on reading from the Old Testament, starting at the very beginning. Jimmy had a pair of steel-rimmed spectacles, and to further his missionary work, he changed bunks with Scouse, so that he could be directly under the lamp, while the big red-head moved into the best bunk in the fo'c'sle right next to an open port.

Jimmy worked his way through Genesis and got well started on Exodus by the time we picked up the S. E. trades. His pronunciation of the hard names was truly wonderful and required much careful wiping of his spectacles. By the time he was within hailing distance of Leviticus we were again approaching the doldrums and once more we unbent our storm canvas and shifted into the easy weather sails.

Australia, one of the most consistent chronologists of the fo'c'sle, working by the brad-hole-and-peg method, using the stumps of burnt matches, pegged a hole around which he had scratched a circle.

"The 'dead horse' is worked off," announced Australia, as we turned out for breakfast one morning, springing a surprise, as it had been more than a week since the subject was broached last in the fo'c'sle. March 5th, three months since leaving the wharf at South Street! It seemed a year in point of experiences.

"Well," ventured Martin, "the boarding masters are smiling today."

"Yes, the lousy squeezers, I'll bet the Front Street House has a good dinner for the boss on my advance."

"I hope he chokes, Joe," chipped in Fred.

"Choking is too good for them; burning is wot they want," went on Joe, almost forgetting his breakfast in the heat of his indignation. "They take in Australia and Martin and Fred and me, and wot do we get? Wot do we get? Why, a few days' grub and a lousy, dirty bed, wot ain't fit to sleep on, and then they send us out. We go down and sign, and the next day out to sea for us in this bloody hell wagon. A half a kit of dog's wool and oakum slops, took from some dead sailor, maybe, and rotten poor oilskins, and sea boots that is no good. A big bargain, and all for six quid—that's all—only six quid for the lot; a mess of fine wearin' rags. And today they collect their hard earned money and all we has to do is to ride down here on a yachtin' toor round Cape Stiff."

"It ain't right. It's hell, that's it—hell!" agreed Australia. "Lookit me and Fred, and Mike, we was only in port two days. Just two days board and no advance money. Said the British Consul would get us sent back to the Ettrick. And that cost us six quid!"

"Nothing ain't right," it was Jimmy who spoke. "You booze, and worse, you sells out your manhood an' your rights to low livin' pigs wot lives off o' the likes o' us. Its principles wot you needs. Young men, take my advice and get principles. 'Ard? O' course it's 'ard to get principles, but they saves you a lot o' trouble an' you can put away a bit. I say live right and you'll be right."

"How old are you, anyway?" demanded Brenden.

"Old enough to know my own bloody business," rejoined Jimmy, scenting a comeback on his reform precepts.

"Well, now that your dead horse is worked off you can start in and save until you hit New York again."

"Well, if I do save a bit, it's none o' the likes o' a Dutchman like you wot'll 'elp me spend it," and Jimmy hopped out of the fo'c'sle at eight bells sharp. The mate was so surprised to see him leading the watch aft that he promptly sent him up to the fore skysail to loose sail, for the night had been squally and the second mate had taken in the kites, a thing he was prone to do, while the mate always promptly set them again.

After the argument about the advance, we all made up our minds to work off no more dead horses. As Australia put it, "A year at sea and a week in port, and nothing to show for it."

Most of us had slop accounts to clear off with the skipper, and then the velvet would pile up at the rate of eighteen dollars a month, at that time standard wages out of the port of New York for deepwater sailors.

None of the men had shaved for at least a month, and the crew forward presented a truly deep sea appearance; "Rooshin Jews on a ocean picnic," was the comment of Jimmy, who never shaved, and whose whiskers also failed to increase but rather diminished in their moth-eaten way.

On the first Sunday of real fine weather, when the bushes were beginning to get uncomfortable, the fo'c'sle barbers got busy in both watches. Frenchy and Australia were the tonsorialists of our watch and after taking on all hands, Frenchy shaved Australia and trimmed his mustache. Hair cuts were had by all and the effect was good. Perhaps the feeling of cleanliness due to the trimming had something to do with the desire for a "field day"; at any rate, two of the men, Old Smith, of starboard, and Frenchy, went aft and got permission from the mate to have a celebration.

The coming Wednesday was named, and as we were then on the edge of the S. E. trades, the day broke fine. Accordingly after breakfast that morning the watch on deck, all but the helmsman, were allowed to go forward and assist in removing the contents of the fo'c'sle.

The watch below also turned to, and green and blue sea chests with wonderful "tumble home" sides and fancy canvas tops; plain canvas bags, "the sailor's round-bottomed trunk"; bags with fancy eyelets and elaborate grommets; well-worn blankets; knobby straw mattresses, the "donkey's breakfast" of the sea; and all of the humble furnishings of the fo'c'sle of a deepwater merchantman, were hauled out on deck in the light of day. The fore rigging, the bottoms of the upturned boats on the forward house and the fo'c'sle head, were littered with these things as box and bag yielded up their contents to the purifying action of the sun. All of our salt encrusted gear was rinsed out in a barrel of rain water, saved for the purpose, until free from salt, as most of our clothing was so highly hygroscopic that the least fall of dew would make them damp and clammy.

We then rigged the water spar, and with a liberal supply of sand and canvas and with "ki-yi" brooms we scrubbed our home until the place fairly radiated. The scuttle butt was cleaned out and re-charred, the fo'c'sle lamp taken down and polished, and two hands got busy and gave the ceiling a fresh coat of white paint, brightening up things to a wonderful extent, for this had not been done for some years.

All doors and ports were left open to allow the fo'c'sle to dry out, and at noon both watches lunched together, "al fresco," under the shade of the fores'l. A hamper of chicken sandwiches, a case of cold beer, and a box of cigars would have delightfully rounded out our dinner of pork and pea soup. However, we were in a merry mood and the unaccustomed company of the other watch made the simple fare and weevil-ridden tack taste particularly good. Besides, relations with the after-guard were becoming more and more pleasant. The fight between Tony and Mr. Stoddard had faded from mind in the trying weeks that had intervened and the feeling of anticipation, as we neared the end of the passage, helped to make us receptive to better things.

By gradual stages, without in any way compromising their dignity, our experienced officers assumed a less harsh way of speaking; orders were mandatory to the last degree, of course, but less liberally spiced with profanity. An occasional joke on the part of those aft would send a ripple of laughter among the men pulling at sheet or halyard. The cook also felt the mysterious balmy influence of the Pacific sunshine, and every other day we would be delighted with a big pan of ginger bread in the fo'c'sle. On Sundays we would have duff with real raisins in it.

Honolulu was drawing near; none of us had more than a few dollars of pay on the books, and crews among the island and coast traders were hard to get, with pay correspondingly high. Perhaps this had something to do with the change of atmosphere. Even those who had the most reason to complain were beginning to cheer up and forget their troubles of the past.

A clean fo'c'sle, dry, well aired bedding, and smiling skies, ushered us into the region of the equatorial rains. The flying fish began to zip through the air again with increasing frequency and the mates as usual gathered them up, but, strangest of strange things, the cook was told to send half of the catch forward. The daily thunderstorms came with their accustomed regularity. At about eight bells in the afternoon watch it would cloud up suddenly, any sails spread out on deck, in the course of repair, would be hastily dragged to the sail locker or under the fo'c'sle head, and presto!—a rumble of thunder would follow the first faint flashes of lightning. Then several bright jagged discharges would come in quick succession, a clap of Jove's artillery, and a douse of rain, followed by the golden rays of the sun streaming through such rainbows as are seldom seen anywhere but in those latitudes.

During a tropic storm at night, just after leaving the trades, we were roused out at midnight and ordered aloft to take in the t'gans'ls. The yards and rigging were soaked with rain, and, as we got to the tops, St. Elmo's fires started to flicker on the yard arms with a pale blue light. The night was black, and oppressive with the hot humid wind, we were wet and clammy, and the sleep was in our eyes when—

"And sudden breaking on their raptured sight,
Appeared the splendor of St. Elmo's light."

Jimmy Marshall, fear clutching at his heart, refused to mount the futtock shrouds; springing to the forward leg of the main topmast backstays, he slid to the deck while the rest of us went aloft. The stoutest of us, however, were touched with superstitious feelings. The "corposants," as the men called them, started us on a series of ghost stories in the night watches on deck. A few days later we were becalmed in a dense fog, such as sometimes is encountered in the warm, damp region bordering the line. Joe went aft to relieve the wheel just after listening to a gruesome tale. A giant man out in the fog over the quarter reached for Joe when abreast of the open door of the wheel house. Joe nearly fainted with fright, at the sight of his own shadow thrown on the fog wall by the naked binnacle light that the helmsman had taken from the cowl to trim.

CHAPTER XII

MAKING PORT

One hundred and seven days out from Sandy Hook, we crossed the line for the second time in longitude 122° west from Greenwich. The grooming for port then started in grim earnest. Holystones were brought out and the time-honored couplet of the sea,

Six days shalt thou labor and do all that thou art able,
And on the seventh holystone the deck and scrape the cable.

became a matter of routine on board the Fuller. Captain Nichols had never been in the islands before, in fact none of us had, and we were to make our acquaintance with them dressed up and polished in Yankee form.

The art of holystoning, as practiced on American deepwater ships, deserves a special niche in the archives of the sea. No more thorough proceeding can be imagined. To the steamship hand who holystones like a gentleman, at the end of a long handle, the art has lost its fine points. On the Fuller we dug into the work in deep sea fashion. Our knees became sore from constant "praying" and the skin on our hands was worn down thin, making us tender in hauling at the braces or going aloft. To overcome the hardness of the deck, we rigged up pieces of board to which three cleats were nailed and a strip of old canvas stretched over them. This afforded a yielding cushion to kneel on and kept our legs out of the water swishing about with the rolling of the ship.

We worked in gangs, sawing away with the stones and wearing a scum of wood from the deck. Each man soon became jealous of the work done by his shipmates and we were careful to keep all hands going, as there was a certain amount of deck to be gone over, and the sooner finished the better. In holystoning we used two sizes of stones, the larger ones called "bibles" and the small pieces, useful for getting into the corners and along the edges of paintwork, known as "prayer books."

From the time of commencing to holystone, and slick up for port, there was no more watch below in the afternoon; the watch coming on deck at eight in the morning would stay on deck until six in the evening with a half hour below at noon for dinner. Going below at six, supper would be had and at eight the watch that had been on deck all day would turn out for the first watch at night.

Thus, every other day, a watch coming on in the morning would have eighteen hours of duty on deck during the following twenty-four. On the other hand, the other watch would merely have the usual watch and watch. Of all diabolical inventions for working men this afternoon on deck was best designed.

While still in the doldrums, and after the holystoning had been completed, we were set to cleaning the sides of the ship where the rust had worked through, and where the dirt from the scum rubbed off the decks had streaked long lines down from the scuppers. We liked this work, scrubbing the black sides, and painting. It always seemed to me like a vacation to get outside of the ship and off of the familiar deck. Scaffolds were rigged and sometimes our feet would dangle in the cool water on the shady side of the hull.

One day there was a commotion as Brenden and I worked away on a plank slung beneath the mizzen channels. The water under us surged up and a great black object rose beneath our feet, for all the world like a submarine boat coming to the surface. Outcries brought all hands to the ship's side. A huge whale had come up in the shadow of the ship. Some hands ran forward, and presently big Scouse came aft on the run carrying a harpoon from the bosun's locker and a coil of heaving line.

As he was mounting the rail the mate jumped after him, yanked the harpoon from his grasp and sent the red head scurrying forward.

"You damned mutton-headed ass!" he cried. "Do you want to send us all to the bottom? That's a razorback. He'll ram us, quick as hell, if we rile him."

The whale sank from sight as suddenly as he appeared, and, razorback or not, we had no opportunity to try his temper.

The sight of the whale started all hands forward looking for ambergris. This was described as a grayish amberlike substance to be found floating on the unsuspecting surface of the sea in large chunks of fortune, the finding of which would set a man up on a cosy farm for life, or enable him to see a snug retirement behind his own bar and beer kegs. Frenchy and Jimmy both had seen ambergris, and for a while regaled us with many tales of its origin, value and uses.

One of the results of the prospecting overboard for ambergris as we lazed along in the tropic seas of the Pacific was the better knowledge we obtained of the abounding life in the sea. In after years when at sea on the decks of swiftly moving steamers, I have often pondered over the sights that were given us of the queer inhabitants of the deep as we slowly worked our way across the ocean in the Fuller. From her low decks, when becalmed, or when sailing along at from four to five knots in fine weather, especially in the tropic seas, the teeming life in the depths below was brought very close to us.

The glint of queer fins, the vivid flash of some big fish rising near the surface in hot pursuit of prey, and the common sight of a school of flying fishes rising from the water just in time to miss the cruel jaws of their pursuers, gave us a faint idea of the ruthless rule of might below. Often the smother of white mist as the cloud of flyers would rise, and the swift black demons in hot chase under them, like avenging torpedoes tearing through the blue, would show glimpses of other and larger fish after the pursuers.

Time and again we would lie out on the martingale and look under the fore foot of the ship to see if there was a pilot fish around. These queer customers would swim along just under the stem of the ship, convict garbed, in thwartship black and white stripes, and about two feet long. The presence of a pilot fish under the bow was evidence of a shark under the bottom of the vessel, swimming along in the hope that something edible would be thrown overboard, or that the vessel would founder and disgorge her human freight into the deep.

Whole flotillas of the dainty nautilus would sail by us for days. These "Portuguese men-o'-war," as sailors call them, spread a shell-like sail to the wind, pink and airy, gliding gaily before the gentle zephyrs of the line. They truly teach us a lesson, as Pope has it:

"Learn of the Little Nautilus to sail
Spread the thin oar, and catch the driving gale."

With the picking up of the N. E. trade wind a few degrees north of the line, we knew that the main haul to Honolulu was on its last stages. There was more easting in the wind than is generally the case, and we made good progress, holding a course well to windward of Hawaii. For a week at a time we cut through the water at an average speed above ten knots, going it night and day. The sailing was glorious and we all felt the thrill of it. Were we not rushing forward to a paradise set in the middle of the broad Pacific for our rest and refreshment? We hungered for fresh provisions and for a decent sleep of more than a shade over three and a half hours at a stretch. The afternoons on deck had worn us down and the cooler winds bringing such speed and hope were a wonderful tonic.

"Will I take in the skysails?" Mr. Stoddard asked of the captain one night as he came on deck to take the midwatch. I was at the wheel turning over the course to Axel, who came aft to relieve me. The Fuller was boiling along, everything taut, the white water in her lee scuppers.

"No, leave them blow away," said the skipper, laughing. However, we found him on deck still at four in the morning and he took coffee with the mate before going below for a nap. But the skysails "stayed put" and indeed every bit of rag was doing noble duty.

"The Honolulu girls have us in tow," was the slogan on board.

At brace and sheet and halyard, we sung our ropes with a will, and a cheerier crowd of weather-worn, under-fed and half-rested humanity would be hard to find. Man is an adaptable animal, more rugged than the beasts of burden, and cheaper than machinery, and in the lesson taught us on the clean white decks of the Fuller is to be found the remaining hope for the survival of sail. It is cheaper, and with the advent of iron boxes rigged by means of screws, and bolts, and nuts, the sailor of the marling spike days will not be needed. Crews can be recruited, and fed for less than it takes to make steam, and men can be found to sail them, to drive them, as we were driven, and if they, too, are past masters at the art, to lull the crews into a state of contentment, and even happiness, after experiences that would cause a revolt in the worst penitentiary of the land.

When in 154 degrees of west longitude, and 21 degrees north latitude, Captain Nichols up helm and shaped a course direct for the northeast point of the Island of Molokai, the leper island of the Hawaiian group. We made the land just before nightfall. Anchors were got over the bow ready for letting go in case of emergency, and the dipsea lead was placed handy on the fo'c'sle head, the line being carried aft, outside of all gear, to the tub at the taffrail, in which the bulk of it was coiled. A small snatch block on the weather mizzen t'gallant backstay was ready for hauling in should we have to take a cast. The hand lead, or blue pigeon, was coiled in the mizzen chains; I was told by the mate to stand by in case we should have to use it, my schoolship training having made me a good leadsman.

All was excitement on board as we closed in with the land, the good smell of it coming out to us as we raced into the Kaiwi Strait, lying between Molokai and Oahu, upon the southern shore of which Honolulu is situated.

At midnight we were abreast of Koko Head, a peak near the eastern end of Oahu. We put down our helm and hauled our wind ahead, bracing sharp, under easy canvas, on the starboard tack, the ship heading north. Skysails, royals, and flying jib were allowed to hang in their gear, while we hauled up the mains'l, and furled the crojik, at the same time setting the spanker.

At four bells in the midwatch, closing in with the land faster than was comfortable to sailors accustomed to large sea room, we wore ship, and headed her back toward Molokai.

We wore ship again before daybreak in order to hold the weather gauge off Diamond Head, and at the first streak of dawn we squared away and the Fuller was put under full sail as we bore down past Diamond Head for the entrance to Honolulu Harbor.

A whale boat put out from the land carrying the pilot, followed by a wheezy tug of diminutive build. We put down our helm, paid a hawser out over the bow to the tug, and as we horsed up on her the Kanakas started a panic cry on her decks, while the captain on the poop shouted rapid orders to both mates and we let our yards down by the run and swayed up on the courses, manning the clew garnets, clewlines and buntlines in feverish haste.

"Take the lead!" the mate shouted to me, and at a nod from Captain Nichols, I sent the blue pigeon shooting out ahead into the clear blue water of the harbor entrance as we ran down between the barrel and spar buoys that mark the fairway.

"And a half, six!" I felt sand. "Hard bottom!"

The pilot came over to me and looked curious. "No need of this, captain," he said.

"Oh, give the lad some exercise, pilot," the skipper answered. "It won't hurt him."

"By the mark, five!"

We were running past the sea wall and the boathouse to starboard. I could see the lighthouse over the deck on the port bow. The tug was whistling, and as we swung to port, into the harbor proper, I noted the marine railway and the Pacific Mail Wharf with a lot of people on the Esplanade watching us come in.

"Mark under water, five!" I shouted.

"All right, Felix, come in; that'll do," said the skipper, and a few minutes later I found myself on the mizzen skysail, furling sail. We were brought to in the stream by letting go the port anchor and casting off the tug at the same time, and, as the chain rattled through the hawse pipes in a smoke of rust, a whistle on a factory ashore blew a long blast of welcome. It was noon, the harbor life suddenly stopped, for we missed the faint rattle of steam winches and the shouting of the Kanaka stevedores at the railroad wharf.

"Now give us a harbor furl, boys," called up the mate. And as we worked away, we noted the captain going ashore in the whale boat with the pilot. Below us stretched the most beautiful city in the world; cool looking green palm trees lined the streets, the fat squat outline of the Punchbowl rose gratefully verdant behind the little city, a restful sight to our sea-weary eyes, and far beyond we looked up into the misty vista of the Nuuanu Valley. Stranger still, on the wharves we noted native and white women in their fresh looking white dresses, and we could hear the cries of children at play.

Laying down from aloft we squared yards, and went below for our dinner of pea soup and pork, with a kid of cabin tack—a piece of strategy on the part of Chow that was truly an inspiration. The sight of weevils, and the near view of the clean sweet shore, would have been too great a contrast.

We opened hatches that afternoon, ready for the port warden's inspection, ripping out the caulking of oakum and taking off the three layers of tarpaulin, but not lifting the covers. We also sent down the fore and main courses and tops'ls, and cockbilled the main yard for a cargo boom, rigging the cargo pendant from the main topmast head, the same being stayed out over the main hatch by a fall from the fore topmast cross trees.

At four o'clock the captain returned with a boatload of fresh provisions, joints of clean red meat, fresh vegetables, onions, green stuff, bananas and pineapples, and a big basket of real baker's bread, the loaves rich and mellow in the sunlight, like bricks of gold. How our eyes popped out at the sight and smell of this treasure cargo from the shore! Our salt ridden senses were starved for something fresh and clean. A dozen hands rushed to the side to help unload the boat, passing the grub up the ladder and carrying it in to Chow.

Captain Nichols also announced that we would go alongside at Brewer's Wharf the next day.

At six, in the evening glow of the harbor, we pumped her out and went below for supper. Vegetable soup, floating with fresh green things and rich in meat extract; steak, onions, and potatoes! Have you ever been without potatoes for three months? If you have you will know how it feels to crave them. The fresh bread and the delicious ripe bananas topped off the meal.

We were too full to speak, all hands together at our feast under the break of the fo'c'sle head. Millionaires cannot buy such appreciation, and our bellies were stretched to the utmost limit.

An anchor watch was set, by lot, of one hour tricks, and I was fortunate enough to escape. Before eight o'clock the fo'c'sle was heavy with slumber as we dreamed away the hours in such heaven sent rest as only the angels can understand; we were one hundred and twenty-one days out from the port of New York, and our first night of unbroken sleep ahead of us.

CHAPTER XIII

IN HONOLULU TOWN

We have had enough of action, and of motion; we Rolled to starboard, rolled to larboard, when the surge was seething free Where the wallowing monster spouted his foam fountains in the sea.

Let us swear an oath and keep it with an equal mind
In the hollow lotus-land to live and die reclined,
On the hills like Gods together, careless of mankind.
**Tennyson.**

"Well, now that we are here, what?" Joe put the universal question. "I hopes we has it a bit easy for a change," he went on, seeing that no one rose to his query, and no doubt some dim, subconscious yearning must have stirred in the recesses of Joe's mind; perhaps the sight of the palms may have wakened this, for in his clumsy way he voiced the spirit of the poet. Indeed we had all of us sensed the languor of that lotus-land in the humid morning vistas of heavy tropical foliage lining the avenues of the city, and stretching far beyond into the blue-green richness of the Nuuanu Valley. After months of deep sea existence, the smell and feel of the ripe, luxurious land came to us with a powerful appeal. All of us felt this, but, sailor-like, the feeling was disguised in various ways.

"I hope them bulls aft gives us a fair deal," went on Joe. We were at breakfast, both watches together, assembled outside the fo'c'sle doors.

"Fair deal!" snapped Old Smith as he speared a spud. "Say, you young heifer, do you think you was brung all the way out to Honolulu for to loll back at your ease and eat the bread fruit, that we reads about, offen the fatness of the land, without no toil nor trouble? You'll get your damned good whack of sweatin' here. I know these ships, and it won't be just because the weather is hot, neither."

This was followed by dire predictions of hard grinding to come, ghastly prospects fathomed from the depth of experience by such masters of discouragement as Jimmy Marshall and Australia.

"Say, shut up, will you! Maybe it won't be so bad," piped Frenchy, who never liked to have his meals interrupted, especially when we were breakfasting on dry hash made with potatoes and onions, a real feed much needed by our hungry crowd. We had turned out at dawn for a hasty washdown, had put the long boat over the side, and rousing out a number of large manila hawsers, had flaked them down in the boat ready for warping. The cable was hove short and the quarter moorings were taken in. In addition to this a number of the men under the second mate had completed the rigging of the cargo gear. The carpenter, with me helping him, had rigged the dolly, wedging it under the pinrail on the starboard side just forward of the main hatch with blocks of wood and a small jackscrew. The large cargo blocks had been hooked and moused to the pendants, and the falls were rove, all for the starboard side, as the skipper had inspected the berth and that was to be our side for discharging at the Brewer Wharf.

Breakfast came as a rest, a breathing and a talking spell with a good day's work already to our credit. The change in routine, however, made the work seem easy enough, for we arose from our full night of rest with a feeling of wonderful vitality. Word came out that an island steamer would hold the berth at the Brewer Wharf until noon, and we were to warp in to the Oceanic Steamship landing to allow the port warden and the agents the opportunity to inspect the hatches and make a survey of the condition of the cargo, at the same time bringing us that much nearer our berth.

A plunge overboard in the early dawn, the last man on anchor watch having called me a half hour before the rest, put me in fine fettle. All hands were eager to get foot ashore and the prospect of tying up to the beach filled us with expectancy. The fresh grub, the full night in, and the electric atmosphere of contact with human affairs, gave us a keen sense of being again in the world of the living. After breakfast we sat around for a few precious moments smoking and yarning as we gazed toward the shore. News filtered out that the battleship Maine had been blown up in Havana harbor on the night of February 15th. War with Spain was imminent and the port of Honolulu was pregnant with impending world affairs, made even more intense by the fact that there was no cable in those days and news came only at intervals with the arrival of the mail steamers. War might be declared at any moment and rumor had it that a squadron of raiders from the Philippines might descend on the port.

The gunboat Bennington lay in the harbor with the old training ship Mohegan and constant gun drills were being gone through.

We "turned to" promptly after breakfast, and while one watch carried out the lines the other manned the capstan bars and broke out the hook as soon as the warp was thrown over a cluster of piles on the Esplanade. When the anchor came up dripping with gray mud, the long warp was carried in over the fo'c'sle head and taken to the main deck capstan and we walked the ship alongside in the good old-fashioned way.

At the string piece of the wharf there was a misunderstanding as to orders. The mate being in command took occasion to deliver his compliments to the second mate in no uncertain tones. So refreshing was the spectacle of wrath descending upon the head of the hated second mate that all hands stood idle grinning at the show. The old saying, "trouble aft; good times forward," at once went into effect. Mr. Zerk, seeing his mistake, ordered Mr. Stoddard to his room, and then turned his attention to "the people" as we hustled out the breast lines and adjusted the springs. We got the gangway over in jig time, to the great amusement of the dock loafers, and crowds of curious citizens, who had heard that a Yankee hell wagon was alongside with the bucko mate in full action.

When the gangway was lowered, Mr. Stoddard walked ashore with as much dignity as he could muster, garbed in a wrinkled brown suit and a rusty, dented derby that struck a ludicrous note amid the straw-hatted natives on the wharf.

"I hope he never come back," growled Tony, no doubt thinking of the day off the River Plate. "If ever I get him ashore—" but the Italian did not finish, for we were hustled about lifting hatch covers and setting things to rights, the deck being littered with long bights of the wet hawsers.

Native boys offered to dive for pennies, but we had none to give, and enterprising Chinamen crowded on board with baskets of fruit and hampers full of bottled pop, the whole gang being driven ashore by Mr. Zerk with his best delivery of picturesque profanity. The Kanakas on the shore started to mock him, and that made matters worse, as none of us dared crack a smile. Later on Mr. Zerk was to learn that the happy, carefree natives were an independent lot, who would work under persuasion, but were stubborn as mules when driven.

Captain Nichols came aboard with the port warden, and the top layer of cargo was examined. We carried a hundred tons of blacksmith coal on top of a general cargo, the coal being separated from what was below by old canvas and tarpaulins. One of the inspectors jumped down and tasted the coal for salt. Indeed it would have been mighty hard to tell whether the cargo had been damaged or not and, in a way, it was a bit of strategy on the part of the South Street stevedores. After some discussion, the state of things seemed to pass muster, and a great many smart looking young men from the offices of the agent came down and looked over the ship. Most of them carried papers of some sort, and in their white duck trousers and their fancy silk shirts, brilliant neckties, and spotless shoes, we seemed to behold some favored species. No doubt they looked at us too, though without interest, we being merely a lot of lean and leathery deepwater sailors dressed in common dungaree.

The captain himself was no slouch when it came to dressing and on this occasion he upheld the dignity of the ship, and the great American Merchant Service, by sporting a wine colored cutaway suit. His shoes were shined like the galley stove on a Sunday afternoon, and his heavy watch chain and fob dangled across his vest, which was buttoned to the very top in spite of the heat. Of course he wore a boiled shirt, and his black derby was of a square topped model, conservative and dignified.

Inspection over and the island steamer out of our berth at the Brewer Wharf, we cast off and again warped our ship across the harbor. This took up the remainder of the first day. The boss stevedore came aboard and we learned that the crew was to work aboard ship, breaking out and slinging the cargo. The "hatch man" and the "dolly man" were to be natives of the shore gang; two important posts, as upon them depended largely the speed of unloading.

**AT BREWER'S WHARF**

Word was passed forward that the captain would allow those of us who wished to, to draw against their pay on Saturday afternoon. In the meantime, it being Wednesday, we were alongside and free to explore the city in so far as such investigation could be carried on without the expenditure of coin. However we found the Chinamen ready to take "chits" for modest amounts.

After pumping out, and before knocking off for supper, the mate called Charlie Horse aft and appointed him night watchman. He was delighted with this billet, and except for a good deal of grumbling about not being told earlier and having a chance to get some sleep in the afternoon, he was well pleased. Charlie Horse had once been mate on a schooner, a fact that he never allowed us to forget, much to the amusement of such men as Australia and Hitchen. Jimmy Marshall resented all mention of it and more than once made cracks about the kind of "schooner" Charlie Horse was most familiar with. Charlie Horse, and no one ever forgot the Horse part of his name, which I believe was Horstman or something like that, never ventured an opinion without a great deal of deliberation, a trait that has much to recommend it, especially when at times he was referred to during heated arguments.

The long night shifts in Honolulu were well suited for one inclined to secluded thinking and deep contemplation. Besides this, Charlie Horse was to have the laugh on us after our second night in port.

That first blessed night of supreme rest while our ship lay in the stream, swept by a cool sea breeze, was followed by a sweltering night of discontent. Most of us turned in early, after a short stroll ashore, and in our ignorance of the customs of the place, slumbered in innocent exhaustion without a thought of the perils of the night.

Parts of New Jersey and Long Island are noted for their mosquitoes. Alaska is also somewhat remembered on this account by unfortunates who have summered along the southern shores, but Honolulu in the historic year 1898 could boast of one of the most vicious swarms of torturers lining the shores of the seven seas. We were ripe for them, our skins spiced with the salt horse and pea soup fluid that coursed through our veins. We were tired from the labors of the day, and slumbered unmoved while the enemy put all that was exposed of us to the bayonet. I lay stripped in my bunk gasping for breath, and in the morning found I was a mass of bumps, red and unsightly. The next day the china merchants along Nuuanu Street did a big business in mosquito bars, supplying us on the strength of our "chits" after the captain had verified the statement that each man was to be paid five dollars, on account, at the end of the week.

CHAPTER XIV

UNLOADING—WITH A BIT OF POLITICS

All hands working together made us better acquainted with the men of the starboard watch. Axel and I developed a lasting friendship, and of course Old Smith joined the higher councils of our watch. Hitchen and Mike and Tommy proved to be a great team of kidders, and with Australia, of our side, formed a dandy quartette, singing such old time favorites as "Tom Bowling" and "All in the Downs." Hitchen, a very superior sort of sailor, an Englishman, reticent about himself, but a volume of information about the ports of the world, was a great addition to our life aboard. In fact the men of both watches were sea worn and tired of each other, and we welcomed the new contact with our shipmates. Add to this the unusual sights of the shore and the fresh provisions, as well as the possibility for rational sleep, and sailors will know what I mean when I say that we were a very happy lot of men aboard the Fuller.

Scouse had a large mouth organ, "Made in Germany," a gaudy tin affair well fitted for his capacious maw. Tony had an accordion, and no one could deny that we were a lively crowd forward. On the other hand the people aft were shrouded in gloom. The mate lived very much alone and Captain Nichols was separated by more than a bulkhead from his first officer. Chips was also a lonesome figure, dining in dreary state at the second table. Tommy said that since the second mate had gone, the Jap boy felt it beneath his dignity to wait on Chips, and the lanky carpenter found the table set with all that he was to have at one load, soup, meat, dessert, etc. "I wisht they'd let me at it once," said Joe, his mouth watering at the mention of dessert.

The second mate did not return on board the night following his racket with the mate, and we were in hopes he would quit the ship. Our wishes were realized, for the afternoon of the second day in port, while we were in the midst of breaking out the coal in the main hatch, Mr. Stoddard came to the coaming and looked down on the grimy crowd shoveling coal. He carried a dilapidated satchel and had evidently been paid off by the skipper.

"So long, you dirty bums!" he called down, sending a squirt of tobacco juice into the midst of the coal-dust and sweat-covered gang.

Tony, who was in the hatch, dropped his round-nosed shovel, and picking up a lump of coal hove it at Mr. Stoddard, just missing him as he dodged back from the coaming.

"Wait until I get you ashore, you dirty —," shouted our ex-officer, shaking his fist at the hatch as he ran over the gangway.

"Thank heaven he's gone," I remarked to Frenchy, both of us looking down at the play from our perch on the fore tops'l yard where we were unreeving the downhauls.

"A good thing he's done with us, and the ship saves thirty dollars a month while we are in port," was Frenchy's wise comment.

That night Tony and Tommy went ashore for the purpose of finding Mr. Stoddard and beating him up. The ex-second mate was boarding in a Chinese house in Beretania Street, according to reports from some of the Kanakas, and the two avengers trailed him from that place to the Criterion saloon.

The true story of what happened was long obscured, for both Tony and Tommy came aboard very late and turned in refusing to say anything until the next morning, when they were given the third degree by the exacting masters of fo'c'sle affairs in the persons of Jimmy and Australia.

The stories did not tally and for a long time it was thought that Mr. Stoddard had given them more than they counted on. The truth came out when Chips told the yarn to some cronies on the beach. It seems that Mr. Stoddard met Tony and Tommy as he was leaving the saloon. Their determined manner, and clenched fists, at once warned him of trouble. With a knowledge of sailor psychology, nothing short of masterly, he advanced toward them in true "come on" style, greeting them with a warmth of cordiality entirely unexpected, and a moment later Tony and Tommy were with him at the bar drinking imported beer at two bits a glass, and wondering how they had ever been so mistaken in him.

No doubt Mr. Stoddard would have got his licking had he remained in port, but we learned that he shipped before the mast on the bark W. H. Dimond bound for San Francisco.

A day at the coal got us rid of that objectionable part of the cargo, and when we took up the tarpaulins we found a large consignment of case oil filling most of the 'tween decks. Case oil, let it be known, is kerosene in large square cans, packed two in a case, and nicely calculated as to weight so that a good husky sailor man can just about lift one of them without straining himself too much. However, I can vouch for the fact that these cases are very hard to handle and get heavier and heavier as the exercise is continued.

The stevedores ashore, so we learned later, were Republicans, a jolly lot of progressive Kanakas, demons for work and constantly chattering like crazy brown magpies. On the other hand, the donkey crew, the man at the dolly, and the hatch man, a lively Kanaka named Nigger, were Royalists of the bluest strain compatible with their swarthy complexions. The Royalists did their level best to send the case oil out on the wharf so fast that the lowly Republicans could not handle it. Below decks, in the stifling heat, we labored in gangs, running the cases to the square of the hatch from two sides, while Old Smith and Frenchy adjusted the slings about the stacks of twelve cases and up they would shoot. It seemed that the cargo hook was constantly dangling in the hatch like a hungry black worm while that demon Nigger raised a hell of sweat and hurry with his constant shouting to "Hook her up! Hook her up!" and every few minutes the mate would bend over the hatch and roar down his bit of encouragement.

My job was to help hand the cases down from the tiers, lifting them to small trucks upon which we rushed them to the hatch opening. A half day of this exertion found us pretty well blown, and when the noon whistle sounded over the harbor we got on deck, bolted our dinner and stretched out on anything that was handy and relaxed. Some of the boys slept, but I was too sore to sleep and had a feeling that it was better to stay awake, anyhow, as the rest would seem longer.

When we turned to at one o'clock the gang on the wharf started to howl defiance at Nigger and his men, and the cruel ball began again with the mate, as king driver, egging along the performance. Being rid of the second mate and with the captain ashore, he was thoroughly enjoying himself.

The cases of oil were hard to grab hold of, and as I have said, got heavier and heavier as the weary day advanced. Cursing and sweating in hot 'tween deck, we strove like mad to keep up our end of the fight.

"Don't let them niggers beat us," shouted Brenden, as he dug in with renewed energy, the sweat dripping into his eyes as he began slinging down the cases like a madman.

"The dirty black bastards!" shouted Jimmy. "I hopes they croaks afore I sees the last o' this place."

By the time the afternoon was half over my arms and back were numb with pain. I had ceased to sweat and every effort was made by super-force of will. We were red-eyed with the labor and the heat; swearing had ceased, and we plugged along doggedly as the damnable Nigger kept up his constant bawling to "Hook her up!" or "Liki! Liki!" (meaning "the same").

Frenchy, who was under the hatch, suddenly brought us to our senses. "Rain, boys! Rain!" he shouted.

In our torture we had not noticed how dark it was getting, and when the first large cool drops pattered down on the 'tween deck hatches covering the cargo in the hold, we knew that relief was at hand. A minute more and the rain came down in tropical torrents while we struggled to get the big strongback into place, the hatch covers on, and the tarpaulin spread. Our black tormentors had fled to cover under a nearby shed, and the donkey engine crew were drawing the fire from beneath their boiler. Nigger, too, had disappeared, for Scouse came up determined to take a fall out of "that black —."

To say that we were thankful for the rain is mild; we were saved by it, nothing less, and as we went to the fo'c'sle that night we were as badly beaten a lot of men as ever cumbered the port of Honolulu.

"Say, Smith!" yelled Joe, shouting through the partition that separated the fo'c'sles.

"Well, what do you want?"

"You was right when you said sumthin' about me workin' here."

"I told you you'd sweat, didn't I?" shouted back Old Smith.

"Say, Smith," in a chastened tone.

"Yes?"

"Was you sweatin', too?"

"Shut up! Shut up!" cried Jimmy in alarm. "If you wants to start a fight, do it tomorrow, an' let your betters get some rest."

CHAPTER XV

HAWAIIAN HOSPITALITY

On a fateful Saturday night, the one when we drew five dollars apiece against our payday, Peter, the boy, and I decided to go ashore and have our hair cut by a regular barber and then indulge in the pleasure of a luxurious bath with plenty of soap and a good big tub of hot water. After the hair cut the bath—and this took us to a Japanese establishment that was conducted upon true oriental lines. As a bath house it was A1, but in addition to the supply of hot water, which was drawn by a female attendant, I found that she (the attendant) was ready to remain and assist in the scrubbing. Being of a modest turn of mind myself, and unable to converse with this would-be helper, I finally made known my desire for her removal by pushing her through the door. The floor was slippery and in my embarrassment I may have given her too hearty a shove, for she lost her footing and shot out in a most undignified manner, "cutting the star" as we used to call it when skating. Peals of laughter sounded through the flimsy walls, the Japs taking the whole thing in good part.

However, in the native Japanese quarter, this sort of thing was considered proper, and, as I afterward learned more of the Japanese, while in their islands, I found that it was all a simple matter of point of view and nothing at all extraordinary.

Of Peter a great deal might be said. He was a type of the young American who will, when circumstances force him into it, go to sea. However, I have only touched upon him lightly, as he in no way represented that bygone breed of sailor that made history on the hard square riggers of that day.

Peter had a delightful voice that passed in Honolulu in lieu of real coin, at least among the Kanakas, where his wit and general good nature won him many friends. We attended a luau up in the Nuuanu Valley, a real native feast where we were received royally because of the high regard in which Peter was held by the Kanakas. Poi, one finger stuff, and none of your poverty stricken watery three and two finger poi of the stevedores and little island traders, was on the bill of fare. Pork, fish, and fruits of all kinds afforded by the islands were served to us on ti leaves, while swipes flowed freely.

Peter sang "Hawaii Ponoi" over and over again with our hosts, and we wound up late at night with the native girls dancing the Hula Hula. All very decent, of course, but calculated to impress one with the broader range of vision accorded simple strangers traveling in that land of song and sunshine when without the stodgy hall mark of smug respectability to hamper them in their enjoyment. Peter astonished the natives by sleight of hand tricks with a pack of worn playing cards, and before we left them had dated us up for another engagement. My head the following morning was something to be remembered with respect, and I swore off all further indulgence in the Kanaka's wonderful hospitality.

On board, our routine became more established. After the consignment of case oil was put over, we found the work less trying and were better able to meet it as we accustomed ourselves to the new labor, although the Republican-Royalist feud continued to the end of our stay. In the main hold, directly below the hatch, we carried a locomotive boiler. Getting this overboard called for some seamanship on the part of the mate. He strengthened the main yard support by extra tackles, and hoisted the fish fall up to the cargo pendant, which in turn was backed by several parts of wire rope. The yard purchase was replaced by a fourfold tackle rove off with new gear. Once ready, we sent the boiler over the side in good style, setting it squarely on a flat car.

While this special gear for getting over the heavy freight was being rigged, the remaining running gear of the braces was unrove, coiled and marked for stowing while old stuff was sent up to take its place, as all such untarred rope deteriorates rapidly when exposed to the dust of the port for any length of time. Following the discharge of the boiler we roused out a large number of cases of heavy machinery, all to be assembled as a complete locomotive. The Fuller was stowed with a very mixed cargo, her manifest containing every kind of agricultural and household implement imaginable. Castle and Cook, a large importing house in the Islands, got a lot of our cargo and as we would unload a consignment of stuff for them they would run an advertisement in the daily papers—

CASTLE AND COOK, Large assortment of the best fruit jars with patent screw tops just received from the States by Ship A. J. Fuller.

Had we been wrecked on a desert island, our freight would have set us up as a very respectable lot of Robinson Crusoes, for we brought the most general of general cargoes.

After a week in port, my mosquito mottled face having subsided to normal, I presented a letter of introduction to Mr. William H. McInerny, at his place of business on Fort Street. Mr. McInerny, his mother, sister and brothers, were most kind to me, and I enjoyed their hospitality with an appreciation made extra keen by the life of the ship. Clean table linen and all of the ordinary necessities of civilized existence seemed extra good. On the other hand I had sense enough to appreciate the life aboard ship. This was never dull, and was soon destined to become particularly strenuous.

Mr. McInerny called for me frequently of a Sunday and took me driving behind a pair of fast horses. His first appearance on the ship aroused the gravest sort of suspicions in the mind of the mate. He eyed me critically when I went ashore in my best Sunday suit, pressed the night before by a Chinaman on Nuuanu Street. As we drove off, so Peter told me afterward, the mate shook his head as much as to say, "Another young fellow gone wrong."

The next morning there was considerable coldness in the manner of the mate, but nothing actively malignant. He gave me no harder work to do than before, but he did not condescend to his customary gruff camaraderie.

When Mr. McInerny called for me again on the following Sunday with a different rig and another pair of high steppers, Mr. Zerk became thoroughly disgusted. On Monday he called me aft just before we turned to after the washdown, and made some very sarcastic remarks about my "dude friend."

"I suppose you will be getting out of the ship?" he ventured.

"I have never thought of getting out," I answered.

"Well, I was just thinking that you might have a chance to get out. Maybe your friends with their horses and carriages would not like to see you working too hard."

"I suppose they would hate to see me work hard, seeing what an easy time I am having now."

"Damn your hide, they will hate to see you work before I get through with you. Call that thick ass Scouse aft and that — Joe."

When these unfortunates arrived they found Mr. Zerk under a heavy pressure of bottled-up wrath. The whole silly business had so exasperated him that he fairly sizzled with madness. Heretofore his outbursts were mostly impersonal, at least they always seemed so to me; merely a part of the day's work. We were now turned over to Chips and found that he had received instructions to clean out the limbers of the ship, starting in the fore peak and working aft as the bottom of the hold was uncovered. From that time on until the ship was discharged I was kept at the most disgusting work of the voyage. Bucket after bucket of a thick sludge, the results of a previous voyage to the Orient, when the Fuller loaded some filthy cargo in Hong Kong, was lifted out. Of course she was never cleaned in New York, where the crew was always discharged as soon as the hook went down, and no longshore laborer would do the work we were set to.

After three days of this Joe said to me as we came up out of the hold covered with filth: "Here is where I quits. To hell with this. That rotten bull aft thinks he can work anything off on us. Some may be soft an' easy, but," and here Joe came in strong, "I can get thirty dollars a month in the coasters, an' I won't be leavin' much. To hell with the rotten skunk, says I."

That night Joe found a chance to go out on the barkentine Irmgard due to sail in two days for San Francisco. Like most of the craft trading to the Islands from the coast, the Irmgard was glad to pick up a deepwater sailor. Joe agreed to work his passage to Frisco and would then sign on regularly before the U. S. Commissioner. Joe wanted Scouse to join him but the big fellow shook his head as Joe urged him, during the next two days down in the bilge dirt. All conversation on the subject of Joe's departure was taboo in the fo'c'sle, though Joe worked hard to have Scouse join him, even going so far as to see that it would be all right for him to ship in Frisco.

"No, Choe, I don't do no more pilge cleaning when I ged back. Dere ain't no rotten pilges on farms, ant you never knows what rotten backets you ship on. I stand dis ant, den, no more."

The night that Joe left we got his clothes ashore over the bow. All he had was a round bottomed sailor's trunk—a canvas bag. Joe was a favorite with all of us, and his bag bulked large with parting gifts of clothing. In addition to this we all chipped in, at the suggestion of Old Smith, and at a tarpaulin muster, though it was near the end of the week, we managed to find five dollars. Let it here be said that after the first generous advance of five each, the Captain cut us down to two dollars each week, and held down on the slop chest. Of course five dollars was out of the question, as the pay per month was only eighteen.

Also, in the details of Joe's departure we had to keep everything from Charlie Horse. As watchman he would undoubtedly be blamed for not reporting the desertion. As it was, Charlie Horse was given a hard call by Captain Nichols, and later on he thanked us for keeping him in the dark. Charlie was a decent sort and said he was glad he did not have to lie about the affair when called aft.

"Joe's going," Frenchy whispered this to me. It was near midnight and Joe had returned as he promised, after depositing his dunnage in the fo'c'sle of the Irmgard, only a few wharves away.

"Good-bye, boys."

"So long, Choe. Goot-luck. Goot py," the last from Scouse. Joe slid down one of the bowlines and we watched his dark figure walking along the wharves. Under a street lamp on Nuuanu Street Joe waved back at us on the strength that we were watching him.

**Charlie Horse**

We all felt sorry to lose Joe. Scouse was especially gloomy over his departure, and I missed the happy-go-lucky fellow in our work below.

Next morning when Joe failed to show up at the wash down, Mr. Zerk was furious. Charlie Horse came in for a round of abuse and all hands in general were cursed fore and aft and athwartship. In it all I seemed to detect a certain note of insincerity. In fact the mate was glad that Joe had left; it seemed to please him that the drill in the limbers was tough enough to have had that result.

No one was assigned to take Joe's place, but after a week of it Scouse was relieved and Tony became my partner in filth.

"I suppose we will have other deserters," said the mate, coming down and looking us over. His words were evidently intended for me.

"I don't think so, sir. Scouse doesn't mind this a bit," which was a foolish remark, but at least resulted in giving the red-head a relief.

I kept fit by getting up an hour earlier each morning than the rest of the crowd and taking a plunge overboard as a bracer, swimming about the ship. In the evening, being too dirty to give a hand in pumping out, I had the pleasure of a plunge into the cool waters before supper. I always washed out my dungarees as soon as I came up, and alternated, leaving the ones last worn to have a good sunning.

Captain Nichols saw me one noon looking rather dirty. He may have remarked the fact that he had seen me in the same state some ten days before, when the grind first started.

"What are you doing?" he asked.

"Cleaning out the limbers, sir."

"How do you like it?" grinning.

"Fine; wish the ship had four instead of two, sir."

This seemed to tickle the old man, and whatever he did I don't know, but the next day the mate came below and lifted a horrible fuss about the way things were dragging, with Chips at his heels saying "Yes, sir, yes, sir," so fast that the mate turned on him and asked him if he had St. Vitus's dance. "Yes, sir," answered Chips, before he realized his mistake. "Well, then, get the hell out of here and let me finish this." Four extra men were sent down and the job cleaned up the next day.

I was mighty glad when the drill was over, for to tell the truth my health was beginning to suffer from the nasty grind and the constant breathing of foul air. In the fo'c'sle, too, the boys were more than decent about it. "Well, you stuck it out," was the opinion.


CHAPTER XVI

HONOLULU OF THE OLD DAYS

Honolulu harbor in 1898 retained more than a trace of its old time flavor of romance. In later years, when I again visited the port, the improvements had entirely eliminated many old landmarks that spoke so clearly of the historic past. At the time we were there in the Fuller, the remains of the hulk that once was the famous, or perhaps I should say infamous, Hawaiian man o' war, Kaimiloa, lay bedded in the mud flats at the delta of the Nuuanu River, a shallow part of the harbor between the railroad wharf and the waterfront of the city.

The Kaimiloa, a vessel of 170 tons, had once been called the Explorer, and was then engaged in the copra trade. King Kalakaua purchased her (she was a wooden steamer, by the way) for $20,000, and had her refitted as a ship of war. On the 17th of May, 1887, she was dispatched to Samoa to strengthen the hands of the embassy. Robert Louis Stevenson wrote, "The history of the Kaimiloa is a story of debauchery, intrigues, and waste of government property."

On this memorable cruise she was under the command of a half-pay British naval officer who must have been possessed of a keen sense of humor. "The Primacy of the Pacific" was King Kalakaua's dream, and the H. M. S. Kaimiloa was the apple of his eye. Her armament, so far as I could find out, consisted mainly of a heavy silver service boasting several large caliber punch bowls. In every way she was appointed with a view to the pleasure of the monarch.

In Samoa she got into difficulties. German men o' war in the port refused to recognize her colors, or return her salute, and she finally departed, returning to Honolulu by way of Pago Pago (what's in a name?), where her half-pay commander exchanged her small arms for gin, and had a month's debauch, as a sort of bracer, before reporting home to the Kanaka Admiralty. This cruise is said to have disgusted

King Kalakaua with his navy, and further support was withdrawn. What became of the silver service, the armament, or the half-pay commander, cannot be recorded by the writer.

The forlorn remnant of this royal hulk, with planks bleaching in the sun, centered upon an interesting sector of the harbor. Here in the shallow weed-grown water numerous native women, wearing extremely proper Mother Hubbard wrappers (when dry), were always fishing industriously. No lines or nets were used, but the finny unfortunates were caught between the toes of the fishers. The fact that the natives of the islands relish live fish only added to the fascination with which we observed their operations. The harbor was also the scene of much active fishing by the Japanese, who employed a seine and several small sampans. So changed was all this when the writer returned to Honolulu, some eight years later, that it was with a pang of regret he recalled those old romantic, inefficient days.

Not far from the Fuller was the berth of the Morning Star. We could look over her decks as our ship rose higher with the discharge of her cargo. This famous missionary craft was a yacht-like three-masted schooner with auxiliary steam, the mizzen being built of steel and serving her as a funnel. The comings and goings of the missionary folk, male and female, for they busied themselves mightily on board the pretty craft, furnished us with something to look and wonder at when we were not otherwise engaged on board.

We established friendly relations with her crew, meeting some of them ashore at the concerts. Frenchy made the acquaintance of her cook and the "doctor" presented him with a can of curry powder. But no matter how friendly the crew of the Morning Star might be when ashore, they were careful to never go aboard the Fuller; also the moral atmosphere of this vessel was so strong that it pervaded the clothing of the whole ship's company, for none of them ever was seen in any of the barrooms frequented by sailors. However, Peter had met them while attending lauas and they were as fond of swipes as the next man, quite human, even to the extent of getting gloriously drunk.

One class of visitors on board the Morning Star, who seemed in the majority, were the army officers. And by the word "army" as generally used in the capital of the Hawaiian Republic at that time, was meant the Salvation Army. The Salvationists were very influential in affairs along the waterfront. We had been in port about a week when their advance guard came over our rail, sort of spiritual Uhlans descending upon us, after dusk, as we sat about between the time of clearing away the supper kids and lighting our pipes for a stroll ashore. And let it here be said that whatever good they may do in other fields, and there is no denying this, they were working in ground already fairly moral when they boarded the Fuller. My observation has been that the moral index, if I may coin a term, is inversely proportional to the amount of work. Hard workers, physical and mental, are as a rule fairly moral.

On the ship Fuller was gathered at that time as decent a lot of men as ever sailed the seas. I have listened to more obscenity in a short space of time among men who held themselves educated than fouled our ears during the whole voyage about which I am writing. For one thing, we always had something interesting to talk about, and our few leisure hours were too precious to throw away.

The head scouts of the army were no doubt attracted by the rather cheerful noises coming from our band, an organization making use of all the typical sailor instruments, the accordion, several mouth organs, a jew's-harp, and a drum made by Jimmy Marshall out of a small paint keg with canvas stretched on both ends. The missioners from the good ship Morning Star were very much interested, no doubt scenting talent for their concerts, and the party came aboard on what might be called a cutting out expedition.

"Yes, we were getting lots to eat." "No, the ship was not particularly hard. The captain was all right." "Yes, the mate did swear a lot; in fact he was a bad man, but we had seen worse." "Yes, the life of a sailor is a hard one. We all liked Honolulu. Etc. Etc." Old Smith had the party in tow, and acted as spokesman while the parley was going on. Jimmy in the meantime buzzed around, all eagerness to get in his fine work at panning the ship, the grub, and everything else.

One of the visitors noticed this. He was a tall thin man wearing the fatigue uniform of nothing less than a Major, and was evidently a student of the genus sailor, that is, a student of the sailor man going through his paces ashore; a down trodden unfortunate, sleeping in a bunk innocent of woven wire springs, without clean linen sheets, and having to wash himself in a common deck bucket, all of which of course is true enough. The tall man was drawn aside by Jimmy, his grizzled monkey face working like a nutcracker. Jimmy talked to such good purpose that the tall army officer handed him a card and asked him to call when ashore. Our band then struck up, and nobody could help but notice that Jimmy Marshall was a most proficient drummer.

The upshot of this was that a week later Jimmy took to his bunk sick. "Contusion of the liver," he called it. "Too much work an' the rotten grub 'as got me at last." There was much groaning in his bunk, and when Captain Nichols looked him over he shook his head.

The following day several army authorities came aboard to visit Jimmy, a mighty fine looking captain among them, for we all admired her. Two days after this Jimmy rose from his bunk with great effort and went aft while the captain paid him off. Kanakas came aboard for his dunnage, and Jimmy Marshall joined the Salvation Army. We saw him on the corner of Fort and Hotel Streets soon afterward beating a brand-new drum and utterly ignoring us. How the army did it remained a mystery until a young man from Brewer's office let fall the hint that army influence was exerted through the agents. Whatever it was, it worked, and for many a day we missed Jimmy. His "beef" on a rope was negligible, but he was clever at every sailor art and his singing was in a class by itself.

Scouse summed up the fo'c'sle opinion when he said, "Dot's a smart feller, dot Chimmy."

While the efforts of the Salvation Army were directed with vigor and enjoyed the support of the powers that were in the city, the devil was also well represented in the thriving little nest of humanity, way out there in the middle of the Pacific. This was before the time of the great fire that swept away the Japanese quarter, and before the yoshiwara had been established. Saloons had a pleasant ingenuous fashion of advertising in the daily papers. Such items as, "Drink at the Criterion Saloon," "Visit the Louvre Saloon, for your rickeys," were displayed in bold type. Intoxicated men reeled along the streets at night in the region bordering the waterfront, and assaults of various kinds were not infrequent. All nations were represented in the motley crew who formed the floating cosmopolitan conglomeration drifting about the port. The new republic being the eddy in the middle of the transpacific lanes where human flotsam gravitated, like Hong Kong and Port Said, it had become a nodal point of adventure.

Of course Honolulu itself rose serene and beautiful above this mess of wreckage that washed up on her beach. Beautiful homes were there, on the long avenues lined by royal palms, set in fine grounds, bordered by hibiscus hedges alive with flaming red. The date palm and the fan palm all added to the natural beauty surrounding her public buildings and her dwellings. The solid worth of the place far outweighed the ribald doings of the beach combers, not all of them, let it be said, in dungaree. Well-dressed adventurers were even more numerous, and no doubt far more dangerous, than the unattached sailors of the port.

The life in the Chinese and Japanese quarters, with their hundreds of small shops supplying the modest needs of their countrymen, was most interesting to us. In fact we were compelled to do most of our trading with these merchants, as two dollars per week was of little account in attempting to go shopping on Fort Street in the American or English stores. As for having a regular blowout, with drinks of civilization, at two bits per glass, it was simply not to be thought of. Watermelons, bananas, pineapples, soda pop, and ginger ale were our refreshments after an evening spent at the concert in Emma Square, or Thomas Square, and very often I went to a small Chinese coffee house on Beretania Street for a cup of Kona coffee and a plate of sinkers. If a steamer had arrived it was the custom to have a concert at the Royal Hawaiian Hotel; the band, by the way, being a particularly fine one under direction of Professor Henry Berger, and supported by the Government. King Kalakaua during his famous tour of the world conceived the idea of having such an organization in Honolulu. It was composed of native Hawaiians, all excellent musicians, and he secured Professor Berger to lead it. The frequent concerts inaugurated by King Kalakaua have been continued ever since. Bad as the old king may have been, the band will always remain a large item to his credit. Without it, Honolulu would be a bad place in which to live; many a poor devil has enjoyed the treat of the best music under conditions calculated to conserve its influence, who would otherwise have spent his evening in some hideous dive.

The concerts in the grounds of the Royal Hotel were a sort of dual function so far as I was concerned. When attending them in the company of Mr. McInerny I walked boldly into the lobby of the hotel and lolled about on the verandah like a gentleman. When out with Hitchen, Frenchy, Axel, or Tommy, and on the single occasion when we induced Old Smith to forsake the waterfront, I stopped on the lowly outskirts of the crowd among the natives, and the groups of Chinamen, Portuguese, and Japs. We enjoyed the music and had as good a time as the folks on the verandah; in fact we were more comfortable, for we dressed in cool clean dungaree with our cotton shirts unstarched and open at the throat. Pipes were always in order, lavish conversation was indulged in, and we got to be accepted on an equal footing by many of the natives. Nigger, the hatch man, a sort of top boss among these people, was one of the best of Kanakas, which is saying much; a white man under his skin, and a gentleman every inch of him. He introduced us to as exclusive a society as there is in the islands, and we always swore by him in spite of the way he treated us the first few days of our stay in port, but then, as he explained, it was the Republicans he was after, and of course us white fellows could look out for ourselves.

On Sundays, when I was not out driving with Mr. McInerny, Frenchy and Axel and myself would wander about the city looking at the strange sights. Tommy got to be one of the sightseers later on, and in our different excursions on foot we covered the place pretty well. The Palace (from the outside), the statue of Kamehameha I, the Museum, and the cottage in which Stevenson lived at Waikiki, were some of the points of interest visited. We also made a long hike out to the Pali. All of this is uninteresting but simply spread upon the record to show that the sailor-man of the old deepwater days, of which I write, was liable at times to enjoy many of the milder forms of dissipation now almost exclusively indulged in by Cook tourists and the winners of voting contests sent abroad by enterprising newspapers.

CHAPTER XVII

A DINNER ASHORE

With all due respect to Chow, and he moved in the best silk-shirted circles of oriental society, we could never say that his regular bill of fare on board the Fuller was exactly epicurean. He was bound to remember that sailors were the ultimate destination of his efforts and he guided himself accordingly.

When the ship was at the end of her discharging, and my trials with the mate had come to a close, so far as the bilge was concerned at least, Frenchy suggested that we have a dinner ashore. I felt like celebrating and readily agreed. At first we thought of having this feast alone, but after due deliberation, and consideration of all of the questions involved, we decided to invite a third shipmate. Frenchy figured this out on the basis of the size of the bird that he held to be the necessary central feature of the proposed banquet. The kind of a bird Frenchy had in mind was a three-man bird—indeed many a family of twice that number would have considered it sufficient. Then again, in his way the Frenchman was quite a philosopher, and realized that in a three-cornered celebration the whole affair would take on a better air. Three may be a crowd under certain circumstances, but where shipmates get together, three of them generally manage to have a better time than when they travel in pairs.

Now as to the third man. I suspected that Frenchy had already selected him when we went out on the fo'c'sle head to talk the matter over, a few nights before the event was to come off. He urged me to suggest candidates. I did, possibly more on their merits as sailors than anything else, forgetting that the man who knows best how to stow a fore t'gan'sl may not be the handiest shipmate with a knife and fork. Hitchen or Axel were named by me.

"No, Felix, that Hitchen always laughs at me when I tell about the way we cook things in France. Axel is all right but he eats stock fish. Let us ask Tommy. Tommy knows a good dinner when he smells it. Let's ask him."

Thereupon Tommy was asked, and of course accepted. We were to pool our week's allowance, two dollars apiece, and by the ready way in which Tommy and Frenchy got together on the proposition I knew that they had already thrashed out all the details. Frenchy merely started the ball rolling my way by true fo'c'sle diplomacy, the boys imagining perhaps that I would want someone besides Tommy as the third man, for somehow or other Tommy and I had never chummed to any extent since our arrival in Honolulu.

The matter of Tommy disposed of, Frenchy took the arrangements in hand, going ashore with Tommy Saturday night to perfect the details, for these archconspirators had already selected the place at which we were to dine. It transpired that Nigger, who was a warm friend of mine host, had highly recommended the place, so I agreed to put myself in the hands of my friends after the time-honored custom of more exalted candidates, turning over to them the two silver dollars received from Captain Nichols, and that night I followed my routine of many other evenings of enforced economy, and repaired to the reading room of the Y. M. C. A.

When I came aboard Frenchy and Tommy were there to meet me. They had seen the proprietor of a little restaurant on Fort Street a few doors north of Hotel. A table had been reserved for Sunday, at one o'clock, and the final specifications of that dinner minutely laid down. Frenchy was enthusiastic. I would now see what a real dinner was like; I was to tell him frankly if it was not better than the dinners I had had ashore with my friends. The proprietor, a Portuguese, was a man of taste ready to welcome us as friends of Nigger; his wife was to cook the dinner herself. Clean white tablecloth, napkins, and everything right, had been ordered by Frenchy.

We did not tell the rest of the crowd forward of our plans, for like enough they would only ridicule the idea. As a matter of fact it did seem like an extravagance, but we were having so much fun out of it before we ever came to the actual disposition of the dinner, that it was well worth the sacrifice entailed. "A man likes to have things good once in a while," was the justification of Frenchy.

Sunday morning, after the washdown, which was always particularly thorough on that day, lasting an hour or so longer than usual, we partook of a very light breakfast. We then shaved carefully, that is, Tommy and I did, and got out our best clothes, brushing them with great care.

"Are you going riding today?" asked Martin with a grin.

"No, Mart, I expect to dine at the Palace with President Dole."

"Is Tommy and Frenchy going with you?"

"You guessed it. By special invitation, Mart, Tommy and Frenchy have been asked up to dine and to advise the President as to the cut of his whiskers. Some say he should shave like Tommy, on account of the heat, others contend he should let them grow like Frenchy, on account of the mosquitoes; so you see he is asking us up to dinner in order to settle the matter," at which both Tommy and Frenchy expanded perceptibly, and Mart, muttering "Rats," went out on deck to escape the jibes of the crowd. It was certain that something unusual was up, but after the manner of a free fo'c'sle, the men kept their own counsel, only such goats as the wood-turner Martin having the crust to edge in.

Frenchy broke out his best—a blue suit, very square cut in the shoulders, double breasted, and of substantial cloth, rather heavy, but undoubtedly good. He told me proudly that it had been made to order in Dunkirk two years before when he was home on a visit. He also polished the leather visor on his blue cloth cap, a petty officer's cap, a relic of the old days in the navy. Of course Frenchy had on a stiff white shirt, one with a very small bosom, which made it necessary for him to keep his coat buttoned, for he decided not to wear a vest. This shirt was a work of art, hand made by sister Madeleine, and having collar and cuffs attached. In place of a tie he wore a loosely knotted scarf of black silk.

Tommy had a gray sack suit, not new, but well brushed and neat. The edges of the vest, which he insisted on wearing, were lined with black braid, and he had worked black silk triangles at the corners of the pocket slits. Tommy wore a very shiny boiled shirt, a low wing collar, a fancy butterfly tie of the very latest South Street pattern, held in place by an elastic band, and a gray felt hat.

I donned my visiting clothes, and the three of us turned out in the height of perfection, scrubbed, polished, and rubbed down to the last turn; Beau Brummel, had he ever shipped deep water, would have had nothing on us.

"Well, I hope you has a good time," called out Brenden as we headed aft for the gangway, just as the smelly kids from the galley were coming forward, in the hands of Fred and Tony, masses of greasy potroast unappetizing and uncouth.

The mate sighted us as we went over the gangway. He stood in the shadow under the after awning giving us a thorough looking over.

"Three gentlemen of Verona!" he cried after us in derision, for let it be known Mr. Zerk was something of a scholar in his way and not without a sense of inaccurate but racy humor.

Glad to be clear of the ship, we headed up Nuuanu Street to King, put our helms hard to port and ran east under the shadow of the substantial concrete stores and offices, with their heavy iron shutters closed for the Sabbath day. From King Street we turned northerly into Fort Street and, with yards squared, and three abreast, we bore up to the haven in which we were to dine, as well pleased a trio of low degree mariners as ever sailed.

The proprietor, swarthy, stout, and smiling, and wearing a white apron, greeted us at the door; while his wife peeked from behind a curtain in the rear, as he ushered us to a nice round table next to a window overlooking a cool shady garden. We were the only diners in this cozy room, the private parlor of mine host. The trades were blowing rather strong that day and a pleasant breeze came in through the open window. The lace curtains still linger in my memory, with other details of the feast, and I had to tuck them back, for they threatened the soup.

When I say that a small vase of flowers decorated the white linen, or perhaps it was only cotton, but at any rate fresh and clean, the fine hand of Frenchy will be recognized, for, let us say so again, and if necessary, again and again, he had planned the dinner from first to last in every detail.

The soup, for of course we started with soup and not with any of the exotic indigestible frippery often attempted by ambitious but ill-informed caterers, was cold consommé! "Hey, wot's this?" demanded Tommy, "are we late?" "No, Tommy, you eat this cold. Try it." "Say, that's all to the all right!"

Well, it certainly was "all to the all right," and real cold, in fact chilly would be the proper word. The host fluttered about; he was doing things right, and to entertain guests such as we, who knew and demanded that every detail be carried out; for such appreciative guests were rare indeed in the vicinity of Fort Street, not far from Hotel.

The fish course was a dainty morsel of some native species, flaky and white. It would take a connoisseur, and few of them shipped at sea in those days, to describe that meal.

The roast was a fat fowl, but not too fat, a plump bird of the genus chicken.

When this rare bird appeared on the table Frenchy insisted upon congratulating the cook, the proprietor's wife, who blushed with pleasure at the gracious compliments showered upon her, and the bird, with equal facility. Of course Frenchy carved. He carved exactly as he had often carved before in the long hungry night watches off the coast of North America when we first chummed together. Only now he was dismembering a real plump drumstick done to a golden brown, and not one of the imaginary mouth-watering tantalizers of the cold high seas. Dressing was there too, and mighty good, and a big dish of mealy mashed potatoes, white and satisfying.

"Have some gravy," said Tommy, passing around the gravy boat, a vessel he was well able to command.

We wound up with a salad of lettuce, and Frenchy mixed the dressing at the table. It will not stretch the imagination of the reader to believe that by this time our shipmate was in a highly satisfactory mood. Tommy and I were having the time of our lives, and as far as dinners go I have never enjoyed a better. Since then it has been my fortune to kick heels beneath the same table with a prince of the royal blood, to have broken bread with school-men and with men of the old world who feel themselves of noble strain; I have speared spuds with the fishermen of the north and have shared my bacon and corn pone with the niggers in the swamps of Florida; I have dined in state and have taken my chances in a college commons, but never can I remember a better or a merrier meal.

Some guava tart and cream cheese, the latter served on small green leaves, and large generous plebeian cups of clear Kona coffee, completed the dinner.

Our host had a surprise for us. He opened, and passed around, a box of good cigars, urging us to help ourselves to extra ones, which we did. He then took off his apron and, drawing a chair up to the table, joined our well satisfied company. We talked of all things under the heavens and upon the land and waters. More coffee was called for at intervals, and when our host learned that I had been in Horta, his native town in the Azores, a new bond of interest was established.

Finally, with regret, the time came to depart. A fine touch worthy of that finished sailor, Victor Mathes of Dunkirk, God rest his soul and grant him all prosperity, was the fact that the meal had been paid for in advance and we left our host without the sordid jingling of change or offering of a pauperizing tip, this worthy bowing us to the door, three contented sailors, with extended belts, and empty pockets, and nothing but a ship to call our home.

CHAPTER XVIII

BRITISH NEIGHBORS

The memory of our famous dinner ashore, a feast that was enjoyed over and over again in reminiscences during the succeeding months of the voyage, brings to mind, by very contrast, the sad picture of a body of men who were constantly hungry. These unfortunates were the crew of the iron ship British Monarch. We became very friendly with the crowd on the Britisher during our stay in port, finding them there when we came and leaving them behind when we put to sea. These poor devils talked of food, thought of food, and dreamt of food; they did everything but eat it in anything like satisfying quantities.

They were a typical English ship's company in this case, carrying a larger number of Britons than was generally the rule. The Dutchman, that is anything hailing from the north of Europe, of course predominated.

"Bli me if she ain't the 'ungriest bloody tawnk hout o' Lunnon. Arsh thy calls hit. Sye, hif arsh hever tysted like that, so 'elp me. And they arsts me to heat me fill, the rotters! Blarst 'em! The bloody rotters!"

The speaker, a native of parts near London, a vivacious and interesting lad named Parker Tweedy, treated us to this and much more in the same vein. Tweedy elected himself a "Hextra 'and" at our mess and helped clean up the kids on many an occasion. In fact many a pocket full of tack and many a half pan of dry hash went from the Fuller to the British Monarch.

Two very youthful apprentice boys, fair haired and rosy faced, with china-blue eyes, were among her complement. These children, they were nothing more, gloried in the most awful command of profanity. The boys were to be seen wandering about ashore of an evening, their faded blue uniform caps proclaiming them the sons of doting parents who were willing to pay a bonus of fifty pounds in order that their boys might learn the rudiments of seamanship and navigation on the clipper ship British Monarch, late of the China and Australia trade. "Uniform is worn—meaning the caps—and the young gentlemen are berthed in separate quarters in the cuddy house." So read the tale that snared them. However, nothing except hunger ever seemed to happen to these lads, and as they flattened their noses against the confectioner's windows ashore, they were unconsciously absorbing lessons that might be of value to them in after life.

Like most English ships of this class, the British Monarch was a disgrace to the sea and in no way representative of the best traditions of the English service. The system in vogue in ships of her kind may be epitomized as one of least work and less food. Day after day the crew would sling a scaffold plank over her side and chip her rusty plates in a languid, melancholy way, interspersing their half-hearted labors by lengthy discussions. Small patches of the chipped surface would be coated with red lead and the British Monarch looked like a tattered sea rover wearing a very much torn coat through which patches of red undershirt were visible.

Her gear aloft was most slovenly, Irish pendants hanging from every yard, and her spars taking any direction in which they happened to be at the time the braces were belayed. Her skipper, a youngish man and very unassuming, would scull about the harbor in a small jolly boat visiting his friends. Why the crew stayed by the ship was a mystery, with good billets going begging for sailor-men to hold them; however, when we learned that they had a year's payday on the books and were looking forward to some happy distant time when that rusty ark would drop her anchor in the Thames or Mersey, the reason for their staying by was plain.

Hitchen and I went on board of her after we had been in port for several weeks and I was surprised to have him take me aft into the cabin. All he would say was that he had met Mr. Gore, the mate, back in England; they were old friends, "so what's the difference if I am before the mast so long as it's in another ship?" which was true enough. The cabin of the ship was very elaborately appointed, though not well taken care of. The British Monarch had been in the East India trade at one time and was fitted to carry a limited number of cabin passengers.

Mr. Gore, the mate, was a taciturn man of about forty, much given to study and reflection, for which he had ample opportunity, as the care and working of the ship never seemed to bother him. The second mate, Mr. Hauton, a lad of less than twenty, was most hospitable. He was a graduate of an English schoolship, and as I was from the St. Mary's, we had a lot to talk about, comparing notes on all matters relating to the profession of the sea. He was a "Wrinkles" fan and exhibited a thumbed copy of the first edition. As I had a copy of the latest, much enlarged, Hauton made me promise to loan it to him.

One thing that was notable was the fact that they had the run of things aft, going into the captain's room for books, and freely inviting their friends on board to partake of such hospitality as the vessel afforded. The social equality aft was better balanced than in the Fuller, and deservedly so. On the other hand, our mate was a far better sailor than either of these men, yet he was as far removed from the captain, as we were from the sacred shelter of the forward cabin.

Hauton and I made a number of interesting excursions about Honolulu and its vicinity. We visited the Oahu prison, whose white walls loomed over the green meadows beyond the railroad wharf. Another trip took us out to the great Ewa Plantation. Hauton was keen on visiting the coast traders as they came in from California, and having more or less of a fixture during the long stay in port of the British Monarch, he was able to make many friends. His reason for staying by the ship was the fact that the time in port, he being signed on as a regular officer, was telling toward his sea service. On their return, if they ever did return, he would go before the examiners of the Board of Trade as a candidate for the First Mate's Certificate of Competency.

They do this sort of thing much better in England, and in fact in all of the European countries, than we do. There an ambitious lad of seventeen, who has had his service and possesses the necessary knowledge of navigation, can pass for second mate. In the United States the young man must be twenty-one, an age at which they commanded ships in the good old days, before the Local Inspectors of Steam Vessels can examine him for a second mate's license.[6] This foolish rule kept me roughing at sea, in subordinate billets, for three years before I could qualify and go to sea as an officer, that is, three years more than were necessary, as I was qualified by service and knowledge at the age of eighteen.

[6] *Changed in 1916 to admit men of 19 years, having the required sea experience, to examination for third or second mate.*

Another thing, and here is as good a place to say it as any, the whole system of examining merchant officers is wrong. The U. S. Local Inspectors of Steam Vessels are earnest, capable officers, but must work with the laws and regulations as they find them. The examinations are even less rigid now[7] than formerly, owing to the great need for officers to man our ships.

[7] *1918.*

One of the worst features of the thing is the fact that they give a man a "license." I have no desire to quarrel about mere words, but why not be consistent? As we "license" our merchant marine officers, let us do the whole thing in the same hayseed fashion and give our naval officers "permits" instead of "commissions," or perhaps include them in the scheme of licenses. An old sailor once told me that he would rather have a liquor license than a license to sail the oceans as master. Dog licenses, peddler's licenses, and what not, all confused in the average mind with merchant officer's licenses are the result of ignorance founded on a political system, that, originating ashore, has bungled the laws governing our sea service since the fatal time when it was taken under the present system of control.

To end this "backwash of wrath" let us give our merchant officers "A Certificate of Competency" or any old thing but a "license." As a matter of fact the officer's license looks very much like the license displayed in saloon windows, permitting them to do business by virtue of their payment of internal revenue taxes.

The yawl of the Britisher was an able, fine modeled boat, sported a leg-o'-mutton rig and frequently, of a moonlight evening, the breeze being fair, Hitchen and I would go out sailing with the mates of the British Monarch. On one occasion Hauton and I took the yawl out through the harbor entrance and beat our way as far east as Waikiki Beach, expecting to sail back before it with a fair breeze. It fell calm and we were compelled to beach her and leave the boat in charge of a native, as she was too big an order for us to row back alone, especially as we carried only one oar. This taught us a lesson, for we had to walk back, not having a cent in our pockets. The next night we went out by car with the two apprentice boys and a number of our Hawaiian friends, who brought their ukuleles. The sail back into the harbor was most enjoyable. These people have excellent voices, as a rule, and sing with a haunting plaintive strain of sadness that can never be forgotten.

In the undertow of human flotsam that circulated about the wharves and waterfront saloons, there was considerable talk about the smuggling of opium. It seemed a profitable business to engage in, judging by the talk we heard. A leak in the customs, or some loophole in the restrictions on the trade, allowed a lot of the drug to get into Honolulu. Often, as we sailed about the harbor in the evening, we would notice the small schooners coming in and out, many of these being consigned to Chinese and Japanese merchants. The cleverest of the smugglers would come into the port with their shipment of opium slung under the keel of the vessel. Bearings would be taken at some point, perhaps some time before letting go the anchor, and the contraband tripped to the bottom. All that was necessary then was to deliver the bearings; the consignee could go out and pick up his freight in a fishing net when most convenient.

Going to sea breeds a garrulous curiosity among sailors. The shipping in the harbor was a constant source of discussion aboard the Fuller. Of fine trim sailing craft, Honolulu held more than her share in those days. Such craft as the barkentine Irmgard, the bark Nuuanu, and the Foohing Suey were a delight to the eye. The bark Rhoderick Dhu was also one of them, and eight years later I saw her come slambanging into the broad harbor of Hilo, all sail set and a crowd of gaily dressed women on her poop. She was still popular as a passenger carrier, and came to anchor with the precision of a man-o'-war.

The island steamer, a typical product of Hawaii, is a cross between a steam schooner, only shorter, and a New England boarding house and factory combination. A black tin smokestack rises above the front porch, two stump masts are fitted with leg-of-mutton sails to steady her, and a large crew of Kanakas complete the maritime mess.


CHAPTER XIX

THE MATE KEEPS US BUSY

News that war with Spain had been declared reached us on April 27th, coming by the U. S. Mariposa from Sydney. On the same day we discharged the last piece of cargo in the hold of the Fuller and hauled into the stream to get ready for our return loading of sugar. This ended our shore liberty for a few nights, but it really came as a relief to us. Three busy weeks along shore, weeks that seemed like months when we thought of all that had happened, sickened us of the dust and smell, the latter emanating largely from the Chinese houses with their peculiar odor of rancid sweetened grease. The chatter of the Kanakas wearied us and the mosquito pest along shore was enough to discourage even the most pronounced optimist. We were glad, indeed, for a few days of comparative quiet while in the stream; at least it was three days of quiet that we looked forward to.

Before hauling away from the wharf we took aboard a lot of rough pine and spruce lumber, material to be used in lining the ship. Shore carpenters came out, men thoroughly versed in the work, and in an incredible time had fitted a complete inner skin throughout the hold. This was kept at least a foot away from the sides of the vessel and some two feet above the bilges, and the ceiling next the keelson, the ceiling being at the bottom and not at the top of the hold, as landsmen might imagine. The boarding of this inner skin was cleverly laid, clinker fashion, like the clapboards on a house, so that any sweat or leak water in the hold would be shed and run down clear to the bilges without wetting the precious cargo.

A cargo of sugar such as was to be carried by the Fuller was worth at that time in the neighborhood of a quarter of a million, and the greatest precautions were taken to safeguard it. In addition to guarding against wet, all places where the sugar bags might, by any chance, come in contact with iron, as the bolt heads in the heavy knees that jutted through the inner lining, were wrapped with extra thicknesses of gunny sack. When this job was completed the lower hold looked like the inside of a gigantic melon, nicely hollowed out. There was a clean sweep from the fore peak to the lazarette, only interrupted by the mainmast and the upright water tank, a simple hold such as was considered safe and proper in the days of Columbus and of Drake.

WATCHING THE SHORE WHEN IN THE STREAM

The 'tween decks of the Fuller was rather fancy. Her voyage previous to the one we were on had taken her to China and while in Shanghai the 'tween decks was scraped bright. The under side of the spar deck, the lining, knees, and waterways, were all in natural wood and coated with a varnish made of shellac and oil. The heads of bolts, and all iron work, had been painted with aluminum paint and then varnished. When we first noted this it brought forth some caustic comment.

"They do the cargo a damn sight better than they do us," remarked Australia. And this was right and proper. The cargo pays freight and should be considered, whereas we were a part of the expense, to be cut down as low as possible both in numbers and wages.

Captain Nichols, too, was glad to get away from the wharf and all the annoyances incident to discharging. The dust and unavoidable dirt tracked aboard ship by the people from shore were a constant vexation to his soul. I have often seen the skipper bob up from the companion and chase some unsuspecting visitor ashore without ceremony; some poor deluded mortal without a proper reverence for the sacred character of those spotless after decks that we had holystoned and scrubbed so carefully every day of the voyage.

When we got in the stream a comfortable deck chair was brought out for the captain and placed on top of the cabin and several times we saw him actually recline at his ease in this concession to luxury. The skipper also wore wonderful white clothing with double blue stripes; this was really silk, but looked for all the world like the standard pattern for bedticking. It must have been cool, and after all that is why he wore them. Coming out to the ship a few days after we had hauled out, the captain had his boatman row him around the vessel while he eyed her carefully. Evidently everything was right aloft, yards square and all gear snug, for of course the mate had seen to that, but he was not pleased with the appearance of the hull. The following morning we got busy and all that day half of us were over the side scrubbing her. We took long brooms and cleaned off the high wall of copper, for being light she showed some six feet of it, and when we got through, the Fuller looked something like her old self.

During all of our time in Honolulu the mate remained very much to himself. I only remember seeing him go ashore a few times and none of us ever met him when off the ship. He led a lonesome life, and after the hard day of driving us with all duties devolving on him alone, I have no doubt he was pretty well done. Thinking it over, I have since come to the conclusion that the terrible Mr. Zerk, the bully and the slave-driver, with a curse always ready on his lips, and a heavy fist prepared to enforce his mandates, was a sort of Mr. Hyde to a very domestic Zerk saving his payday at the rate of a paltry sixty dollars a month against the time of his return home to the wife and kids. His supply of home-made jams and preserved pickles, so sparingly given me on the passage out, confirms this conclusion. True, I hated him cordially during those trying days in Honolulu, but then I was very much of an ass, and no doubt deserved all that was given me. When we went into the stream, things got better; the mate slackened up to the extent of allowing me to tally aboard the lumber for the lining.

About this time talk in the fo'c'sle was much concerned with speculation as to who would be our second mate. Martin said he had overheard the mate tell someone from the shore that a man was coming out from Frisco to take the billet.

"Not on yer life," said Australia; "they will pick something easy from forward. This mate likes to run things hisself and all he wants is some boy to stay awake nights to call the captain if a squall blows up. They will pick one of us, but whoever he is, he will be a fool."

In fact not long afterward judicious soundings were taken forward by that left-handed diplomat, the gloomy Chips. Whoever sent him on his fruitless errand must have received an enlightening message. Chips cornered one man after another and in a deliberate fashion got his ideas as to who was willing to go aft. We were all of one opinion as to who was most fitted for the billet; Old Smith of course was the man. Although he was known as Old Smith, it was more a matter of respect, his age being only about forty or forty-five. He had sailed before the mast since boyhood, most of this time deepwater, back and forth around the Horn, sailing as second mate many times but always going back to the fo'c'sle as his choice.

Smith never drank to excess while in Honolulu, was a clean-cut, able seaman, a type as scarce in those days and unknown now.

Some hitch ashore occurred in regard to our cargo, for we lay in the stream three days after we were ready to load. In the interval the mate hit upon a brilliant idea. Why he thought of this piece of hazing, for such it was, is merely a guess on my part, but the growing cheerfulness forward must have annoyed him. The band was particularly active after we left the wharf, the concerts on the fo'c'sle head, of an evening, lasting well into the night.

The day after the hold was finished we were horsed about unmercifully at the washdown. Fred, Martin and I had put large batches of clothing to soak the night before, expecting to find time during the day for scrubbing, as we looked forward to a rather easy time.

"Hey! Put them swabs up. Never mind that, Smith; break out a couple of barrels of sand. Leave the water spar," this last to Frenchy and Charlie Horse, who were about to unrig it; for Charlie Horse always helped at the morning washdown after his night of watching, "to give him an appetite for breakfast," as the mate said.

"Wot in hell is the racket?" asked Australia in alarm. "So help me—is that busher going to start something new?"

"Dot's it. Something's new again. Maybe the 'bear' in port, or something," chimed in Scouse.

"Get your breakfast!" shouted the mate as soon as the sand was on deck, and we went forward with the whole ship in a mess—gear on the pins, deck wet, and two barrels of mysterious sand at the main hatch.

"By —, he's got me," confessed Hitchen; "whatever the bloody bitch has up his sleeve is a new one."

"Joe was wise; that's what he was, wise. And say, that little hipercrite Jimmy, was he wise? Well, ast me, will you, after tonight? I'll bet something is doing, and something very fine. We been having our fling too much. The hell with these American working wagons!"

"Aw, shut up, Brenden, will you? For Gawd's sake, have some feelin's for us. Look at Fred; he's too tired to eat."

The reaction from our high spirits of the last few days was complete. We sat around dejected after breakfast, and it was with a feeling of relief that we heard the bull-like roar of the mate urging us to turn to. This summons reverberated across the harbor, and must have advertised us as a packet of strife.

Things were not long in abeyance. We were ordered to wet down decks again and spread the sand on the main deck as far forward as the windlass. Old Smith, Frenchy, Brenden, and Martin were told off to lend a hand to Chips. The first lengths of the chain cables were stoppered just abaft the wild cats, and by means of handy billys and chain hooks we roused up long bights of the rusty cables and ranged them along the deck, constantly wetting down and sprinkling sand to protect the planks. This was no easy job; in fact we worked like slaves at the back-breaking labor, having something like a hundred fathoms to handle on each anchor. The night after this started our band went out of business, for we all turned in.

Mr. Zerk was positively cheerful during the second and last day of this job. When we had completed hauling out the chain, made of great links a half foot long, and strengthened by a heavy stud, he descended to the chain locker, while I went with him carrying the lantern. We found very little dirt in the locker, and that also seemed to please the mate. The whole operation, aside from furnishing us considerable exercise, did no particular good, nor for that matter harm.

I was glad of the opportunity to see the thing done, an interesting piece of work from the standpoint of the student of seamanship. The ends of the cables were passed through heavy ring bolts on the keelson and then were carried up and secured by a stout lashing to rings in the knight heads. This method of securing made it possible to slip the cables by casting off the ends and letting them go by the run, as the ends are always in sight. The necessity for slipping cables comes very seldom, but when it does have to be done the safety of the ship and all on board depends upon the ability to let go quickly and without a hitch. During this work we examined the markings on the chain. At the links next to the shackles, that separate the different shots of the cable, turns of wire are placed on the studs so that in running out the cable the shackles can be examined as they go over the wild cats, and the length of chain out determined. Large swivels are also provided for taking out the turns when a vessel swings completely around in a tide way. Where two anchors are out, and the chains become twisted, we have the necessity for "clearing the hawse," an old time honored operation performed by the voyagers in the days of Columbus when hawsers were used. The hawse pipes still retain their name though great chain cables are now employed.

The labor of stowing the cables was less painful than that of rousing them up as gravity worked with us.

On the night we finished this job we received word that the ship was to go alongside again the next day, and again we were glad of the change. That the system on board was a good one cannot be denied. We were always glad that some disagreeable piece of work was done, and, except for the croakers, who were always predicting trouble—and were always right—we were a very contented lot of men. It also happened that in the scheme of things no part of the ship was ever neglected, and the owners received full value in the care of their vessel for the wages that were slowly accruing to us.

CHAPTER XX

THE LAND OF LANGUOR

The month in port had pulled us together in a remarkable manner. The ship's company forward were as one large family gathered by strange chance from the ends of the earth, and, because of the wonderful adaptability of human nature, we were working and living our life in pleasant harmony. Of course it might as well be said that if anything otherwise had occurred, if constant fighting had taken place, our well trained masters of the cabin would have put the disturbances down with little delay.

On the Fuller we mustered an imposing array of nationalities; besides Americans, we had Norwegians, a Swede, an Italian, two Germans, and an Englishman. The mate, an American, had "Blue Nose" written all over him. He was one of those hard men, originating in Nova Scotia, who have added their bit to the consummate seamanship of New England and New York. The Chinese cook, and Japanese boy, and later on our Kanaka sailors, helped to make us as conglomerate as any melting pot. The one man we lacked, and it was the only place in my career of much work and poor pay, that I did not find him, was the Irishman. We missed Paddy; he should have been there.

The amount of the pay day coming to us, some time in the distant future, was a constant source of computation. Figuring the time since the working off of the dead horse, and deducting the slop chest account, also the money advanced while in port, and while the figures were often disappointing, there was still the possibility of a tidy pay day looming far ahead. Unlike the poor whaleman with the prospect of nothing but his "Iron Dollar" and escape from slavery, we did have a show to collect. The captain in American ships is allowed to charge a profit of ten per cent on his slop chest account. I doubt if Captain Nichols did even this. He had the steward serve out such things as were wanted, and the prices were lower than the cost of similar articles on South Street. When Peter dipped in too strong, getting, or rather attempting to get expensive things from the slops, the captain refused to let him have them. Peter once wanted some tobacco, he was going very heavy on this item as he regularly gave it away. Captain Nichols shut down on him and after that handed him cigars whenever he happened to see Peter.

Scouse was one of the principal calculators of the pay day. He had a frugal mind and was planning great things with his money when he should once more get back to New York. With Joe gone, Scouse became a different man. He was a sobered Scouse, a deep thinking plodder who gave himself up to day dreams that must have been of vast extent. Scouse announced that he intended to get married. He planned to meet and marry some good obliging German girl, "Just over; dot's the one." A girl not averse to a big lumbering Dutchman with a shock of coarse red hair, and a terrible appetite; however a man not afraid to work. His idea was to go west. "No more from dis rotten sailor's humbug by me. I was going to be somepody ant get respect ant lif like decent people." Also he figured on a nest egg of a little over one hundred dollars. But then, families have been founded on less, though of course the founders were not destined to be welcomed home by a band of crimps and blandishers.

Frenchy too had great plans. He was going back to Dunkirk. To be sure he even talked of going back to Havre, in the French Line, paying his steerage passage. Then he planned to get spliced, and his scheme was to go out in the fishing fleet, or else back to New Caledonia, where he knew the country, and start life afresh.

Axel was going back to Sweden, to Stockholm, so he said, and never more out on the briny billows of discontent. Fred was also a prospective homeward bounder. Trondhjem was his destination, and the fishing fleets of the town the means for his living. Tony and Charlie Horse intended to join Scouse in so far as they were bound for the interior of the U. S. A.

During these many discussions, the wise sailor-men like Hitchen, Brenden, and Smith, the seasoned shellbacks, full of the cruel furrows of time spent before the mast, and God alone knows what other outlandish callings that roving men may follow, kept their counsel and smiled.

"Sonny, I guess I am down on the books of some ship that sails a few weeks after we get back. Another crowd, another skipper and mates, and another voyage." Old Smith was as nearly sentimental as it was possible for him to be, and still be Old Smith. "Yes, I like this ship, but how in hell are we all going to sign on again when more than half the crowd is going to get married?"

It was strange how thoughtful the hard days of hauling that chain made all of us. Besides this, the Honolulu climate was gradually getting under our hardened hides. They can say what they like about the Hawaiian Islands being a "white man's country." It is if you mean a white man who never has anything harder to do than to tell a Kanaka or a Jap to lift the burden. The trades do blow, and it is lucky for the inhabitants that they do, otherwise, the Isthmus of Panama would be duplicated out in the broad Pacific. In spite of the pleasing winds and the beautiful clear weather, things are a bit too balmy for continued physical exertion. Lifting a gin rickey is good enough exercise, and if you lift them often enough, out at Sans Souci, for instance, you can imagine anything you like about the Islands.

Working men stay home, if you are white, let the coolies shoulder the physical burdens; but if you are wealthy and also lucky, you will very likely own stock in a sugar plantation. They were paying seventy-five per cent dividends in those days, and this is so even now, I believe. Also if one is ambitious to put pep and fire into things, seek a cooler clime. It is a fact that the white people of the Islands, who can do so, spend a part of their time on the coast and whenever possible, prospective mothers go to the coast during the time of their pregnancy, as the Hawaiian climate seems to rob them of much of the necessary vitality for the ordeal of birth.

But the Islands do hold a magic, all pervading charm, they are as unlike any other islands as it is possible for them to be. Honolulu, with its beautiful villas, with its modern setting amid a glory of tropical verdure, springing from an age old fertile humus, bathed in tropic sun, cannot be duplicated.

On getting alongside the railroad wharf, which we did by the economical and laborious process of warping across the harbor by use of a kedge anchor, we found that the greater part of the day had gone by, a day that started at four o'clock in the morning with the regular washdown to begin things, when we were ordered to carry out the kedge and pick up our moorings.

Time was plentiful with us in those days, for the eight hour schedule had never been heard of. Mr. Furuseth and Senator La Follette were not there to shield us from cruel fate, and besides, whatever extra drilling was done, was simply at the expense of sleep, a thing under the complete control of the mate. We got up when we were told to by the mate, as Charlie Horse went aft for his orders each evening, and when extra work was to be done he was instructed accordingly.

Once alongside, we took aboard the long hardwood sugar chutes, worn smooth by endless polishing of the gunny sack, in which the partly refined sugar is shipped. These chutes were arranged very cleverly by Nigger who came aboard with a shore gang of stevedores. The inclination must be just right, and the chutes must be placed just so, in order to prevent spilling, where it is necessary to cut corners in order to reach the farther parts of the hold. We were glad that natives were to stow the ship; in fact this work is mighty technical, and we never would have been able to do so with our crew. Working with the natives, we picked up a lot of knowledge about the handling of sugar, points that were to be of much use to me in later years when I returned to the islands as mate of a steamer.

On the Railroad Wharf there were several lines of track and some turnouts carrying short flat cars loaded with sugar bags all safe under huge tarpaulins. We also found the warehouse pretty well stocked with it, and were told that when we once started to load, the sugar would pour into the ship in a constant stream.

That night we again put up our mosquito bars against the enemy from which we had mercifully been saved during the few days in the stream. Tired but strangely content, we sat on the fo'c'sle head in the evening glow or walked out on the stringpiece of the railroad wharf, which then jutted far into the harbor, and watched the lights aboard the U. S. S. Bennington. Except Peter, we had made no friends aboard the gunboat. They seemed like men of a different world, as indeed they were. The sounding of "taps" over the water, the clear plaintive notes of the bugle, ended our day. We were to load on the morrow; at last we were to start on the final half of our voyage, with the taking aboard of our first bag of sugar.

## CHAPTER XXI

## LOADING SUGAR

Loading a deep water ship with sugar in the port of Honolulu during the golden summer days of the young Republic was a lively business.

"Hi there! On the dock! Bear a hand with that sugar! Shake it up now! Shake it up! Do you think we have a year to load this ship? By —! I'll shake you up! Yes, me! You lazy black —!"

"Pau! Pau! Kaliopoulie! kaue Ki! Ki! O—ooo maloue baue Pau. Likee Pau—! Pau! pau! pau! Oh—ee hakau! pau! pau!" or words to that effect, according to the phonetic rendering. A violent protest of many tongues, bristling with exclamation points, and heated Kanaka epithets, rose from the indignant dock gang. Glances of the utmost withering scorn were shot up out of the hold at the mate standing abreast of the main hatch, and all over the dock shirts were being slipped back onto the silky brown backs, stripped in readiness for the work to start, The uproar of indignation was spontaneous, and on the outskirts of the racket the stocky Japanese coolies from the sugar plantation gangs, and from the railroad gang, stood around in sullen enjoyment of the situation. Aboard ship we of the crew were circumspect, but our appreciation of the situation was keen.

"What's this?" A smart looking chap in a suit of khaki, and wearing a panama hat, stepped out of the office on the dock. He was sun browned and efficient; springy in his movements, a natural commander of men.

"Pau —!" cried a dark skinned perspiring stevy, pointing at the mate, and sending forth another shower of island rhetoric. The gang foreman of the shore crowd was explaining, brown face shining and eyes flashing black and white.

"All right! I'll see about it." The railroad superintendent climbed aboard and took Mr. Zerk aft, out of earshot, where they got things settled. Then the superintendent went back on the dock, the gang foreman got an earful of second hand apologies, explanations and promises. Important details of same were passed on to independent Kanaka citizens by their boss, and the steam winch started as the shirts again were slipped off of the silky brown backs of the workers. We are off. The first sling of sugar bags shot over the bulwark and landed on the platform abreast the hatch and four Kanakas started sending it down the chutes like lightning. Bing! Another sling dripped on the platform, and down it went. The action became automatic, the brown bodies swayed rapidly, surely, and on the wharf we heard them shouting as the Jap coolies inched along another car with their crow bars. I was stationed at a point where two chutes met at an angle, and the yellow bags passed me in rapid succession, slapping the chute with a smart patter as they jumped the corner. Soon the whole thing became a matter of easy routine. This was living! What an easy job! The dusky gang below, working in the half light of the hold, and assisted by the crew, were placing a bottom layer of sugar bags and forward stacking and stepping back the tiers, "boulking" it, as sailors say, for the ends of the hold to be kept clear.

The Hawaiian sugar is only partly refined, and of a dull golden color when the sun strikes it. It is largely granular, the particles being almost the size of a small pea. The sacks, made of gunny, are stamped with the names of the various plantations; Ewa, Laie, Halawa, Holua Loa, Kilauea, Makee, Wailuku, and a dozen others, all of them the mystic symbols spelling wealth to their fortunate owners.

They weigh in the neighborhood of one hundred and fifty pounds of the limpest, deadest, weight in the world and without decent "ears" at the end of the sack to afford a hold. Frequently a sack would break, and we would help ourselves to the sugar. The taste is pleasant at first, and we were remarkably liberal in our indulgence, perhaps no more so than a crew of girls would be if they were loading a cargo of chocolate creams.

The sugar as it comes from the island refineries is about twice as sweet as the white granulated article. To a crowd accustomed to black jack molasses as a sweetener for their coffee, the sugar was a wonderful delicacy, for a time. Soon we became cloyed with the taste, and for weeks after my first gorging of sweets, I took my coffee and tea without it, though we always had a small keg of the stuff on hand forward during the remainder of the voyage. The sweet overpowering smell of the sugar soon permeated the ship, and in the heat of midday, became nauseating to us who were not used to it.

The Kanaka workers, splendid specimens, would toss the heavy sacks with apparent ease, the muscles rippling under their smooth skins as they worked. The greatest good feeling prevailed in the hold, and the men constantly referred to our mate amid sallies of laughter for it was considered a great victory for them when the superintendent smoothed matters out.

On deck, at the hatch, and on the wharf, the tally men checked the loading of every sling and bag of sugar that went into the hold. The plantation, the railroad, and the ship's agents had their independent checkers. These chaps, mostly sedate older men, well educated, apparently well paid, kept the neatest tally books I have ever seen. They made the cleanest little marks with very sharp pencils, which they were always sharpening with very sharp pen knives; little marks four in a row, and a cross for every fifth bag. Before the end of each day's loading these very independent tally men would get together under the fo'c'sle head, or behind a convenient freight car on the dock, and reconcile all differences, thus proving themselves brothers under their skins to independent folk in higher stations. Years afterward, I recognized some of these same tally men, still at the job of making very neat little marks and crosses, an easy job no doubt and well worth while if it contributed toward the upkeep of a happy family; most of them looked like settled benedicts.

As we cleaned out the warehouse, the sugar began to come in on the railroad and was slung right aboard from the cars, the Japs sending the loaded cars along by pushing, getting them started by short crow bars, used as levers under the wheels. These Japs were a husky lot with very able bodies, small heads, black cropped hair, often wound with a red or white head band. Most of them had dazzling white teeth which they constantly exposed by expansive grins; altogether they were a testimonial to a rice and fish diet, so far as physical wellbeing is concerned.

The days at the sugar wharf were among the most pleasant of our stay in Honolulu, and like all good things they raced away with disquieting swiftness. Having lighter duties to perform, we were not so dog tired at night and enjoyed our leisure that much more. Peter continued to make progress with the native population and on one eventful night was presented with a large jug of swipes, as a token of esteem.

Brenden, Axel and I were up on Nuuanu Street, in the vicinity of Merchant, watching the shifting crowds as we wandered aimlessly about. Presently we spied Peter, coming toward us, carrying his jug. The street was fairly crowded, and going ahead of us, toward Peter, was a one-legged man; a pugnacious individual who brought down his iron shod peg with loud determination. The wooden leg yawed badly, sailing at least three sheets in the wind, and the flag sidewalk was none too wide for him. Coming up to

Peter, he lurched suddenly to port, taking our shipmate squarely on the bow, and the three of them, all carrying cargo, Peter, the Peg Leg, and the Jug of Swipes, rolled into the dusty gutter.

A fight started right there. The Peg, to give him a proper name, attacking, and Peter defending himself from the strange fury of the indignant cripple.

"Separate 'em! Don't you see the man's got only one leg?"

"Hi! The bloat wi' the wooden pin is fightin'! Blarst 'im!—look at 'im!" Sailors, beach combers, natives, and Orientals were gathering and taking voice.

We closed to render assistance as the crowd formed under the circle of light from a street lamp. The two combatants sat back in the gutter after a second exchange, both having fought sitting down.

"What are we fighting for?" cried Peter, covered with dirt and sweat.

"I dunno," admitted the stunned Peg.

"To hell with this, let's quit!"

"Naw. I wanna fight!" Peg was getting back his belligerent wind. "Wash in that jug?" he demanded, seeing the prize.

"Swipes!" cried Peter, trying to retrieve the jug.

"Lesh fight fer swipsh. Al ri! Fight fer swipsh!" he screamed with enthusiasm.

The Peg made another lunge at Peter, as our boy jumped up with surprising energy, and we grabbed our shipmate and hauled him out of the crowd of riff raff that was rapidly increasing. Some blue-jackets from the Bennington came up, scenting fun, and Axel was just in time to beat them to the jug of swipes that lay neglected in the dust. He passed this to a Kanaka standing near, a boy we recognized as one of the loading gang, who rapidly departed with his unexpected present, while we hurried off with Peter in the direction of Fort Street. What became of Peg is unknown. On Fort Street we were attracted by the melody of Salvation Army music, and to wind up the night, watched our famous Jimmy rouse things up in his new uniform, his chest expanding visibly as he ignored us and pounded his drum with added zest.

On nights such as this, warm and sultry, when the trade wind was not over strong, the smell from the Chinese and Japanese stores would come out into the streets with added intensity. The Chinese merchants, in the shadow of their open front stores, would entertain their families and friends of an evening with interminable jabberings that must have been mighty interesting to them. I used to wonder what these industrious law abiding citizens found to talk about; now I realize that, except to those who were blind or deaf, the Honolulu nights could hardly be long enough for them to discuss half of the peculiar doings of the daffy white people residing in that busy little town, in those stirring days of the Republic.

To a foremast hand, a common sailor in the fo'c'sle of a deepwaterman, the point of view is almost on a level with that of the perpetually unassimilated Oriental. The sailor sees, he hears, and if he is gifted with brains that think, he must needs wonder at the strange ways of folks who dress themselves so well, who live on the most appetizing foods, perform very little hard work, and who do themselves to the height of their ability. That we had a few philosophers among the crowd forward goes without saying; men who had lived, and who had had their fling, and for all I know to the contrary are having it again. I wager Hitchen, if not killed by this time, has mounted to more enlightened planes; perhaps back to a station from which he temporarily stepped down to sign articles in the ship A. J. Fuller for the voyage around Cape Horn.

We did a lot of swapping of books and magazines among the craft in the harbor. The poor starved crowd from the British Monarch were first over the side with bundles of old magazines, paper covered novels, and mind destroying sheets called "Tit Bits," and "Snappy Bits," periodicals of a peculiar type. After reading one of them for an hour (and the funny part is you keep on reading and reading), it is a sort of mental dope, nothing remains but a vague idea of a lot of short paragraphs full of piffle.

We got a number of Clark Russell stories in this exchange, though we really had little to give in return. All hands read these yarns and while there was much grumbling about "too much skirt," the sailor was recognized.

Hitchen and Old Smith were the best read among the crowd, with Australia a close second; leaving out of course that biblical student, the dear departed Jimmy. Frenchy also was entitled to a place among the intellectuals of the fo'c'sle; he read Voltaire, had several copies of his works in the original, as well as shopworn copies of Les Miserables, and the Toilers of the Sea. Frenchy read English with difficulty. Axel also was handicapped in literary discussions by his lack of English though he waded through books in that language, having been taught it at school; of course he spoke English well, as indeed all did, barring a bit of slack here and there, that merely served to give the fo'c'sle individuality.

One thing I will always remember with a great deal of pleasure is the fact that Axel was the first one to give me a definite story of the Andree North Pole Expedition, he having tried for, and almost succeeded in going along. A university professor took the place he wanted at the last moment, the scholar going to perform the duties of a common jack in order to be with Andree. I recall the fo'c'sle discussion of this ill fated venture, the final outcome of which was still in doubt. I felt at that time that Andree had a good chance to accomplish his end, and I still think so; the luck simply ran against him. Nine years later it was to be my fortune to have a part in a similar expedition under Wellman, except that a dirigible balloon, of which I was navigator, was employed. We were more fortunate in so far as we got back. Andree, Strindberg, and Fraenkel were not fools as some think, but fearless scientists who took a legitimate chance to explore the unknown polar regions; fate was against them, but even so, they have left the memory of a brave deed inscribed on the bright scroll of Swedish honor.

Old Smith had a dog-eared copy of Marcus Aurelius that had served its noble duty in discussions with Jimmy Marshall, while the latter was deep in the wisdom of King Solomon. I don't know what Brenden read, but he was a great letter writer, and often received mail. When taking pictures one day, Brenden asked me to take a picture of him reading a letter from his girl Hilda. The Letters of One Brenden, Able Seaman on the ship A. J. Fuller, would certainly make quaint reading, could they be got at and translated, for Brenden conducted his correspondence in German.

**BRENDEN READING LETTER**

Mike, and Martin and Fred were mere fillers in. Beef on a rope, and able eaters, they remain as memories, indistinct and still quite clear; they never succeeded in making an impression on the life of the ship but were the background of that distant time, seldom saying anything that was listened to. Of Tommy, or the more dignified Tom, we will learn more later on. He was a man with a past, and I hope a future, for he certainly earned the right to a very bright one while on the Fuller; that future, however, did not lie on the sea. As high admiral of a pickle barge and fleet commander of a whole flotilla of shelf jugs full of vinegar and preserved edibles, in his own delicatessen store, he may have risen to success.

Scouse never read anything; he was too busy thinking, and as he did less and less talking as the voyage lengthened, we concluded he must be a very deep fellow. Scouse had points, and I have no doubt after all the hazing afloat and skinning ashore, he learned and digested lessons of the utmost value.

Peter, of whom so much has been said and so little told, was in a way the most interesting character on board. He was, and no doubt still is, one of the most generous souls alive. If he is rich, it is certainly for no lack of a wild desire to share his last cent with any unfortunate that might cross his path. Peter started to sea in deep water sail for reasons that do him credit. He saw a way to recoup his health and at the same time bring to a conclusion an intense amour that seemed to lead directly to an early grave. He shipped on the Fuller, leaving a large wash behind in the tender care of his sweetheart. No boarding master captured part of his advance, and for a week afterward at least, so Peter said, two coffee pots must have stood on a certain N. Y. kitchen window, as a signal that his laundry was ready to be taken away. The lady's husband was a night clerk in the post office.

The career of Peter would serve as a theme for a first class psychological novel with the plots of half a dozen red-hot problem plays added by way of good measure. He started life with the curse of good looks, of the romantic type, dark and interesting, his rather long silky locks, curled slightly, and his regular features were classic. Deep brown eyes, and a very fine, rich voice completed his downfall. As reporter on a country paper, Peter told us how he would write up the stories of the socialist meetings, by sending a boy around to the local hall to see if the lights were lit. His adventures as foreman in a corset factory, as cadet in the American Line, and as a social worker in the humble ranks of those who uplift the sailor ashore, were chapters in the start of a busy life.

CHAPTER XXII

## GOOD-BYE TO HONOLULU

As the hold began to fill up, the top of the sugar was brought inboard from the wings to an apex, and the lower cargo space not quite filled. The 'tween deck was then loaded in order to carry the dead weight sufficiently high to prevent the ship from being stiff; to make her more "sea kindly" as sailors say. Theoretical questions of metacentric height, of the center of buoyancy, and their relation to stability never bothered the captain or Mr. Zerk. But as the loading progressed they paid a lot of attention to her trim and in the placement of the last part of the cargo, the mate assumed complete charge. The Fuller sailed best trimmed a few feet by the stern, but in the final loading this extra depth aft was cut down to a single foot as a matter of experiment, the mean draft loaded being seventeen feet eight inches, giving her the usual freeboard of about four feet or three inches to every foot of draft, according to the old rule. Draft is shown by figures cut into the stem and stern post; these are six inches high and the figure rests on the mark it indicates.

In addition to the sugar from the railroad, we had steamers of the inter-island trade come along side and discharge their cargoes right onto our deck. These craft have been touched upon before. The Mauna Loa, one of the largest at that time, was quite a passenger carrier. As I think of the inter-island steamers they always appear to have been somewhat out of drawing, when compared with the beautiful sailers of those days.

During the final week of loading, when we had closed the 'tween deck hatches to the lower hold and were putting down the finishing tiers of cargo, we paid our last visits ashore. I bid "good-bye" to Mr. McInerny and the good friends I had made, both in society and out. We went over to the British Monarch, Hitchen and I, for a last visit. The mates had a bit of a "blow" for us, hot toddy, which tasted right in spite of the warm weather, cigars, and some Huntley and Palmer biscuits broken out of their stores for this special occasion. Of course we promised to write, and never did, and Mr. Gore gave me an old copy of Raper, he having two of them, as a parting gift. To Hitchen he gave a tin of navy cut that had been sent out to him from England. They were hoping for word of a charter to be on their way, and thought they might load sugar for New York, when we planned to meet again as sailors sometimes do.

**Jack Hitchen**

With what little change we had left, we laid in a few stores for the voyage home, a few bunches of bananas, odds and ends of clothing, and the like. I purchased a pair of mittens, after a search in that tropic city, as mine had worn out in hauling at the gear. The most startling addition to our life forward was a green parrot that Frenchy brought aboard, having swapped him at the Union saloon for a small brig, rigged in a bay rum bottle. This brig had been a long time making, and Frenchy only let go of it when he was assured of a prize. The bird, hailing from God knows where, as I don't believe they are native to the islands, was to be a present to his sister Madeleine. Frenchy named him Jaques, at once vulgarized to common Jake, and he was hung in his wooden cage under the fo'c'sle head.

Just before hauling into the stream, Captain Nichols shipped three Kanakas to take the places left vacant by Mr. Stoddard, Jimmy, and Joe. This made it certain that someone from the crew would be taken aft as second mate. The Kanakas were a rare assortment. Kahemuku, a lanky, poetical looking fellow with long hair and dreamy eyes, hailed from Tahiti. The two others, both of them short and somewhat stout, were from Honolulu and should have known better than to ship around the Horn. John Aahee was assigned to the starboard watch; he was clean shaven and dull, a poor devil who merely existed after we got to sea. Black Joe, so the mate called him, since his name was beyond ordinary understanding, was fully whiskered with a bunch of fuzz that looked like the stuffing of an old hair mattress. Joe had a peculiar idea about the relation between officers and men, and never could get this straightened out. Black Joe and Kahemuku were assigned to the port watch to take the place of Jimmy and Joe.

Some of the men thought that I would be called aft as second mate. Ambitious as I was for preferment, I realized that the billet would be about the worst thing that could happen to me. Whatever the captain may have thought about it, the mate was against me, as we remained at loggerheads while I visited with my "dude friends," which I did at intervals as long as we were in port.

Old Smith was the logical candidate for the job, and the mate wanted him. Others were like Barkis, but the strange part was that the real sailors in the crew, the men who knew enough to stand a watch at sea and work the ship, were the most anxious to side step the honor.

Having loaded our sugar, the chutes were sent ashore, and we again hauled out into the stream, this time for good. We at once battened down the hatches, putting on triple tarpaulins, and, having taken down the cargo pendants, we again rove the seagoing running gear; after a day of scrubbing, during which the spars were washed clean of dust, we then began to bend sail. This took us the greater part of two days while we sent aloft the fine weather canvas. Then followed another general washing down and cleaning over the side, and the ship A. J. Fuller looked herself again. Loaded to her deep sea trim, with yards squared to a hair and canvas furled with a harbor stow, we were as flash a ship as ever hailed from the port of New York—clean, and seamanlike in every detail. Fancy manropes were got out for the gangways, the galley smoke stack was given a coat of black paint, making "Charlie Noble," as this piece of humble but necessary sea furniture is called, as sporty as any part of the old girl.

In the meantime, while our busy little ship world revolved within its restricted orbit, events of historic importance were happening in the great arena beyond the seas. Dewey had captured Manila and the first troops to go out from the United States were expected in Honolulu, en route to the Philippines. Preparations to welcome them of a gigantic nature were carried out by the enthusiastic citizens of Honolulu, the American element being in the ascendant. A tremendous flag was got ready, to be raised over the railroad wharf, and huge stores of sandwiches were made and held in readiness for the soldiers. Also every barrel and bottle of beer in the place was put on ice against an emergency. The citizens were determined that hunger should not outflank the U. S. forces, if by any means it could be prevented, nor was old General Thirst to be allowed to down a single man. It was also decided that U. S. legal tender was not to be accepted when offered for refreshment by a man wearing the uniform of Uncle Sam, showing how war fever (for a time) upsets the commercial mind.

The transports City of Pekin, City of Sydney, and Australia, came into the harbor on June first carrying twenty-two hundred troops. These vessels were under convoy of the U. S. S. Charleston. The day was a gala one and in the midst of the excitement we received our orders to sail for Delaware Breakwater. This came as a surprise as we expected to be sent to Frisco because of the possibility of our being picked up by a Spaniard in view of the uncertain state of affairs in the Atlantic. We were then in the stream, wistful gazers at the harbor activities and the glimpses of great times ashore afforded by the pier heads and the esplanade.

With the coming of our orders, Captain Nichols sent out such fresh provisions as deep water ships usually take to sea with them. A potato bin had been constructed under the fo'c'sle head in a place that would be fairly dry and having a good circulation of air. Into this we put about a ton of the tubers. Some fresh meat was sent aboard, and a few bunches of bananas strung in the after wheel house for the cabin mess. A number of our men had been offered billets on coasters, and this was specially so during the last few weeks of our loading. The pay day of close to fifty dollars already on the books, and the prospect of landing in New York with almost eighty dollars added to it, was a prospect hard to leave, especially since the plans for great futures depended absolutely upon these prospective nest eggs. The fact, however, was that we were a well selected crowd and liked to sail together. The captain was absolutely square and the mate was a sailor from his toes to his truck; we were too much accustomed to the routine on the Fuller to want to change. As far as I was concerned, I was happy to remain on board and work back around old Cape Stiff again. Mr. McInerny had offered to have me released from the articles and wanted me to take up my residence in the islands, telling me of the many advantages, much after the manner of Robinson Crusoe's old father, when that wilful lad determined upon the sea as a career. I, too, had old Crusoe's trouble pretty well soaked into my system. I was really an enthusiast about going to sea, in spite of the hard knocks, so I made up my mind to complete the voyage.

On Sunday, five days before we sailed, the captain called Old Smith aft and formally offered him the billet as second mate. Old Smith refused to move out of the fo'c'sle, and came forward with a fat cigar in his teeth, saying, "The skipper's all right. He sure is all right."

After that we were too busy to think anything more of the vexed problem, being horsed about at bending sail and preparing for sea. On the eve of our departure we were sitting on the fo'c'sle head watching the crowded harbor, the comings and goings from the men o' war and transports, and listening to the bugle calls. We had washed up after the day's work, and the mess cooks had gone to the galley for the kids.

"We'll sleep our last night in, tonight," ventured Frenchy, as we perched on the heel of the starboard cathead. It was a thought that came to all of us.

"Grub O!" called Fred from the space about the fore pin rail, where both watches ate together while in port. We sat around the kids, under the tall gear of the foremast rising overhead, the faint peppering of stars showing between the yards as we began our supper.

"Here comes the mate," said Martin, who was perched on the short ladder leading to the fo'c'sle head, from the port side of the house.

"Wot of it, let him come."

Presently Mr. Zerk stood in the gangway looking at us, he bulked big, and smoked a strong cigar. This was the first time he had ever intruded upon our meals during our stay in port.

"Where's the second mate?" he asked pleasantly.

Most of us looked around anxiously, half expecting the old second mate would bob up from some dark corner.

"Come on, where is he?" The mate was evidently enjoying his little game. "Where is he now?" came the question again, but in a sharp tone such as we usually associated with coming trouble. "Come on, where is he?" Suddenly he started to laugh; of course we all joined him in a sort of nervous chorus.

"Ho, there he is hiding behind the kid! Our new second mate, Mr. Morstad! Well, well, well!" and this is how Tommy, most unexpected of candidates, became Mr. Morstad, second mate of the ship A. J. Fuller.

"Lay aft," said the mate, as he turned to go, "the steward has your dinner ready, and don't forget to bring your napkin."

Tommy was choking with astonishment, speechless, and miserable. None of us laughed at the last cruel thrust; in fact we felt sorry for Tommy, but as soon as we saw him stop eating the fo'c'sle grub, with the quick perception that better things awaited him aft, a lively discussion arose.

"Call him Mr. Morstad!" thundered Australia. "I won't have no disrespect here just because Mr. Morstad ain't had the bringin' up you an' me has. No, sir, I have some respect for the officers of this ship, I have."

There was a lot more in a similar vein. Volunteers offered to carry his chest aft, and did every thing but lift it, poor Tommy having to drag it along the deck until he got to the waist, when Chips came out of his den and helped him the rest of the way. It was dark then, and the gong for the second cabin table no doubt compensated Tommy for all the tortures of his departure.

"I'm damn glad he ain't in my watch," said Brenden, and all of us to port felt the same way. Before Tommy had time to adjust himself to his new condition, the kicking started to starboard.

In this particular episode of the voyage Mr. Zerk departed as far from the traditions of the sea as it was possible for him to go. The next morning, as we got under way to sea, Captain Nichols made it a point to show public respect to the new second officer. It was "Mr. Morstad, this," and "How do you head, sir?" all of which pleased Tom immensely, and was the right and proper thing to do.

CHAPTER XXIII

HOMEWARD BOUND

*And we're off to Mother Carey*
*(Walk her down to Mother Carey!)*
*Oh, we're bound for Mother Carey where she feeds her chicks at sea!*
**Kipling.**

Bare feet, gripping the cool deck of the fo'c'sle head, still wet with the washdown, pattered in rhythmic circles to the music of the pawls, sounding over the early morning stillness of Honolulu Harbor. We were heaving up the anchor, having already taken in our quarter moorings. The pilot was aboard; Captain Nichols stumped the poop with his characteristic jerky stride, all business; second mate Tom was aloft with a half dozen hands, and the pleasant swish of falling canvas, and the rattle of blocks and running gear, sounded above as they cast off the long sea gaskets. About us in the harbor the men o' war and transports lay silent to their moorings, sleeping off the effect of a day and night of revelry ashore. Mr. Zerk stood out over the bow on the port cathead, his hand on the catfall, as he leaned far over.

"Five fathom shackle at the water!" he sung out.

"All right! Bring her short!" came the order from the poop.

"Aye, aye, sir! Walk her up, up, boys! Walk her up, and wake her up."

Old Smith got the tune and presently the dirge of an anchor chantey echoed across the water as we bent our weight against the capstan bars.

"Paddy come back and turn in your slack,
Heave round the capstan, heave a pawl, heave a pawl.
We're leavin' Honolulu girls, and never will come back,
Heave round the capstan, heave a pawl, heave a pawl.
An' happy days all lie behind, good-bye to swipes and rum,
Heave round the capstan, heave a pawl, heave a pawl."

"Short stay, sir!" bawled the mate, and we stopped our song. The faint echo of a cheer wafted across the harbor; we recognized the hail from our friends on the British Monarch, watching to see us off.

"Break her out, sir!" answered the captain, sending his voice along the length of the ship in sharp, snappy syllables.

"Aye, aye, sir!"

At "short stay," I was ordered to the wheel and as I slipped the spokes from the beckets, the crowd at the bars again put their beef to the cable, and the anchor left bottom. The tug fastened to our quarter got her signal from the pilot; we heard the jangle of bells in her engine room; we commenced to move.

"Hard a port!" ordered the pilot.

"Hard over, sir!"

"Steady so! Steady so!" We were heading toward the old marine railway, the line of the Esplanade having swung under the jib guys with remarkable swiftness, as I turned the wheel to meet her.

"Port handsomely!" I gave her wheel. "Port, I say! Hard a port!"

"Hard a port, sir!" Again the shore shot past her bow, and then the blue water of the harbor mouth lay fair ahead.

"Steady! Starb'd a point! Steady so!"

We were pointing out through the narrow entrance of Honolulu Harbor. Forward they had hooked the cat and the fall was brought "two blocks" while the great hook hung upright, dripping the slimy harbor silt.

The mate then assumed charge of the deck, sheeting home and hoisting away as fast as the men could man the ropes. A light off shore breeze on the port quarter bellied out the canvas. The buoys, barrel buoy to starboard, spar buoy to port, slipped past us. Presently the tug started to drag her head to port, as the ship's way increased, and I had to give her wheel to meet her.

"Guess we are all right now, Pilot."

"All right, Captain. All clear ahead and plenty of water from here to the Horn. Good luck and a quick passage."

They shook hands, the pilot waved a farewell to the mate down in the waist, then jumped onto the wheel house of the tug from our mizzen channels. A few squeaky toots by way of a salute as she cast off, and the tug swung sharply about and headed back to port; the last link binding us to Honolulu had been severed.

At eight bells, breakfast time, I was relieved and, on my way forward, I stopped for a parting glance back at Honolulu. What was my surprise when I found it well down on the horizon, the Island of Oahu stretching a mere blur of bluish green across our wake. A lump rose in my throat for I did wish to have another look at that fair city of dreams, but it was already a thing of the hazy past; a figment of memory; the port of phantasmagoria; a jumble of many colored people, of smells, of music; of green and restful bowers, of feverish energy and of indolence, of days of dirty, sweaty labor, and of nights of romantic adventures. And what of Jimmy Marshall, I wondered, left behind with his uniform and drum?

Yes, we were out to sea again, the cool breeze wafting us along, out on the restless ocean as before, months and months ago too numerous to remember, when we sailed to the eastward with the Navesink Highlands dropping far behind us in the sunset. Now the only difference was the fact that the Island of Captain Cook, the first port of Stevenson on his retirement to the Pacific, and that vivid stage upon which Father Damien lived and died, was fading away far to the north.

At breakfast we again separated into watches but with orders to turn to again, as the first day was to be one of "all hands." We were glad to a man that the homeward passage had commenced. The drop in temperature put snap into us and Australia celebrated our departure by tearing down the dingy mosquito bar triced above his bunk. He balled this up and hove it over the side with the remark, "Here goes me night cage; good-bye forever."

The breeze was blowing strong, a splendid northeast trade, and the smooth sea made our progress something very cheering. At two bells I was called aft and, with Brenden and Frenchy, helped heave the log chip under direction of Captain Nichols.

The log line, soaked with water, was wound on a large reel. Brenden stood on one side of the wheel house and held this over his head, each hand gripping a handle of the reel as he faced squarely aft. He was far enough forward from the taffrail so we could tend the line. The log chip, a small quadrant of wood weighted on its circular side to make it swim upright in the water, was attached to the line by a triple bridle, the two parts from the ends of the circle being seized to a small wooden plug that fitted snugly to a wooden socket seized to the part of the log line running from the apex of the chip. This arrangement holds the chip upright and perpendicular to the direction of the log line; when the line is given a sharp jerk, the plug disengages, the chip capsizes, and can be easily hauled aboard. It is really a sort of miniature sea anchor.

Captain Nichols stood by with the sand glass. Frenchy was told to cast the chip overboard, while I stood at the rail to see the line run clear. Twenty fathoms of the "stray line" went over first, the end being marked by a piece of red bunting. As this ran over the taffrail the skipper called out "Turn," at the same time turning the glass himself. He was greatly pleased with the whole proceeding and danced around much after the manner of a small boy with a new kite. The sand glass was a twenty-eight second one, and the captain had dried it out in the galley that morning and then compared it with his chronometer.

The line was tearing over the rail like wild and as the captain called, "Up!" Frenchy grabbed the line.

Examining the line we found we were making 10.2 knots.

At the time of shouting "Up!" Captain Nichols stepped over to the Bliss taffrail log trailing on the weather quarter and noted the dial. An hour later we again hove the old-fashioned log and checked our reading on the patent log. For the information of landsmen, it may be well to say that a knot on the log line—and here is where the term comes from—is a distance of forty-seven feet, four inches (for a 28-second glass), the same proportional part of a sea mile or "knot" of 6,080 feet that 28 seconds is of an hour. The different knots along the line are distinguished by fish line tucked into the strands and a knot cast for each mark away from the start. Tenths are estimated, the length between knots being divided by shreds of white bunting into five parts. If sailing fast, as we were, a short glass is sometimes used; this registers fourteen seconds and the readings on the log line must be doubled. In passing it may be well to mention that the old-fashioned log chip, where speeds are not over, say fifteen knots, is the most reliable method of measurement of rate of speed through the roster ever devised. Also, the fact that the sea mile or "knot" is six thousand and eighty feet, and not five thousand two hundred and eighty feet as ashore, is due to the fact that in navigating a ship over the sea it is necessary to have a standard of measurement bearing a simple relation to the size and shape of the earth. One sea mile is the length of one minute of arc measured on the meridian, 6,080 feet. This is the mean value, for, owing to the flattening at the poles, the minute of arc varies slightly from the poles to the equator.

Ten knots and over is fair going for any sailer, and extra fine for trade wind sailing. Our hopes for a quick passage were high. The water boiled past us in a smother of swishing foam, a cheerful chatter when homeward bound, while aloft every inch of sail was doing its full duty. Before noon we got the anchor scrubbed clean and at once unshackled the cables and sent them below, bowsing the jackasses into the hawse pipes, as on the passage out. Both bower anchors were then secured inboard and lashed to heavy ring bolts on the fo'c'sle head, the cat and fish falls were unrove, stopped up and stowed below.

We put in the afternoon rousing up this rope and that, tautening every stitch of canvas to its full extent. Our new second mate was given his first lessons in the handling of a watch at sea, and did well enough, considering the fact that Chief Mate Zerk kept the center of the stage, as was his habit whenever anything transpired on the deck. At four bells the starboard watch went below, and we stood the first dog watch. In the second dog watch we sat around yarning, still being too full of rational rest to seek our bunks. We watched Tommy handle things alone—but for all that Captain Nichols was always to be seen far aft, stumping the poop, and keeping a mighty watchful eye on the progress of events. During the night watches he was particularly in evidence. Tommy gained confidence faster than he did experience and assumed a certain air of superiority that was galling to his former watchmates. Old Smith was the one to carry things along by setting a correct example to the men. Often when Tom did not know just what to do, Old Smith would start things by jumping to the proper rope and the order would tally along afterward. On the other hand, things got so that when Tom gave the wrong orders the watch would disregard them and do what they thought was right. Old Smith, Hitchen, Axel and Charlie Horse knew as much about sailing as any second mate, and the result was not disastrous, although at times a trifle ragged.

The captain shaped a course due south, magnetic, running along the meridian of one hundred and fifty-eight degrees west from Greenwich. This carried us to the eastward of Karatoo Island and we then put more easting in the course and sailed past the Walker Islands, crossing the equator when five days out from Honolulu; a fair bit of travelling for a vessel of the latter sailing ship days. Here the trades failed us and again we were to wallow in the stagnant latitudes that try the spirit and vex the soul. But the ship's company forward were in excellent humor and anything but sea weary. We employed the time below, not given over to sleeping, in sewing our much worn clothing, in scrubbing clothes, an art in which we were expert, and in yarning about the times gone by.

As the days spread into weeks we thought more and more of the times to come, and of course discussed them at great length. Much of our mental intercourse had a hopeful, speculative trend. Being wholly human and with all the weaknesses that sailor flesh abounds in, it is not to be wondered at if the ambitions of that voyage never fully materialized; judging by my own, I can say they did not. I wanted to command another such ship as the Fuller, to stump to windward and set the course, to have all night in, and eat delicious viands at the cabin table. Stranger fate was to await me before I cast my anchor in the fair cove called home, with kids to crawl upon my knee and call me "Dadda," and a wife to remind me now and then that I am not captain here.

CHAPTER XXIV

HAWAIIAN SHIPMATES

"Damn these rotten oilskins. By — what's this?" "Oh, hell!" It was black as a pocket on deck and a sudden douse of rain sent us scrambling for our oil clothing. "Damn it I'm lousy, sure as you're born. Ugh!" and similar forceful if inelegant expressions punctuated the night as we struggled into these smelly, sticky rags. They were as paper to the rain; we were wet before we knew it. In the pockets and in every fold millions of cockroaches, whole nations of them, debouched upon the streaming decks. Some of us stole forward and in the light from the fo'c'sle examined things. On the fo'c'sle deck, where we had knocked them in hastily, unhooking the oiled clothing from the bulkhead behind the water butt, were several regiments of roaches.

During our two months in Honolulu we had never used oilskins, and, sailor-like, left them hang. In the warm atmosphere the bugs multiplied amid luxurious surroundings with unlimited supplies of delicious linseed-oil to thrive upon. Fortunately we were in the tropics and a wet back did not matter, especially as we always doused ourselves with a bucket of salt water after a wetting by rain, a sure way to prevent colds. As for the evicted roaches, they were no doubt as mad as we were. In the next fine spell we rubbed our oilskins with fresh mixtures of raw oil and a little melted beeswax from the sailmaker's stores.

The first job of any magnitude started, after leaving port, was to scrape all bright work, that is, all varnished woodwork, masts and light spars. We then rubbed them down with boiled linseed-oil. This work was done from bo'sun's chairs, using pieces of broken glass as scrapers. The fine shavings fluttered into every crook and corner of the ship, lodging in the coils of rope and providing a constant job of cleaning while the work was under way. Scouse was again elected to the drudgery, but in this instance he became a man of some importance, for Kahemuku and Black Joe were assigned to work with him. He jollied them in a rough, uncouth way and they sat at his feet in respectful worship. They were permanently constituted the knockabout gang of our watch and cleaned out the head every other morning when we were on deck for the washdown. Getting up coal for the galley of a Sunday morning was one of their regular jobs, and after the washdown they were the boys who handled the big deck swabs while the rest of us got the gear off the pins and stowed the washdeck utensils.

As for myself, a change had come over the mate, or I too would have been of this crowd. Our relations were fairly cordial again, becoming increasingly so when I loaned him copies of "Midshipman Easy" and "Commodore Junk," books given me by my father when I left home.

Of the three Kanakas we had the prize winner in Black Joe. In the first place Black Joe never said "sir" to an officer, but he applied this mark of distinction to every hand forward. At first some of the boys wanted to make Black Joe permanent messman of the watch. He was willing enough, for he knew nothing about a ship and felt his shortcomings and wanted to help out.

"Be fair with him. How would you like that job regular?" Frenchy put in the good word and we decided that Black Joe was to get a square deal forward anyhow.

His failure to properly respond to orders from aft caused a lot of suppressed amusement. The mate bawled him unmercifully but to no purpose, for Black Joe simply had things set in his mind and there was no changing him. Finally, the mate worked out a satisfactory solution of the problem, so far as he was concerned, though Black Joe could hardly be termed a third-rate success as a sailor.

"Here you! Fred, take that baboon and loose the fore upper tops'l!" was his method of horsing him. In working the gear on deck he would shout, "Get that Kanaka coon and hook him on the lee fore brace!" In working ship Black Joe was pushed and pulled from station to station. He could not coil down a rope properly no matter how often the trick was explained to him; every other time he would lay the gear down left-handed as like as not. If he hitched a coil on the fife or pin rails it was an even chance that a fid would be needed to get it down. Black Joe was all thumbs and his slow mind worked backward. His best performance was at the kids, but his table manners would have disgraced him at a luau.

Kahemuku was of a different type. He was sentimental, a dreamer and all for himself when aloft. The way he would strangle the stick when out on a yard was a sight for the angels. His long arms were as good as three turns of a sea gasket, and his bare feet would grip the foot ropes with brown prehensile toes. Life was made more bearable for him by the fact that he was constantly looking forward to a shining goal.

"Pilladelpia" was the burden of his song. He intended to see the great city of "Pilladelpia" and asked interminable questions about it, sitting on the edge of his bunk, a great dusky six footer, with the wistful brown eyes of a trusting child. When told we would probably go to New York, he would answer, "No, I wanna go Pilladelpia." Poor Kahemuku, whatever became of you God only knows. You most certainly never fell from aloft, but your passage around the Horn in the Antarctic winter must have prepared you for any fate.

Sailors, like other mortals, are as jealous of their little rights and privileges as any of us ashore. To stand a trick at the wheel in regular turn, to see that everyone stood his lawful share of this duty, was a strong incentive to silence on the part of those who were wise to the fact that Kahemuku and Black Joe knew nothing about steering. They could not box the compass, and in fact knew nothing about the action of the helm or the use of the wheel.

Black Joe stood a trick nevertheless between Australia and Fred, and Ivahemuku followed Fred and was relieved in turn by able seaman Brenden. That these three worthies, Australia, Fred and Brenden, knew about the Kanaka's lack of proficiency was proven by the fact that they always passed the course over the head of the Kanaka to the man following. For the first few days out of port the steering was easy. The wind held on the port quarter and the sea was smooth. It also happened that the blacks had their tricks during the day watches while the captain slumbered. The mate, as was his custom, seldom bothered with the course during the day, devoting all of his energy to directing the work on deck.

On the third day out Australia went to the wheel in the first night watch and at four bells Black Joe headed aft to assume complete charge of the steering, being shunted on his way by watchful shipmates. Presently a terrible commotion aloft startled us, we were brought by the lee with a slamming and slatting like thunder. Mr. Zerk jumped to the break of the poop and started to bawl orders.

"Hard up, hellum! Weather fore braces! Lively there!"

Everything was shaking, with the yards pointing into the wind, and the ship started to roll. "How do you head?" There was no response. "How do you head, damn you!"

Forward we were swinging the head yards, and she started to box off, while aft a secondary commotion centered about the wheelhouse, with Captain Nichols acting the part of Satan, in yellow silk pajamas, and Black Joe performing duty as the Butt of All Evil.

"What are you steering?" roared the captain. "Mr. Zerk!" never had we heard him so sharp before. The mate was already aft, and to change the course of wrath, he grabbed Joe and tossed him headlong out on the deck, holding the wheel himself while he added to the din. "Lay aft! Lay aft, a man!" Frenchy responded. In a few more moments we were back on the course again and the captain held a drumhead court at the break of the poop.

"Keep those black monkeys forward," he ordered, "and don't let this happen again. By God, sir, these waters are full of coral reefs, and I have got to hold my course, sir," he added, turning to the mate.

The next morning the three Kanakas were mustered in the waist and the captain found that none of them had the least idea about steering, either by compass or by the wind. John Aahee of the starboard watch was denser even than Joe. Later on these simple fellows made up for their lack of steering by doing additional turns at the back-breaking bilge pumps.

After the generous way in which we lived in Honolulu, the return to sea grub was sudden and disappointing. A week or so saw the end of fresh provisions and we were back again on the salt horse of the passage out. Lime-juice was given us at noon, and with the exception of spuds, we were on the regulation lay. The tack was weevily, the tea even more flavored with roach content than before, and the old drill of cracker hash, slumgullion, salt horse, and pea soup, with occasional helpings of applejack, or rare treats of Chow's gingerbread, carried us along.

About this time the parrot, Jake, came in for his share of attention. Frenchy planned to take the bird home to Madeleine, and as his sister would have no use for him otherwise, our careful shipmate guarded the moral tone of the green bird with great care. He also made a screen of ravensduck for the cage and was much worried over how the bird would weather the cold in high southern latitudes. A month of this care on the part of Frenchy was rewarded by the usual result in cases of that kind, whether with dogs, birds, or children. Jake cut loose in a most extraordinary manner, after one of his French lessons, and the outburst would have been a credit to Mr. Zerk. Frenchy was grieved beyond all hope of recovery and one and all we swore to our own innocence. The upshot of it was that Frenchy lost interest in the parrot and the profane Jake became a prime favorite with the crew forward. He was really started on his downward path by Hitchen, of starboard, who took him in hand while his master slept.

"Here comes the grub!" was one of his respectable parts of speech, varied later on by "To hell with the grub," under the tutelage of Australia.

After crossing the line, and working our way through the doldrum belt of daily showers, calms and baffling winds, we held a course that carried us between the Marquesas and Tuamotu, or the Low Archipelago. During this time we kept a special lookout at night and sighted several islands, giving them a wide berth. We were instructed to keep our eyes peeled for "white water" and had a number of false alarms. On a dark night, in this region, the sea is particularly black, of a blue blackness that defies description. The seas are very phosphorescent, especially so under a cloudy sky, and the breaking of a number of rollers leaves a white wake that is disturbing to a lookout on the edge for breakers. One imagines that breakers are ahead every few minutes.

Light rain squalls and brilliant floods of sunshine alternating in the neighborhood of the Marquesas resulted in our witnessing the most remarkable phenomenon of the voyage. We lay becalmed late in the afternoon of a humid hot day, odd jobs were going on all over the ship, iron work was being chipped, service renewed, and Australia and Brenden were rattling down, everyone being busy. Frenchy and I, for we usually worked together at "nice" jobs, were cutting and fitting the canvas for a new mast coat on the mizzen, the old one having cracked and started a leak into the cabin. This was a job that required expert fitting and we were all attention to the work. All hands were so occupied that we did not notice the black rain squall that suddenly came upon us in a puff of cold air. A few minutes of this, while we manned the weather main and lee crojik, to get whatever push there was in it, was followed by the sun breaking through more scorching than before, while the wind, such as was left, was distinctly up and down. A beautiful rainbow formed under the receding cloud, and then we saw that we were near an island, close aboard off the starboard bow, while the rain pall drifted rapidly to port. We came upon it with such suddenness that for a moment most of us lost our heads.

"Hard starb'd!" shouted the skipper, and then there was a laugh on deck in which he joined heartily. We were as stationary as the island except for the little way upon us given by the passing rain squall. "Lay aloft and take a look at that." Captain Nichols addressed Frenchy and me, and we skinned up the mizzen while he went to the companion and took the long glass from the rack. That land certainly looked strange!

When going over the top, I stopped. Frenchy was ahead of me and almost at the crosstrees. He was looking around in a bewildered sort of a way; he was glancing around the entire horizon, thinking the ship had changed her head. I too looked all about but could see nothing.

"What do you make out?" called up the skipper.

"Nothing in sight, sir!"

"All right. Lay down!"

It was a fine mirage; a remarkably clear one. When we got to the deck the "island" had assumed grotesque shapes: the green faded out and the palm trees began to look like young waterspouts. Suddenly the whole picture melted from view.

CHAPTER XXV

DRIVING SOUTHWARD

The mirage served as a subject for conversation during many succeeding days and the captain warned us to be more than ever on the lookout for islands. He seemed to take especial pains with his navigation, testing the patent log repeatedly by use of the chip log, and coming up at all sorts of hours during the day and night when by any chance the lubber line was as much as a quarter point off the course. When on a wind, during this period, he practically lived on deck, turning in "all standing" for short naps during the day.

A lookout on the fore t'gallant yard was also stationed during the daytime. Several more small islands were passed, the distant palm trees seeming like a low broken comb upon the horizon, for we gave them plenty of offing as the atoll formation often throws its reefs far out. Several times our course was altered to do this.

In the fo'c'sle we had a round of mystery stories about islands mainly. One by Frenchy took the prize for heavy ghost atmosphere and when told in the dusk of a last dog watch with only the stars overhead to wink at its absurdity, the effect was all that could be desired. This tale had to do with an invisible island, situated somewhere about the Loyalty Group near New Caledonia. The island was invisible by day but could be found by a night landfall, and indeed was so discovered by that tight little brig the Père Duchêsne, owned and sailed by no less a person than the notorious Jean Ravail, who did not, as Frenchy assured me, perish in the sewers of Paris, as was supposed. Ravail was a pirate, of course, though he sailed as a peaceful trader, exchanging cognac and rum for bêche-de-mer, through the southern islands of Polynesia. Driving onto the ghostly island in the blackness of the night, anchor was let go just in time to prevent the brig from running up the beach, and then, to the tune of entrancing music, the whole crew, led by Ravail himself, were decoyed ashore by women in flowing robes of white. They left to a man, even old Pouly, the mate, who held out to the last until a scantily draped siren came aboard and carried him ashore in her canoe. The story is supposed to have been found entered by Pouly in the logbook of the brig when she was picked up by the frigate La Perouse, drifting with her cable chafed through by the coral reef. Many weeks of cruising failed to locate the island. I always liked this story, for Frenchy enjoyed telling it and did it remarkably well.

The starboard watch also stirred uneasily after the mirage and as a direct result of it Charlie Horse got religion. Not that he had not always had it, but these singular events merely brought it to the surface as it were. Charlie Horse began where our late shipmate Jimmy left off. He was extremely rigorous in his beliefs and did not hesitate to preach infant damnation, advising all of us who had not been duly baptized to rectify this mistake as soon as possible. He paid special attention to John Aahee of his watch, and to that simple-minded native the awful creed of Charlie Horse was a throbbing reality. The existence of purgatory was assured; hell was a positive fact, a hot and terrible place of torture. Often during a brief dog watch of a Sunday, the port side would get some of the overflow, which we listened to with varying tolerance; his own watchmates had arrived at the point of active protest.

With Charlie Horse preaching religion of the hell-fire-and-damnation brand, Frenchy and other less expert story-tellers filling the intervals of the night watches on deck with ghostly discourse, and adding to this the appearance of St. Elmo's fires at the yard arms after one of the tropic disturbances, it was no wonder that we were a bit on edge where anything that smacked of the supernatural occurred. Talk had been rather reminiscent in one of the last dog watches, the weather was fine and we were sailing along before a gentle quartering breeze without having started a sheet or brace for several days—calm of spirit prevailed on board for a time, there was little hazing and, except for the growing rottenness of the tucker, we were content. The mind must therefore cast about for something new to seize upon. The name of Jimmy Marshall had been mentioned a great deal during the watch referred to, Axel having told of meeting Jimmy on his last night ashore, while returning to the ship. Jimmy was sneaking up the dark side of Nuuanu Avenue—there was a moon out—and bumped into Axel before he knew it.

"What! Down to the ship, Jimmy?"

"Naw, jest took a look at 'er. I 'ears you was sailin' an' jest walked down past the Monarch an' looked over. 'Ow's 'ell on board?"

"Same old wagon, Jimmy. How are they treating you?"

"They's slowly killin' me, Axel, so help me Gawd, they is. Talk erbout yer rotters! Say, if you knowed as 'ow they does me along of some other poor Gawdfersooken fellers. Well, what ov it? They looses Jimmy afore long, that's wot they does."

"I'll bet they prays the liver out of him, and starves the little faker to boot," was Australia's opinion.

At about one bell, in the first watch, we had just got to the stage of half sleep, and were dropping off for our precious three and a quarter hours, when we were all sitting up as well as we could, in our bunks. Fred was terror stricken. "By — It's Jimmy. I see him!"

"What in hell's bitin' you?" Australia demanded.

"Jimmy Marshall's in here! He spoke to me!"

"Spoke? Say, you big stiff, if you don't shut up I'll speak a few words you'll remember!" Australia was mad clean through. There was a silence. Something stirred over Australia's bunk, next to Fred's.

"Who's that?"

"Jimmy Marshall?" shouted the thoroughly frightened Fred, and then a voice near the top of the fo'c'sle, in the familiar tones of our late shipmate, very cracked and lifelike, added to the fear.

"Gawd have mercy. Gawd have mercy!" came the words.

"It's Jimmy! Take him away! Take him away!" shouted several, Martin and Scouse among them. We were all tumbling out of our bunks. Frenchy shot through the open door of the fo'c'sle and Scouse close after him. Suddenly there was a wild mixture of screams and screeches and Australia exploded in a loud, whole-souled oath of relief. He held the struggling Jake by the tail feathers. The parrot had recently been about the only consistent listener to the doctrines of Charlie Horse, and his appearance in our fo'c'sle at night gave him a chance to retail some of his new line of talk. Someone had evidently left his cage open and he came in to get out of the draft. From this time on the bird got to be a nuisance as well as a reminder of our folly. Frenchy sold him to Chips for a suit of oilskins.

During these days of the voyage we overhauled our best suit of sails preparatory to bending them for the heavy weather off the Cape. I had by that time become fairly proficient in the use of the palm and needle and could sew a presentable flat seam, or round seam, as occasion demanded. Frenchy was the best sailmaker in our watch, and with Brenden and myself, constituted the sailmaker's gang to port. Old Smith, Hitchen and Axel were the starboard complement in this kind of work. We had our benches in the most comfortable part of the deck and of a morning, after the washdown, while we were getting the canvas out, the rest of the crowd would wipe the deck dry with pieces of old sugar bags, getting right down on their shin bones and rubbing the planks. We put in new tabling, renewed lining cloths, sewed on new leather at the clews, wetting it so that when dry the leather would shrink tight, gripping the bolt ropes so the strands would show through. In some of the older sails we sewed an extra line of stitching down the middle of the double flat seam where the cloths join.

I learned to properly work the reef and head holes. The canvas was cut with a "stabber" and a small fish line grommet laid over the edge, the hole then being finished off with a fencing of heavy waxed and double laid twine. In these later degenerate days, a brass eyelet ring is often crimped around the hole, a much quicker job and about one-third as strong.

In all of the lore of cutting canvas for sails, and we made a set of skysails on the voyage, the mate was a past master. The "roaching," the proper way to allow for gores in the cloths, the fact that "square" sails are anything but square; all such old-time knowledge was handed down and eagerly assimilated. We talked of the "hoist" of this sail, meaning sails that spread by hoisting the yard; and the "drop" of that sail, referring to the courses and lower tops'ls.

On the Fuller the mains'l and crojik (corrupted from the "crossjack" of the ancients) were fitted with "cross leeches" and a "midship rope." These were stout hemp ropes sewed to tabling cloths on the forward side of the sail, the cross leeches running from the head earings to the middle of the foot, and the "midship rope" from the head to the foot of the sail also on the forward side. This left the after side of the sail smooth so as to draw best when flattened on a wind. At the foot of the sail, and hooked into a stout thimble where the cross leeches and midship rope joined, the "slap line" led aft, and the "midship tack" led forward. With wind a point or two on the quarter, the weather clew garnets of the main and crojik would be hauled up and these sails set perfectly by the midship tack and the weather cross leech, in this way allowing a good share of the breeze to distend the great foresail for all it was worth. Sailors who have not been shipmates with this method of fitting the after courses will appreciate the utility.

One thing Mr. Zerk always harped upon was the necessity of making canvas set flat, whether on the wind or before it.

A large sail, the main course, for instance, is fitted with what at first blush appears to be a useless amount of gear. The sail being bent to the yard by means of the head earings and robands is handled by use of the following ropes: the tacks leading forward from the clews, the sheets leading aft. When before the wind the sail is held to the deck by the two sheets, the tacks being idle. When on a wind, that is, close hauled, the weather tack is boarded and the lee sheet hauled aft. To reef, the tacks and sheets are started and the reef band hauled up on the yard by the reef tackles. To furl, the clews are hauled up to the quarter of the yard by means of the clew garnets while the body of the sail is gathered in by the leechlines and the buntlines. Add to this bowline bridles for steadying out the weather leech when on a wind, slap line for keeping the foot of the sail away from the mast in light winds and calm, the midship tack used when sailing with the weather leech hauled up, and we have a very respectable lot of rigging on our sail. Upper tops'ls are almost as bad. Now this means nothing to the landsman, but a lot of queer names, yet the gear has come down through long ages of elimination and represents the utmost efficiency in handling sailing canvas. A main sail is a mighty spread on a large modern ship and may show to the wind as much as four thousand square feet of surface. Our mainsail on the Fuller was approximately of this size. Given a heavy press of wind, say twenty pounds to the square foot, and we have the sail urging our ship along to some purpose.

To get back to the voyage, after a reminiscent ramble with technicalities for which we ask forgiveness, though old, and perhaps new, "shells" may read it, I will add that the working of canvas is one of the best jobs aboard ship. We were excused from jumping up at every order to do some bit of pulling or hauling, and knowledge of the tricks of palm and needle stamped a man as of the real salt.

Australia, Charlie Horse, Tony, and a few others were kept busy renewing chafing gear, fitting sword mats and helping Chips, who was constantly employed about the ship at repair and renewal of the wooden fittings. The battens on the "swifters" were always being broken by the clew garnets, and had to be renewed, the pump leathers were overhauled at frequent intervals, hatch wedges were constantly inspected and "set up," and Chips was the man to do these things.

Martin, Mike, Fred and Peter were given a large job of overhauling all spare blocks. The pins were knocked out and turned over so that the least worn side of the pin would bear against the bushing. Iron straps were chipped and red leaded and all the deck and emergency tackles were treated in the same way, the blocks, thimbles, and falls being put in fine shape; nothing was spared in the quality of the material with which we worked. Whips and gear aloft might be turned end for end, but after that they were unrove and put to humbler uses; never spliced except in an emergency. On a ship, the odds and ends of rope yarn, oakum, and old wornout gear is headed up in barrels and sold as "shakings." This is often the perquisite of the mate.

Scouse, as usual, was in for the drudgery, with Kahemuku and Black Joe tailing along as his assistants. He did not seem to mind it and got on famously with the Kanakas. It was always "sir" to Scouse, from Black Joe, who looked upon the big Dutchman as a sort of hero. The red thatch may have had something to do with this attitude, but whatever the cause, Scouse would have got at least two votes had he ever become a candidate for President of Hawaii.

Just before shifting sail, this taking place during a lull between the S. E. trades and the counter trades, we sent down the main lower tops'l yard and rigged and sent up a spare spar that we had on deck. This was a regular seaman's job and called for all hands during an entire day. The old yard had a slight spring, a fault developed in the heavy weather off the Cape on the passage out. We unbent the sail, leaving it stopped on the main yard, all the gear, clewlines, buntlines, etc., being carried into the top and the quarter blocks hooked to the main cap. The yard was sent down by means of a stout burton from the topmast pendant, and the upper tops'l sheets, downhauls, etc., were unrove and carried into the main top. The upper tops'l was hung in its gear and the yard steadied out by the braces alone. As we had a fair sailing breeze, the t'gan's'l and upper canvas was kept set.

As soon as the long yard was down, we unhooked the burton and fastened onto the new stick, swaying this aloft, when the braces were hooked. The lifts were then attached and, as soon as the yard was up, the standard was keyed, and all running gear rove. We bent sail in record time, had everything shipshape again and sheeted home before two bells in the afternoon watch.

A few days after this, on a Sunday, of course, we shifted sail and we knew that we were in for some more dirty weather. "Well, this will be the last," was the feeling voiced more than once by the men in the fo'c'sle.

During the time of many jobs, of fine weather, and much activity of a sailor kind, the Kanaka Kahemuku astonished us by his skill in tattooing. Of a Sunday he was always busy. His first subject was Scouse, and we watched the progress of art with great interest. Kahemuku offered to fix me up, but I had in mind the advice of my father and decided to remain undecorated by anchor or star.

"You are wise, kid," Australia agreed. "Them marks never come off and they are a hard thing to get by with. Many a poor bloke has gone to the gallows because he carried a bright red star of hope tattooed on his chest."

While not altogether complimentary in his allusion, Australia was right. Scouse, however, showed his honest contempt for this point of view by having a Hula Hula dancer done on his chest. For a while he looked as if he had been crusted by a growth of barnacles.

As we ran past the little islands of the South Pacific, that lay sparsely scattered along our track, Kahemuku would gaze at them with intense longing. His desire for "Pilladelpia" alone compensated him for their loss. But, after a while, the increasing chill overcame all thoughts of that wonderful city of "Pilladelpia," and Kahemuku, Black Joe and the melancholy Aahee turned a shade of ghastly gray. They lay shivering in their bunks during the watch below, objects of compassion to the rest of us who were hardened to the cold sea.

The rapidly dropping temperature, it was then the last week of June and the middle of the Antarctic winter, served to remind us that we might expect a colder and perhaps stormier time of it than on the passage out when we rounded Cape Horn in the middle of the southern summer. One thing that would be in our favor, and all of the old sailors mentioned this, was the fact that for the most part we would have fair winds, the prevailing storms coming from the west, sweeping eastward along the edge of the Antarctic Continent, Cape Horn shoving its nose into the very center of the storm path.

The sting of the cold, crisp nights, as we increased our latitude, warned us that we were in for weather not far ahead. The Kanakas became more and more inert at each drop in temperature. They were so poorly provided for in the way of warm clothing that all hands dug into chest and bag, contributing from wardrobes none too large. The Kanaka boys did everything they could to show their gratitude. Our two of the port watch worked at the bilge pumps each night until they were utterly done. "It keeps them warm, and no one died working yet," said Brenden. "As long as they keep going they're still alive," added Australia, and this was true enough, so we were ready to accept their sacrifice at the back-breaking job.

CHAPTER XXVI

CAPE HORN AGAIN

As the strength of the winds increased and we were mostly always before it, Captain Nichols concluded the ship would sail better if she was a trifle further down by the stern. We had loaded on an evener keel in Honolulu than on the passage out and now it was decided by the skipper to shift some weight aft. This was done by breaking out two hundred bags of sugar from the fore part of the hold and dragging it aft to the extreme end of the lazarette. The weight shifted, about fifteen tons, certainly made her steer better than before.

On June twenty-third we rove off a new main tops'l halyard purchase, and overhauled the tops'l tye. The weather was getting more and more severe, and we ran before it under fore lower tops'l, close reefed fores'l, reefed main upper tops'l, main lower tops'l, and mizzen lower tops'l, all other sail being on the yards and furled with the exception of fore topmast stays'l and jib, both hauled amidships as a precaution against broaching to. The seas rose gradually and the ship rolled heavily. On June twenty-fifth our cargo shifted in the fore part of the 'tween deck, giving us a nasty list to leeward of about five degrees, and all hands were called at two in the mid watch to trim cargo. This was a devil of a job, except that it was warm, and kept us steadily employed for a stretch of twelve hours with only a short spell for grub. Captain Nichols himself came into the 'tween decks, and later on Mr. Zerk, myself and two of the men, Frenchy and Axel, if I remember right, went through the lower hold on top of the heaped-up sugar, where the sweet, sticky smell, slightly sour, mingled with the odors of the riled-up bilge, and the complaining of the hull. I carried a lantern and the rays, against the knees and beams, cast weird shadows. The hold was a fearsome place, pitching and rolling as if in mortal agony.

We found it increasingly necessary to keep the pumps going as the water worked in rapidly when running. A ship under such conditions of wind and sea is alternately lifted with her midship section carried on the back of a roller, her ends more or less tending to droop, or she is in the trough between two wave crests with her ends buried and the midship section hanging. Oftentimes a poorly built craft becomes "hogged," that is, the midship is permanently lifted up and her sheer thrown out.

A constant repetition of stresses such as we were experiencing on the Fuller, made intense by the dead weight of the cargo and the urge of the masts carrying their spread of sail, is bound to result in damage to the vessel. While working in the hold, the complaining of her timbers seemed worse than ever before on the voyage. We often wondered if she was going to pieces, as indeed many unreported ships have done. The sensation below gave one an impression of being at sea on a very uncertain proposition; a great leaky wooden box, with every solitary frame, scantling, hook, knee, and plank, complaining bitterly at the hard fate that had wrought them in the shape of a ship.

"I wish the bloody owners was down here for a day or two," said Old Smith, as we were shifting cargo in the hold, and I heartily agreed with him.

A few days later, when on deck, we forgot the forbidding pandemonium below; purposely forgot it, as so many people do with other things, and, as the ship did not wrack herself to pieces that voyage, we at least were saved a lot of unnecessary worry.

On July first we were still plowing before it under reefed canvas. All work on deck was at a standstill except that required for sailing the ship, and by way of exercise and safety, the "farmers" dragged the "bear." Cape pigeons were everywhere and we caught a number of them for their wings by trailing a fish line overboard and hooking them. These birds are beautifully marked and when taken on deck invariably vomit their dinners; it almost looks as though the motion of the ship made them seasick. High overhead gray molly-hawks and fulmar gulls soared white-bellied and noisy against the leaden sky.

Oil bags were trailed over the side as the high seas surged past us like race horses, their white crests crinkling dangerously under our transom, and along the full sweep of the bulwarks, slopping aboard as we rolled, filling the gangways and main deck with tons of cold, blue water. Often, at the braces, we would be buried in these seas, a strange sensation that for the moment, as the weight of water lifted the feet from the deck, gave one the sensation of being detached from the ship, of being out in the midst of it all thousands of miles from shore; a funny feeling is this, entirely devoid of fear, though, of course, one held on like blazes to whatever was most handy, usually the pin rail or other substantial deck fitting.

Much has been written about the height of waves, and as we approached the southern limit of our course and headed to the east, well below the parallel of Cape Horn, we got the full benefit of those constant westerly winds that blow around the world. Here the heaviest straight line gales are to be met with and the great fetch of deep water helps to produce magnificent waves of the first magnitude.

Lecky, in his "Wrinkles," a book no sailor should be without, and a book no lover of the sea who likes to "be up" on things nautical should neglect to read, quotes Mr. Thomas Stevenson as the authority for an empirical formula that approximates the possible maximum height of waves, the same being considered as a function of the "fetch."

This is given as a matter of interest, for working it backward it shows how tremendous the sea spaces through which the rollers that followed us had their being. The Stevenson formula is as follows:

Height of wave in feet equals the square root of the "fetch" in nautical miles multiplied by the constant 1.5.

Or, backward: the distance a wave has come equals its height, divided by 1.5, and the quotient squared.

As the wind increased in strength the waves mounted until immense billows were formed that measured from 50 to 60 feet in a vertical line from hollow to crest. This was easily determined by mounting the shrouds and watching until the ship was in the trough, then noting the height of eye on a level with the wave crests. In reversing the Stevenson formula we find that for a 60-foot wave a fetch of at least 1,600 miles is necessary.[8]

[8] Dr. G. Schott, as the result of studying the form and height of sea waves, claims that under a moderate breeze their velocity was 24.6 feet per second, or 16.8 miles per hour, which is about the speed of a modern sailing vessel. (Some speed!) As the wind rises, the size and speed of the waves increase. In a strong breeze their length rises to 260 feet and their speed reaches 36.0 to 36.4 feet per second. Waves the period of which is 9 seconds, the length 400 or 425 feet, and the speed 28 nautical miles per hour, are produced only in storms. During a southeast storm in the southern Atlantic, Dr. Schott measured waves 690 feet long, and this was not a maximum; for in latitude 28 degrees south and longitude 39 degrees west, he observed waves of fifteen seconds' period, which were 1,150 feet long with a velocity of 78.7 feet per second, or 46-1/8 nautical miles per hour. Dr. Schott does not think that the maximum height of the waves is very great. Some observers have estimated it at 30 or 40 feet in a wind the force of which is represented by 11 on the Beaufort scale (the highest number of which is 12); and Dr. Schott's maximum is 32 feet. He believes that in great tempests waves of more than 60 feet are rare, and even those of 50 feet are exceptional. In the ordinary trade winds the height is 5 or 6 feet. The ratio of height to length is about 1:33 in a moderate wind, 1:18 in a strong wind, 1:17 in a storm; from which it follows that the inclination of the waves is respectively about 6, 10, and 11 degrees. The ratio to the height of the waves to the force of the wind varies greatly.—Scientific American.

Note on Above by Author.—It would seem that the late Dr. Schott, if quoted correctly, did not consider the "fetch" as an element in the process of wave formation at sea; but his maximum waves were observed at a point where there was plenty of sea room.

Enough sail had to be carried to give the ship ample steerage way when the walls of rushing water passed us, for incredible as it may seem to those who have not had the experience, the waves of the sea run at a speed far greater than anything afloat that sails. The tidal wave, theoretical at least, must have a speed of one thousand miles per hour in order that the tides may follow the attraction of the moon and girdle the earth each twenty-four hours; some speed even in these days of rapid travel. Here we have a vertical translation of motion and not a horizontal shifting of water at that terrific speed. In the sea waves caused by wind friction, there is also simply a translation of up and down motion, except for the rearing crest; if the sea waves moved bodily it would be extremely dangerous to live near the seashore and the coasts would soon be worn away; also, ships would not dare venture upon the ocean.

This statement about the possible destructive effect of the sea waves were they to move bodily started one of the hottest arguments ever contested in the fo'c'sle of the Fuller. Tired and worn as we were, the greater part of an afternoon watch below was taken up in assailing my position. Australia could not see that I was right; even my staunch pal Frenchy doubted it. Finally I brought out my trusty "Wrinkles in Practical Navigation" by that sailor's friend, the late Captain S. T. S. Lecky, who added laurels to the name of the English merchant sailor that will never fade, and put them all to rout. The passage on Great Sea Waves is worth giving, and I here include it.

"The term 'Great Sea Wave' is used in contradistinction to 'Great Earth Wave,' which latter is the name given to the disturbance experienced on land.

"An earthquake may have its center of impulse either inland or under the bed of the ocean. In the first case, when the 'Great Earth Wave,' or superficial undulation, coming from inland, reaches the shores of the sea (unless these be precipitous, with deep water) it may lift the water up, and carry it out on its back, as it were; for the rate of transit of the shock is sometimes so great that the heap of water lifted up has not time to flow away toward the sides.

"At Arica, in Peru, and other places, this sudden going out of the sea has made bare the bottom of the bay, and left ships aground which only a few minutes before were riding quietly at anchor in several fathoms of water.

"As soon as the shock is over, the body of water thus forced out to sea returns as a huge wave, and, on approaching a sloping shore, rears up like a wall, and breaks with overwhelming force. Sometimes, however, its volume, height, and velocity are so great that it comes ashore bodily, and breaks far inland, causing even greater destruction to life and property. At Arica, the Wateree—a 'double-ender' belonging to the United States Navy—was carried inland quite a distance by the reflux, and remained as evidence for many years. If the writer's memory is not at fault, she was carried clean over the railway embankment.

"When the seat of the disturbance is beneath the ocean, the 'Great Sea Wave' rushes in upon the land as before—with this difference, that it is not preceded by the water retiring from the foreshore, as in the first case....

"About the most notable instance of a 'Great Sea Wave' occurred during the stupendous and ever-memorable eruption in August, 1883, which had for its center the Island of Krakatoa, in the Straits of Sunda. On this occasion the loss of life amounted to 37,000, caused chiefly by the sea waves, one of which attained the almost incredible height of 135 feet. Its effects were traced to all the principal tide gauges of the world, and were even observed at Havre, some 11,000 miles from the source of origin.

"A full account of this eruption, which was investigated in detail by committees and sub-committees of the Royal Society, comprising many of the leading scientists of the day, has been published in a volume of nearly 500 quarto pages, under the editorship of Mr. G. T. Symons. In this book every branch of the phenomenon and its effects have been most thoroughly dealt with, and is consequently well worth perusal."

What Captain Lecky has said may well cause us to pause and wonder how a "Great Sea Wave" would affect Coney Island of a hot Sunday in midsummer.

However, on the ship Fuller, to get back to our muttons, we thought of no Coney Island. We were very much at sea, and thankful for the fact that the waves could grow no larger. For it is a fact that the rapid rate of progress of waves serves to limit their height, for as soon as the speed of the wave becomes about half that of the speed of the wind the accelerating effect of the wind action remaining is absorbed by the friction of the water particles, and the waves are at their maximum.

We had a splendid opportunity to study the waves, and it was with a never-failing fascination that I always looked for the occasional grouping of three or four large rollers, rising above the rest, due to a piling up because of differences in rate of progress. On the ships of an earlier day, the fear of being "pooped" was always uppermost in the minds of timid helmsmen, but on the Fuller we were protected in a measure by the wheelhouse. This structure, right aft against the taffrail, served as a shelter, and at the same time housed the tiller, the tiller shackles, and the relieving tackles. The fore part was given over to the wheel and was quite fancy, immaculate white gratings under foot, bright wood panelling inside and brass fittings wherever possible. A sliding shutter overhead was thrown back, when on the wind, to allow the helmsman a sight of the weather cloth of the mizzen skysail. Just forward of the binnacle, and taking in the whole front of the wheelhouse, was a window fitted with sliding shutters. At least one of these was always open, for the officer of the deck never came into the wheelhouse when on duty, merely shouting his orders to the man at the helm. The good sense that finally provided wheelhouses on sailers was amply justified. Comparative warmth and protection from wind and sea helped just that much in steering, and a far better course was held through the long, strenuous watches of heavy weather. The wheelhouse was always one of the most comfortable spots aboard ship.

To my mind, steering was a lot of fun. This was specially so in good lively weather. The direct pull of the rudder, the "kick" and the "feel" of the ship never failed to thrill me with a sense of power. Just as handling "the stick" on a good able boat in fine brisk weather is a sport of never-ending delight, so the trick at the wheel aboard the Fuller always made me feel that I was the man who sailed the ship.

The pointer by old Bo'sun Dreilick, of the St. Mary's, and now of the Newport, that ancient mariner of many, many voyages, filled with the accumulated wisdom of the seven seas, stood me in good stead. "When at the wheel, work the ship in your mind as if you had charge of the watch," was his advice. Doing this aboard the Fuller with such a consummate sailor as Mr. Zerk in charge was an instructive exercise. During daytime tricks I could see where sails needed trimming, or where a shift of canvas would help her, and would often have everything settled in my mind before the mate would notice things. At night it was different. The least shift of wind or the slightest change of weather always found him on the alert. To an ambitious lad, anxious to master the hoary art of conducting a ship across the surface—decidedly, surface—of the many wrinkled ocean, this practice can be recommended; the only trouble is that such ambitious lads are now scarce, and the ships are scarcer still.

Captain Nichols had a pleasant way of coming up, especially during the second dog watch, after the mellowing influence of a Chow dinner, cabin style, and conversing for a minute or two. He would let drop a hint as to where we were and sometimes give me sights to work out. While we were making such heavy weather of it and the wheel was hard to manage, he told a story calculated to make me anything but cheerful. The ship had yawed and the slap of the rudder sent the wheel over against all the "beef" I could bring to bear. Then suddenly, when the pressure shifted to the other side, the wheel came back with the kick of a stubborn mule, and I was bodily lifted off my feet, saving my head by doubling about the spindle.

"Look out, son!" shouted the Old Man. "I had a sailor thrown up against the top of the wheelhouse once and his skull bashed in. That was his last trick at the wheel. You better be careful."

## CHAPTER XXVII

### MAN LOST OVERBOARD

At this stage of the voyage hardship had become a habit; rotten tack and half-cooked cracker hash all went the same way; we were toughened to the grind. A mess of weevil-ridden hard bread was disposed of by knocking the worms out and eating what was left, the crumby, mealy stuff, soggy with damp, was often made more palatable by heating in the galley with a sprinkle of molasses or a coating of our abundant sugar. The working of the ship was done in grilling discomfort of wet clothing, and the cold added its quota to our troubles day after day. But for all that we were living. The scenes of wild fury that only those who have run before it in the latitudes of Cape Horn can understand, spread about us in a fitting panorama to the tragedy of suffering on our half-drowned deck. Surely the angels must have wondered at the vast ambition of men who dared such dangers and lived such hardships; all of which vast ambition could be summed up in one sentence—the pay of an able seaman out of the port of New York—eighteen dollars per month, minus "advance" and the deduction for "slops," leaving the net earning in the neighborhood of ten or eleven dollars.

We were getting our romance in the raw, however, and, like most things in this world, we were paying for the show—working our way—through experiences that only those who go down to the sea in deepwater sailing ships know anything about.

Endless rows of mighty snarling combers, the howl of sleet-laden wind tearing through the glistening gear aloft, and the blind rush of snowstorms, crusting everything with a powdering of white, gave us a real taste of weather such as I had never experienced before.

"Thank God we are going before it, and not trying to beat back," said Hitchen to me one night, as he came aft to relieve me at the wheel.

John Aahee, of the starboard watch, disappeared and we thought he had been lost overboard. For two days we missed him and kept the news from Black Joe and Kahemuku, who were in a state of low spirits, where the loss of Aahee would have well-nigh proved fatal. On the third day after the absence of John he suddenly reappeared, when the boys of our watch heard a loud knocking on the under side of the forehatch. Having enjoyed a two days' sleep on the sugar in the 'tween deck, he climbed in by way of the forepeak, which had been opened in order to rouse up a barrel of saltpork.

The mate threatened to put him in irons for shirking duty and promised all sorts of dire punishment. However, the poor Kanaka was so far gone that it seemed he never would survive, and I believe he was positively numb when the mate made him finish out the last two hours of the watch on deck by bending over the bilge pump, "to get the sleep out of your eyes, you — black."

July Fourth found us nearing the end of our southing. We experienced a moderation in the weather, and set the fore and main t'gans'ls. The fore t'gans'l split during a squall that blew up before it had been set an hour, and we at once got busy in sending down this rag and bending another sail which went with a loud "bang!" during the midwatch, Second Mate Tom being on deck and Captain Nichols pacing up and down on the forward side of the wheelhouse.

"There she goes again!" we heard them shouting out on deck, amid the din of wind and the booming of the seas as they fanned away from the flare of our bows, when her head doused down into the back of a roller. The report as the new canvas split was sharp and characteristic, waking most of us, as it was directly overhead.

"I hope they don't call us out," was the thought expressed by all; we plunked down in our blankets with a will as though we were going to wring every last fraction of sleep out of each precious second of the few hours of the watch.

Our days were becoming more than merely strenuous, they were of that dead level of sustained hardship where the senses cease to register the added kicks, but go on in a sort of merciful anesthesia, no doubt brought about by the toxic action of prolonged fatigue.

On the glorious Fourth, Chow had spread himself to the extent of favoring the fo'c'sle mess with two large pans of gingerbread, nicely cut into squares, so that everyone would get his lawful whack. This gingerbread was a special stunt in baking such as I have never seen its like before or since. The top crust was flexible, and leathery, of a deep seal brown. The bottom was hard and usually well burnt. By grabbing the top crust and the bottom, the middle portion could be made to stretch at least twice its size and then broken apart, but long strings like cobwebs would connect the two halves. We blamed it for the boils that appeared on most of us toward the end of each passage, for Chow liked to bake it, and we had it at least once a week or oftener.

Poor Frenchy was taken sick during those dismal days, and when he mustered aft one dog watch, and promptly swooned, we picked our shipmate up and carried him to his bunk with heavy hearts. If gloom could kill a man, Frenchy would have cashed in his record during the next few days. The fo'c'sle was as sad a hole as a man could think of. Captain Nichols came forward and examined Frenchy during our watch on deck. This was a sort of concession to the proprieties, as he only came forward of the main hatch one other time on the voyage that I can recall. After his professional visit the steward called me aft and handed me a large tumbler full of a dark liquid called "black draft" by Australia; it had marvelous cathartic power. I was instructed to give this to Frenchy at one dose. What it did to him in his weakened state can be imagined.

The next day the mate came to the fo'c'sle and examined the sick man and reported aft. Frenchy had said he was much better, which was a lie, but a wise one. I then prevailed upon Chow to give me some cabin stew that he was preparing, and with this under his belt and a hook pot of coffee, cabin style, Frenchy felt better. I also broke out a set of brand-new underwear that I had been saving against an emergency. It was extra heavy, and with this on him and the good food, he felt like a new man. Chow fed Frenchy for three days, and fed him well, after I had prevailed upon Chips to give him the parrot, Jake. Fortunately Frenchy recovered before Jake got in his fine work in the galley, for in less than a week the latter was back under the fo'c'sle head again, having started his talk about "to hell with the grub," etc. This was more than Chow could stand, and one night his cage shot out of the lee door of the galley amid a series of quirks and screeches, and Fred rescued the bird from a comber that was about to curl over the bulwark.

Our precautions in the way of preventer gear and rolling tackles were employed as on the passage out, and the relieving tackles were hooked to the tiller in the after wheelhouse. Captain Nichols also had two heavy hawsers bighted about the base of the mizzen mast and flaked down on the cabin top ready to pay out through the quarter chocks should we by any chance broach to. At the end of these we had constructed two improvised sea anchors or drags. Under ordinary circumstances we would have been hove to in such weather as we were having, but the wind was fair and the captain determined to run before it as long as possible.

Discomfort and hardship on board were not altogether confined to the fo'c'sle. The after cabin was washed out a number of times and the mate was swamped by the seas backing up in the waist and running over the sills of the cabin doors. Mr. Zerk was much less violent during the stormy days. The hard drive to the south and east put a feeling of common danger into the minds of all; it had a very beneficial effect. So far as the psychic aspects of the voyage went, we were happy.

Also, we were, with the possible exception of Black Joe and Kahemuku of our watch, and the unfortunate Aahee of starboard, a very ready and smart crowd. When I say possible exception in referring to the Kanakas I mean that these unhappy people were always running with the crowd, and while always in the way they bent what beef they had to any gear we might be hauling on. Sailors have a weird wail, or dirge, without words, to which they sway at brace or halyards and Black Joe became proficient in this, throwing his whole spirit into the thing. Even in those days of actuality the perfect picture of glistening oilskins and the splashing sea, with the human cry of labor mounting above the snap of the storm, was driven home to me—and I was mighty wet and tired, too.

On July tenth we were still going large before a heavy sea. Second Mate Tom was on deck in the afternoon watch and, the wind having moderated some, his crowd were aloft shaking the reef out of the fore upper tops'l. Aahee was on the lee yardarm and as the sail dropped a squall of wind slapped along suddenly, and he, holding on to the jackstay with all of his might, turned a complete somersault as his heavy boots shot up from the footrope. He was wrenched from the yard, his body struck the belly of the reefed foresail and dashed into the sea. Some claimed he also struck one of the jib boom guys.

All hands were called and the ship hove to. Mr. Zerk stormed out on deck mad clean through, and Captain Nichols conned the wheel, myself and another man from starboard being at the spokes. A half barrel of oil was broached into the sea as we braced sharp and put down the helm, manning the lee fore braces with great speed. The main spencer was hauled out and reefed spanker set while we braced sharp forward. Mr. Morstad had thrown over two life buoys, but we could not see either one of them. As we hove to the seas swept over us with redoubled fury, the racket aloft being frightful. We then realized how hard it was blowing. Captain Nichols estimated it at from 9 to 10 on the Beaufort Scale,[9] and the Fuller bore down almost on her beam ends.

[9] *The Beaufort Notation, to indicate the force of the wind.*
0   Calm.
1   Light airs: just sufficient to give steerage way.
2   Light breeze. Ship under all plain sail 1 to 2 knots.
3   Gentle breeze. Ship under all plain sail 3 to 4 knots.
4   Moderate breeze. Ship under all plain sail 4 to 5 knots.
5   Fresh breeze. Ship close hauled can carry Skysails.
6   Strong breeze. Ship close hauled can carry Topgallant sails.
7   Moderate gale. Ship close hauled can carry Reefed topsails.
8   Fresh gale. Ship close hauled can carry Lower topsails, courses.
9   Strong gale. Ship close hauled can carry Lower topsails; reefed courses.
10  Whole gale. Hove to, under main lower topsail and reefed foresail.
11  Storm. Hove to, under storm staysails.
12  Hurricane. Hove to, under bare poles.

To launch a boat would have been madness and we watched the sea for a sight of Aahee or of the life buoys, all, however, without success, as no doubt he had drowned at once and the buoys were several miles to windward, while we were drifting off faster than they.

Once hove to we shortened down for the night under lower tops'ls and storm stays'ls. The death of Aahee was tragic in the extreme; Kahemuku cried in his bunk, and no means could be found to stop him. Black Joe said nothing, he ate in silence, and when we went below he turned in without a word.

They were one less to starboard; only a weak brown man gone, a poor piece of human wreckage washed loose from that plaything of the storm, a ship at sea.

CHAPTER XXVIII

AUSTRALIA'S STORY

Following Frenchy's sickness, Australia and I chummed together as Frenchy, by common consent, was allowed to perch on a coil of rope on the main hatch just forward of the mast during the night watches, the mate winking at this whenever the weather was not too bad.

On such nights Australia and I would stump the wet deck and we got to be very good friends. Unlike so many of the crew, I remember his name, John Roth, and from what he told me at various times I knew that he had come from a good family, as such things go, people in easy circumstances. His grandfather had settled in England, coming originally from southern Germany, and his father had taken over and extended a business founded at that time. Roth had received a good education, evidently, though he was of a shiftless temperament and his talk savored of the fo'c'sle and not the schools. He unburdened himself as we tramped the deck and I found him to be a charming companion and much deeper than was my idea of the devil-may-care deserter from the Falls of Ettrick, who had impressed me as a sort of scatterbrained ne'er-do-well, when we first bumped against each other in the fo'c'sle of the Fuller, for my bunk was ahead of his, as we settled down in that first mixup, months before.

**Australia**

"I'll tell you, Felix, there's lots of blokes who have had less chances than me, and is well off today. I always got in the way of trouble and you bet trouble never missed me once."

This sounded like something new, so I kept my mouth closed instead of replying after the usual manner of deck chums making conversation.

"When my father died," went on Australia, after a long pause, "my brother took the management of the business. He was in the building trade and doing very well at it, supporting mother, two sisters, brother and myself. My brother James had quit school and was helping father at the time of his death. I was at school near Winchester, much to my disgust, for I hated school and wanted to go to sea." Australia paused. He was strangely sober and we paced on deck for a turn or two in silence. Then he continued, and I remember how his words came slowly but with a long-forgotten attention to choice and grammar.

"On the settlement of the estate of my father a small legacy of four hundred pounds was left me, and with the business safe in the care of my brother I felt at liberty to quit school and go to sea. I had an idea that I would settle down somewhere with my money and be a gentleman planter, or something like that. At any rate, I cashed in and, with more money in my pocket than was good for me, put to sea in the fo'c'sle of a ship out of London bound for Melbourne. I'll call her the Iverclyde, that's near enough. They shipped me 'ordinary,' and when I handed the mate a five-quid note, as I asked for the job, he was sure he had hooked a fool, or a lunatic. The rest of my fortune I carried in a wallet in the bottom of my chest, a place no one would ever think of searching for money.

"The Iverclyde was an iron ship, a wet ship, if you know what I mean. We was drowned and we was starved, but never overworked. Once the crowd went aft and told the mate they wanted to put the main topgans'l on her, as she was rolling so. The mate he says, 'All right, Bo'sun, set the main topgallant sail,' and that is the way we worked.

"We ran into Table Bay, with a sprung bowsprit, lifted loose of the gammoning when she was taken aback while the mate was sleeping against the binnacle. This was my chance, and by use of another note, I got smuggled ashore with a suit of dirty dungaree and a big bundle of damp Bank of England notes, leaving the rest of my kit behind. I soon got some decent clothes, and put up at the Royal Hotel. The life in Cape Town suited me, I made friends among a fast bunch, spent the filthy, and enjoyed the air of mystery that surrounded me. No one ever suspected that I was from the Iverclyde, though I saw our captain walk by the hotel once; in fact I was very safe there.

"Shortly after the ship left, I found that I was being shadowed. Some bloke was always in my wake. I tried to get him and blow him to a dog watch of drinks and find out his game, but it was no use. When they saw I was on to them, for they watched every move I made, and I was spending free, the gentleman aft gives the signal and I am arrested. It seems that an embezzler was wanted and they had me spotted for the game. Not knowing the lay they was on, I did not get my story straight at first, thinking they was still after me for deserting the Iverclyde. This was bad. They chucked me in jail and kept me there for three months, lifting what was left of my wad. 'I say, is this all that's left?' the officer exclaims, counting the notes. They expected to pick up about ten thousand pounds.

"When the correctness of my story was proved, they let me go. I heard that the blackleg they was after was caught in Calcutta.

"Sure, they let me out and gave me what was left of my wad. Almost half gone, but then I had three months of lodging and tucker free and a little over two hundred saved. I was a wiser one after that, but I was still a fool, which was something I did not find out till later.

"In order to get away from Cape Town, and at the same time follow my idea of settling down in some warm climate where a man can become a planter and have a lot of blacks do the work for him, I shipped before the mast on the Dutch bark Java, out of Amsterdam, bound for Batavia. This craft had put in short of water and several hands who had died on the passage down to the Cape. The Java was unlucky. The most unlucky tub that ever sailed, except the Flying Dutchman, but unlucky enough for any real ship. We winds up in a typhoon, a hundred miles west of the Sunda Strait. The masts went by the board and at the end of the blow, after two days of pumping and praying, a steamer picks us up. She was bound for Singapore. The second mate of the steamer, a young fellow from London, decided he wanted to work the Java into port, his idea being Anjer. The skipper says 'all right' and he called for volunteers. As I said, I was still a fool, so I joined five other men and with the young second mate we was put on board the Java; I was the only one of her own crew and this scared me. Them Dutchmen knew when they were well off; and they stayed aboard the steamer.

"The second mate of the steamer did not know exactly what to do. He said, 'We will get up a jury mast,' but there was nothing to make a jury mast out of. The steamer was far down on the horizon when we found by sounding the well that the old tub was gaining water fast. After that we did nothing but pump. We pumps for the best part of a week. I don't remember what we ate, or if we did not eat. The crowd on board curses our young skipper, and pumps. They kept on pumping because we found the long boat that we depended upon stove in and all of the thwarts smashed.

"At the end of the week another blow comes up from the West. 'So long, good old London Town,' one of our fellows sings out. 'The hell with dyin' tired,' and he drops the pump handle and sits down. We all do the same, and the second mate, who took his trick along with the rest, says, 'I guess you are right; we might as well rest a bit before swimming.'

"We rested all afternoon and till late at night. I had my wad in a pouch at my belt and each of us had two life belts. We ate a little; the young second mate found a small beaker of rum in the cabin and we had some of that, and some hard bread and a hunk of cheese. I drank very little rum; I was afraid of going to sleep.

"At about midnight we caught the beach. We were in the breakers before we knew it and when she struck, the sea breached over her and away we went. I lost my two life belts the first thing and made up my mind to die, but I held my breath. Might as well die with my lungs full of air I figured as I went over and over. The water was warm, and I did not mind it. Before I knew where I was, I washed up on the beach and was lucky enough to get clear of the undertow. All I had on was a pair of torn pants and my belt with the soaked notes. Not a sign was to be had of any of the salvage crew, and the beach for miles was strewn with bits of wreckage. At daylight I was met by a man coming out from behind a clump of small trees. He was dressed in dirty white clothes and had a young beard. I told him the yarn of the wreck and asked him where I was. He directed me to Anjer, about thirty miles east along the coast. I asked him if he could give me some clothes. He said yes, if I would wait where I was he would be back in about two hours.

"Well, to make a long story short, as they say, I waited, being a natural born fool and not knowing any better. Still," and Australia paused in his extraordinary tale, "I don't think anyone else would have done different. I was so glad about meeting this man that I carefully unrolled a wet five-pound note and set it out on a rock to dry, weighting it with a little stone. I wanted to square him for his trouble.

"About noon my man shows up. He has a suit of white cotton clothes that were not any too new, a pair of shoes, brogans, they call them, and a straw sun helmet. He also gave me a half loaf of bread, after I handed him the five-quid note. This took his breath away, so he got reckless.

"About two miles out of Anjer I was met by two constables. They ran at me so fast that I knew there was something wrong and before I could say Jack Robinson they had the bracelets on me, and was going through my pockets for weapons. They got the wad, and that settled me. 'Gawd,' I says, 'what am I in for now?' My clothes was stripped off of me in the jail, and took as evidence, I found out later. When my shoes came off, my left foot, for I wore no sox, was a dull red, like rust—this was blood.

"'You are charged with murdering the keeper of the Fourth Point Light!'

"'Great Gawd!' I cries, 'what next!'

"Well, they has me, and no mistake. I am a British subject and I set up a roar. The Consul was called, and I tried my best to get him to believe my story. It was no go. 'Bally rot!' he says.

"I was sent to Batavia, and held for murder. Fortunately my story about what happened in Cape Town was verified in an unexpected manner or things would have gone hard with me. What saved me was a newspaper story of my jail term in that port, my belt of money, and my hard luck in being taken for the crook. This tallied with my yarn when I gave an account of myself, and the fact that the Java had sailed, as I said, and the story of the salvage crew put on her, sent on from Singapore when the steamer arrived, helped me. The British Consul took up matters, and by spending the greater part of what I had left, funds that were again at my disposal, I cleared myself. However, in the meantime, my people in England had got the story of my being a murderer with full details of the horrible deed. It killed my mother, who was in feeble health. Nothing of the clearing up ever reached the other members of my family and to them I am a murderer to this day.

"I left Batavia on a tramp steamer bound for Sydney, a wiser young fellow than ever before, also a much poorer one, for I had just two pounds in my pocket when I went ashore.

"My narrow escapes had the effect of making me restless. In the next two years I worked at every trade and calling that I could lay my hands to. I tried sheepherding, I went into the bush and tried farming, working as a laborer. I worked as a blacksmith in Sydney after picking up something of the trade travelling with a small circus. In Melbourne I started a very good business in peddling milk. I gave this up as soon as it began to pay me and I could afford the help to make it easier. Again I shipped to sea. News of my mother's death had reached me, and I worked my way back to England. My brother had married and would have nothing to do with me. My name was never mentioned in his home. Both of my sisters had married and moved away, one to Scotland and one to America—Canada, I think. Then I went to Liverpool and shipped on the iron bark Falls of Ettrick. Now that is my story. Rotten, eh? Well, I hope some day to settle down, and quit this thing for good. I have cheated the rope out of a good stiff by helping along the murderer with five-quid, and nearly paid for it with my own neck; I almost got mine a number of times before and since. If I had a decent chance I could make good, if I only could settle down and stick."

"You ought to get married; that would settle you, Australia, old boy," I offered, somewhat taken aback at the recital, for it was poured out from the heart. I knew that a strange sort of adventurer was telling me the things closest to his soul. What I said jarred.

"Married? Say, kid, I've tried that game. Yes, sir, I've been married twice, and I suppose they could jail me for that, too."

"Twice?"

"You bet. Once in Melbourne, and again in London, when I came home and found I was a murderer yet."

"What happened to your wives?"

"I don't know. Guess they are married again, leastways the one in London is. She was no good. Thought I was a rich bushman and wanted to get in on the wad. But the wife in Melbourne was decent. I should have stuck; that was when I was in the milk business." Australia paused. "I hope she sold that for a decent figure. You see she was expecting something, and—oh, rats—what am I saying—"

"Weather main brace!" sang out the mate, and in a moment we were tailing to the rope, and Fred and Black Joe were wailing in the night as we swigged at it. The watch was nearly over and Mr. Zerk was working the sleep out of us. As for me, I was wide awake. Australia never mentioned his story again, except to say in an offhand way that it was all a lie about being married twice. "I just wanted to see how far I could go with you," he said.

Australia was a wiry chap of medium size, full of life and a distinct ornament to the fo'c'sle. He was never at a loss for a witty retort and his sallies at the expense of the mate—during the watch below of course—furnished endless amusement. He always shaved in port except for a diminutive mustache, but at sea he sported a growth of beard, merely trimming this with a large pair of scissors such as tailors use for cutting heavy cloth, a murderous weapon that he carried in a canvas sheath nailed to the inside cover of his sea chest.

Unlike sailors on shorter runs, and that hybrid animal, the deckhand in steam, the sailor on board a deepwater ship has a sense of home. He occupies the same bunk for a year or more at a time, and in spite of the way he is robbed, or perhaps I should say, was robbed, he carried a small accumulation of household goods, things that the crimps and boarding masters did not consider worth while stealing. Every bunk in a measure reflected the personal taste of the owner.

Australia was one of the few men on board the Fuller who owned a mirror. When he wanted to nail this up under the lamp in the fo'c'sle, there was a storm of protest, and the damning implement of an effete civilization was again restored to his chest. A mirror was only permissible on rare occasions when a man shaved; otherwise it was taboo.

CHAPTER XXIX

STORMY DAYS

"Diego Ramirez ahead, a point on the port bow!" This was the news that greeted us as we turned out on the morning of July 17th, 1898. It was Sunday, cloudy, but clear, one of the first days without snow or hail since the fourth of July. Off to the E. S. E. was a sail and by the long time it took us to raise her we knew she too was a homeward bounder.

The morning watch had set all of the tops'ls, shaking the reefs out of the fore and main, and we were sent aloft to loose the main t'gans'l, sheeting home and hoisting away with a will. As we raced along under the lowering gray, the rocky islands of Diego Ramirez stood out with the distinctness of cameos cut against the light skyline to the northeast. The breaking and dashing of the white frothy seas marked them well and served to remind us that we were plowing in a fairish sort of a seaway ourselves. Our added sail made the riding better and we hove the log after getting the t'gans'l on, showing a speed of ten knots.

As it was Sunday, there was no objection to our doing some sightseeing; I got the ship's head from the wheelhouse and went forward and made sketches of the island, the first one, bearing north, magnetic. This gave a continuous line with a cleft near the eastern side. A few minutes more and the cleft opened up, showing Diego Ramirez to be at least two separate islands. My sketches were made on N.; N.N.W.; and N.W.

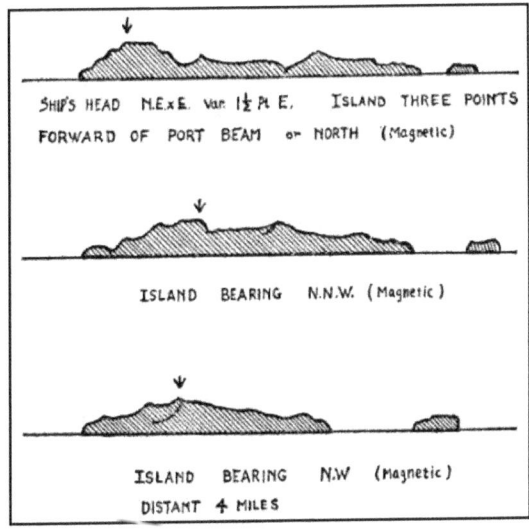

Australia also got busy with his case of crayons, for he was an artist as well as a story-teller, and his sketch of Diego Ramirez is one of the most cherished souvenirs in my scrapbook.

All hands gazed at that bit of weather-scarred rock jutting up from the troubled waters, with a feeling of reverence. It was the turning point, the high tide of distress on many a hard voyage into those stormy waters. Kahemuku and Black Joe watched it with a sort of fascination. No green-capped cliffs with white cataracts dashing into a warm deep sea as at their native islands of Hawaii. Not a scrap of verdure, not a ray of hope, only black-blue water and sullen sky with between them the primal crags rearing their worn heads above the sea.

Since John Aahee was lost, the brown-skinned brothers had merely suffered to exist. They talked much together, and Aahee was mentioned constantly. We did our best to cheer them, though to tell the truth we all felt the death keenly. To starboard they missed him more than we. Second Mate Tom was of course blamed by the fo'c'sle judges, though he had nothing to do with the accident any more than having been on deck at the time.

As we quickly dropped Diego Ramirez on the quarter, we went below at noon for our dinner. The day was incredibly fine for that season and we made the most of it. We were then tearing past the south point and would soon get some northing into the course. Cape Horn lay far below the horizon to the north, and from the progress we were making we had hopes of establishing a record, for the Fuller at least. We had made the run from Honolulu to Diego Ramirez in forty-five days; as a matter of advance information to the reader, it took us sixty-three days more to sail from Ramirez to the Delaware Capes, our passage as a whole merely proving a very fair one of one hundred and eight days, against one hundred and twenty-one on the passage out. This difference of thirteen days in favor of going east can be attributed to the westerly winds off Cape Horn. From this it will be seen that the ship A. J. Fuller was not the fastest craft afloat, and yet she was far from being the slowest.

The sail ahead of us proved to be a Norwegian bark. We came up to her in handsome style, our ensign snapping from the monkey gaff, and as her colors went up, we "dipped" in the long graceful salute of the sea. The bark made her number and asked to be reported. She was droughing along at a slow pace under reefed main upper tops'l, lower tops'ls, and reefed fores'l, showing a leg-o'-mutton sail on the mizzen. We were then under all plain sail to royals, and must have made a glorious picture to the sailors lining the sides of the square-head craft. Moments like that make one tingle with pride at the sight of the colors, a sort of pride that seldom comes to those who sail under the flag in these degenerate days.

From Diego Ramirez we shaped a course to take us well clear of Staten Land; the familiar sound of this name was like home, and I found myself talking about it in the dog watch with peculiar relish. Old Smith of starboard joined us, and told of having run through the Strait of Le Maire on the passage to the eastward. This is safe enough, though careful skippers like Captain Nichols prefer the wider reaches of the Atlantic to the Le Maire Strait, dividing Staten Land from the larger island of Terra del Fuego.

As we brought the wind about two points abaft the port beam, the sky started to thicken and during the early watches of the night we were again treated to real Cape Horn weather. At midnight we took in the lighter canvas, reefing the main t'gans'l. By eight bells in the midwatch we had her staggering under reefed fore and main upper tops'ls, lower tops'ls and reefed fores'l, fore topmast stays'l, and reefed spanker. We were making heavy weather of it, the seas dashing high over the fo'c'sle head as she buried her nose whenever a big roller tumbled in under the counter.

There was no warm breakfast, Chow having been flooded that morning by a heavy sea. The door to the carpenter shop was stove in and poor Chips was in a state bordering on hysteria, with all of his tools wet. To add to our woe, and looked upon as a sign of bad luck by all hands, the parrot was drowned when his cage unshipped from the hook under the fo'c'sle head and he was deposited in the scuppers. He lay there all night and was picked up by the starboard watch in the morning. Poor Jake, of all the sad birds that ever cruised on stormy water, you were the unluckiest as well as the most profane.

Everything was afloat fore and aft. The fo'c'sle was swimming and the after cabin was also washed out when a storm shutter carried away on one of the ports. Brenden, Frenchy and I were called aft during our watch below on Monday forenoon and told to swab up the captain's quarters. We worked the better part of an hour in these palatial spaces, our caps respectfully tucked into our pockets. The captain gave us a large tin of cabin roast beef, and a half can of fine pilot bread, as a reward for our trouble. Of course we shared this forward and we had a rather elaborate spread that noon—a clammy cracker hash which we threw overboard, hot slops, and the grub from aft.

"Give me meat like this and they can take my watch below any day," was Frenchy's opinion of the canned roast beef. At about the same time, no doubt many of our soldiers were dying of this stuff under the hot sun of Cuba,—they called it embalmed beef.

Ramirez is in 56 degrees 29 minutes south, corresponding in latitude to the Wrangell Astronomical Station just south of Sitka, Alaska. When we remember that the Antarctic winter is even more severe than that of the northern hemisphere, it will be possible to get some idea of the state of the sea through which we were racing. Running north between Staten Land and the Falklands we encountered a succession of storms that were calculated to impress us with the quality of the Cape. We were under shortened canvas most of the time, and as the winds became very unsteady, we were compelled to wear ship frequently, the great seas making it difficult to attempt to put her about in the eye of the wind.

My journal entries follow, covering the last two weeks of heavy weather, shifting winds, and great cross seas; a period of cold and wet without parallel on the voyage:

July 18th, 1898. Wind hauled to S.E. at end of day. Yards sharp up on starboard tack. Heavy snow at nightfall. Cold. Saw some small cakes of pan ice. Wind stronger.

July 19th. Snow, hail, and ice, all over decks. Wind moderate, from S.E. as before, veering a point at noon. Braced in yards. Set topgallant sails. Overhauled another homeward bound bark; could not make out her colors.

July 20th. No snow today, but very cold. Are heading N.N.W. Wheel from four to six during washdown, glad to get out of it. Passed between Falkland Islands and mainland today, no land in sight. Wind holding steady.

July 21st. Colder today. Wind freshening. Furled fore and main upper topsails in the midwatch. Heading N.N.W., starboard tack. Looks bad. Rigged life lines today.

July 22nd. Wore ship in morning watch, set fore upper topsail and mainsail. Ship under fore and main upper topsails and two courses, fore topmast staysail and spanker.

July 23rd. Warmer, but still cold enough for my monkey jacket. Weather puzzling. Old Man seems worried. Told me we were a long way from home; I know it.

July 24th. Sunday. Wind unsteady. At braces most of day. Calm in afternoon. Got orders to shorten down to reefed topsails. Caught two Cape Pigeons in dog watch. Let one go and took wings of best one. Glass falling. Got up rolling tackles. Steadied out life lines. All hands forward hope the skipper has made a mistake. Funny sky to south.

July 25th. Wind jumped out of the south last night. Heavy sea running. Colder than before. Sleet in the wind. Under lower topsails and reefed foresail. Running fast. Shipping blue water.

July 26th. Running with wind one point on starboard quarter. Sea came aboard in midwatch and carried away the freeing ports on port side, from mainmast to the poop. After cabin flooded again. Colder, hail all night.

July 27th. Wind abating. Got sail on her to topgallant sails. High sea running. All hands standing by. Ship yawing badly. Took in mizzen topgallant. Blowing up again at end of day, started to shorten down.

July 28th. All hands took in the mainsail at six this evening. Called all hands at six bells in first night watch and took in foresail. Living gale. Under lower topsails and fore topmast staysail.

July 29th. We hove to at daybreak. Got her around in the smooth and used a lot of oil to windward. Under fore and main lower topsails. We took in the mizzen lower as soon as she came around and set the mizzen storm sail. Fore lower topsail blown out of bolt ropes at noon. All hands on deck, aft on poop. Everything streaming to leeward. Captain rates wind at 11. Hail and sleet all night. Very cold.

July 30th. Still blowing hard. Sent down remains of fore lower topsail and bent new one. Set this at four bells in afternoon. Wind moderating. Warmer.

July 31st. Sunday. Gale dropped, day broke fine. Set all sail to royals. Warm. Had plum duff. Drying clothes. Are making ten knots and going faster as sea goes down. Deck wet, rigging forward full of clothes.

CHAPTER XXX

HEADED NORTH

"Well, for one I am damn glad we are through with it," said Brenden during a discussion of Cape Horn weather that went on forward as we cleared out the damp fo'c'sle that wonderful Sunday following the gales. "This makes five times around for me and I hope to God the last."

"How far to Pilladelpia?" chirped up Kahemuku, his face again approaching its natural brown, though lean and worn beyond all resemblance of his Honolulu poi-fed chubbiness.

"Ha! The Kanaka is coming to life!" kidded Australia. "Well, me brown brother and fellow shipmate, if I do call you that, even though you are not white, Pillerdelpia is a long way off yet. The walking is bad and if I was you I would stay aboard a while longer. In fact you will have to ride all the way with nothing to do but work, me hearty, work."

All hands were feeling good. Black Joe hung around the galley all Sunday helping Chow and for supper that night he was rewarded by a large sea pie, one of the bright-red confections made of the mysterious "pie fruit." A chemist might analyze it as a composition of apple peelings, glucose, acetic acid and aniline dye. My, but how good it did taste! The human system demands its poison. Folks ashore prefer theirs in the most expensive form, while we poor sailors on the ship Fuller, on that memorable voyage in the year of the great war with Spain, took our weevils, which are no worse than Roquefort, only larger, and relished them. We ate many cockroaches browned in the cracker hash and dandy funk, and drank their extract in the tea and coffee, beverages, so called, for want of other names. As for the sea pie, it acted as a corrective to the gingerbread. When Shakespeare asked, "What's in a name?" he had certainly never experienced such a voyage as ours.

Following our dose of weather we entered upon a spell of work that carried us well up to the latitude of Cape Frio. The gear had to be overhauled in all of its details; whips of braces shifted end for end, new chafing mats and battens seized on to the stays taking the place of those worn through, and the slack standing rigging set up.

Our own gear, the clothing of the crew, was sadly in need of attention and every dog watch found the fo'c'sle busy with thread and needle. Frenchy was our top notch sailor man at sewing. He could ply a needle with the best housewife that ever swapped a bit of scandal at a sewing bee. He did not use a thimble, but handled a long coarse needle, pushing it through with the calloused end of his thumb, a simple and effective method for those gifted with the necessary toughness of cuticle. I had always wanted a pair of real seagoing canvas pants such as Robinson Crusoe must have worn, before he skinned the historic goat, pants wide in the legs, and fashioned of well weathered stuff, soft and comfortable. My good shipmate constructed them for me. They were not beautiful, but being what was left of an old skysail, a veteran of many voyages, a romantic piece of canvas that had swept the starry paths on many a balmy night, dew-bleached and mellow, they meant much to me. These pants were very homelike, and I never was able to wear them out.

In patching and sewing we managed to do wonders with old rags that at first seemed beyond all hope of redemption. Also, owing to the near approach of the payday, we begrudged the slop chest any further inroads upon the accumulated wealth that was to belong to us; the sailor's pot of gold, sitting so brightly, way beyond to the north, where our dream rainbow ended in cynical old New York.

About this time Peter came in for a lot of joshing by the men of his watch. He had an old long-tailed oilskin coat given him by Chips. Such a garment is never worn by sailor-men who have to go aloft, it being the sole prerogative of officers and idlers who never venture above the sheer pole. However, with Second Mate Tom on deck, many strange things happened in the starboard watch, and Peter, the stiff tails of his long coat sticking out in the wind, would go up the rigging as unconcerned as if it was the recognized and proper thing for a sailor-man to wear.

It happened that during a rain squall at the latter part of his watch on deck, he was sent up to furl the main skysail, and we tumbled out just in time to see him going up the weather rigging with his long yellow tail sticking out above his legs for all the world like a huge pale cockroach. At the same time First Mate Zerk stood aghast at the unusual spectacle.

"Come down out of that! Hey you! Lay down!" Peter heard and obeyed. "Lay aft!" "Yes, sir!" "Hey, Chips!" "Aye, aye, sir!" from Chips. "Bring a knife aft. Cut the tail off of this. Now!" Chips had trimmed a good two feet off of Peter. "That looks fine. Now take off another foot, we want to have this fine fellow in style."

When Chips got through, after a lot of sarcastic criticism by the mate, and laughter by all hands mustered in the waist, Peter looked like a well trimmed bird. His jacket was so short that the drip from its end went into the top of his trousers. He made a move to pick up the discarded tail, no doubt thinking it would do to sew on as an extension. "No, you don't!" shouted the mate. "Throw that overboard, Chips! Now, go forward, watch below. No, you don't," to Peter; "you lay aloft and furl that sail, my fine fellow, and show us what a starboard watch hand can do."

Poor Peter lay up in a dismal manner and after a lot of shouting from the deck, he came down and went below with a good half hour of his watch gone, all on account of the offending garment, showing that even at sea the correct thing in dress is essential; at least it was so in those strict old days.

Officers in the old ships were very precise as a rule in matters of this kind. A number of years after the coat incident, I was serving under Captain Geo. D. Morrison, one of the old-time sailing-ship masters.

We were on the bridge of a fine steamer. Eight bells had just been made and a quartermaster, an important little man, came up out of the fo'c'sle where he had his quarters, and as he walked aft along the forward well deck he drew a huge silver watch out of his pocket as though to verify the correctness of the bells on the bridge.

"Great Scott!" exclaimed the skipper. "What in thunder are we coming to with sailors carrying watches? I suppose they will carry walking sticks next. But, sir," turning to me, "not on my ship! Send that man down to the chart room!"

When Erricson, the quartermaster, arrived on the bridge, I sent him down to the skipper. The old man closed the chart room door, he was a very religious man, and after a short session, the quartermaster came out looking much scared. When we got to San Francisco, he was paid off, and Captain Morrison handed me an envelope to give to the man; this contained a heavy turnip-like object that no doubt was the offensive watch.

As soon as warm weather struck us, the last remnant of our potato bin went bad, and some of them were thrown overboard. This ended a duty that had helped to pass away many an hour for the farmers of the watch when they were sent forward to pick the sprouts off of the spuds and discard those that were too bad. Chow always picked out the bad ones anyway, and for the most part we subsisted on concoctions of half-rotten potatoes. Someone, Old Smith, I believe, said that raw potatoes were good for the scurvy. We all tried eating them. Scouse and the Kanakas were the only ones who could stomach the raw tubers. They always picked out the best sound potatoes and seemed to relish them; at any rate they robbed the cabin table of a good many messes of selected spuds.

When the old potato bin was knocked down, we had a general clean up under the fo'c'sle head, a scrubbing and overhauling of the bo'sun's lockers, the paint locker, and the oil stores. The short half deck forming the fo'c'sle head was not high enough for a man to stand upright under it, the lockers being arranged along the sides up into the bow. In the very nose, next to the hawse pipes, were the toilets of the ship, that is, those for the crew. These were very wet and uncomfortable in heavy weather. They were kept scrupulously clean, however. Large oil tanks were provided above these, fitted with small copper tubes leading into the sea alongside of the forefoot of the ship. Small cocks provided for the release of oil in heavy weather.

The bo'sun's locker contained everything necessary for carrying on the marling-spike work of the ship; fids, serving mallets, iron spikes, and the like. The tar pots were strung along a beam in the top of the locker and the shelves at the sides held the deck stores of small stuff, marline, spun yarn, rope yarn, houseline, hambroline, roundline, ratline stuff, etc. Several new coils of various sizes of rope, untarred hemp and manila were always carried in the bo'sun's locker against an emergency. Another compartment of the locker held the deck tackles, the "handy billys" and all emergency gear. This locker also carried the straps, rope circles used in attaching tackles to spars and rigging. Of such straps we had hundreds, always in apple-pie order. Small "salvagees" for clapping a fall onto a stay, large three-inch rope straps for hooking the rolling tackles onto the mast doublings. The compartment for blocks was also kept in fine shape, so we could lay our hands on things in the darkest night. Great snatch blocks for carrying a tack or sheet to the main or fo'c'sle head capstan, or for taking the fore or main tops'l halyards to the same; secret blocks for bunt jiggers, a small round block about the size of a soup plate, with the sheave completely covered, the whip, for it is a single block, reeving through small holes in the edge of the shell to prevent the canvas fouling between the rope and the sheave as is possible in an ordinary block. Clump blocks, small and "clumpy" like a roly-poly baker's loaf. These are very strong blocks and are used at the ends of the staysail and jib sheets for the reeving of the whips. These sheets, as sailors know, are always in two branches and the clump block makes it easy to haul the weather sheet, block and whip over the stay without catching, as the lee sheet is hauled aft. There are others called sister blocks, double and treble blocks, fiddle blocks, great jeer blocks for sending up and down heavy spars, stepping masts, etc. Many of the blocks aboard ship take their names from the particular use to which they may be put, such as quarter blocks, brace blocks, hanging blocks, clewline blocks.

When we were cleaned up forward, and ready for the last long spell of fine weather, with its round of marling-spike work, chipping, painting, tarring and holystoning, we were treated to a few hours of excitement that was different from the usual thing of that kind aboard the Fuller, as we had a chance to enjoy the show like spectators at the rail, and not, as on most occasions, when we saw the circus in the same way that the performers see it, namely, dangling from the flying trapeze near the top of the tent.

It was on a wet Friday morning; we were scrubbing deck paintwork when the "wheel" sang out, "Steamer ahoy!"

This was unusual, and all hands were astonished at the closeness of a cloud of smoke that was tearing toward us from somewhere to windward. Captain Nichols came out on deck and got the long telescope to bear. He pronounced her a cruiser.

She was coming for us fast; suddenly she altered her course fully four points and came in under our stern. She was a dirty white, streaked with rust, a fair-sized armored cruiser, two funnels with a military mast between them.

"Break out the ensign, Mr. Zerk. Might as well show her who we are." Indeed, the cruiser was reading our name and hailing-port on the broad transom in letters of shining gold.

"She's a Spaniard, one of them has a mast between two funnels," someone said. I remembered this, having in mind the pictures of the Spanish ships in West Indian waters, published in the magazines while we were in Honolulu.

"All out for Barcelona!" shouted the mate. The ensign went up, and we dipped. The cruiser ran up the Argentine colors, answered our salute and resumed her course.

"Hey, you loafers, get back on that paint work; this ain't no Spanish prison!"

Of course we all grinned at the great humor of the joke, and began to rub with our brick dust rags; the starboard watch went below at once, for it was unhealthy to be seen standing around on deck during a watch below. We all knew that the afternoon below would soon be gone and hoped to stall off the day of doom as long as possible.

CHAPTER XXXI

FO'C'SLE DISCUSSIONS

Frenchy, Brenden, Australia, and myself were told off as a special gang, in the port watch, to set up the topmast and topgallant shrouds, worked slack by the heavy weather we had just encountered. We were in the tops most of the watch, as the wind held fairly steady, and passed the time pleasantly, yarning as we worked; talking in sotto voce of course, and busy as monkeys in a jungle. The tops, as some landsmen may not know, are not exactly at the top of things, but they are the platforms about a fourth of the distance up the masts where the heel of the topmast rests on the trestle trees of the lower mast.

The top consists of a platform, semicircular in shape, the curved side forward. The topmast shrouds are led to the edges of the top, giving them a certain "spread." The historic "lubber's hole" is to be found in this piece of ship's furnishing, and one can hardly pick up an old-time volume of sea adventure without some reference to it, or I should say "them," for there are two lubber's holes in each top platform. The lower rigging runs up through the lubber's hole, passes around the lower mast head resting on the "bolsters," which in turn rest on the trestle trees, which in turn rest partly on the hounds and on the bibbs. The hounds are formed on the mast where it is squared at the point where the doubling begins. Just below this the bibbs are bolted on on each side,—now, I suppose we all know how it is done. It is certainly as clear as crystal to a sailor, who knows all about it already but merely likes to read over the familiar names, no doubt recalling many hours spent in the tops of old-time ships. The pull on the topmast shrouds is taken by the futtock shrouds, iron rods running down from the lower dead eyes of the topmast rigging, through the rim of the top, to an iron band around the lower mast fitted with eye bolts, some six feet below the top platform; this is the futtock band.

In an interesting book called "The Sailor," the hero, Henry Harper, "slides" down the futtock shrouds to the deck. As he is still going strong on page 450 and the "slide" occurs on page 48, we conclude that Henry was a pretty tough lad.

The futtock shrouds run up from the mast and out board to the rim of the top. A sailor going aloft must go out on the futtock ratlines hanging like a fly. This is easy enough and the quickest way up. The lubber's hole provides a safer way, but as its name implies, it is considered an unworthy method of going aloft. At least such was the opinion in those good old days.

Where these futtock shrouds pass down between the lower mast shrouds is a stout oaken or hickory batten seized to the lower rigging. This is the futtock staff.

The tops have been getting smaller as the art of rigging has progressed. At one time they were very large, affording room for a numerous company, the topmen, and in the old days they served as fighting platforms for the small-arm men. On the old schoolship St. Mary's, the tops were very commodious; a top chest was provided abaft the mast for the small gear and spikes, tar and slush pots, etc., that might be required aloft. I remember a tired boy going aloft in the fore top on his way to the fore tops'l lookout, and lying down behind the top chest for a nap. A half hour afterward, when he was missed on the yard, a general alarm failed to find him, and the ship was mustered and every crook and corner searched. Finally another hand was sent aloft, and spied the culprit. What happened to him the next morning when he was brought to the mast can be imagined.

In the top we were very comfortable, the shadow of the lower topsail, and the pleasant back draft of the canvas, making it ideal for work. We set up the topmast rigging, the burtons being led to the deck, where the men at work chipping iron deck fittings, or scraping the bright work, would tail onto the falls when we sang out, the mate telling them when to "come up," as we clapped on our rackings and seizings in shipshape style.

Aloft with these men I picked up a lot of the fine points of rigging. Discussions between Frenchy and Brenden were frequent, and not often they differed beyond all hope of agreement on matters that might seem trivial. Brenden had sailed in the Rickmer's ships, the great German drivers that hold so many of the present day sailing records for iron ships. His seamanship was of a more modern type. He was the best wire splicer in the crew, and gave us many pointers. Frenchy, though, was far better on the old-time seamanship brought to such a high state of perfection in the sailing craft of the French navy; vessels used for the purpose of training their naval seamen.

Often when being relieved by Hitchen, Old Smith, and Axel, the starboard watchers, who carried on the work while we were below, we would stay aloft with them during the first dog watch until our supper was ready, spending the time yarning. The second mate never said anything and we were always careful not to let the mate catch us. Hitchen had sailed in the large ship rigged yacht Valhalla when she came out. She was the finest yacht afloat manned by a complement of ex-naval men. Hitchen, however, claimed he had never been in the navy. We often deferred to Hitchen, who was a student of seamanship, and carried a dog-eared copy of "Tinmouth's Inquiry Into Points on Seamanship," a learned book going into the intricacies of throat seizings, or the advantages and disadvantages of turning in cutter stay fashion with reference to the attachment of dead eyes.

But most of our knowledge was not to be found within the covers of books. An enthusiast even then, I retain some of it, still what would I not give to have at hand a stenographic record of our "gamming" in the broad tops of the good ship A. J. Fuller?

**Axel**

Of the merits and demerits of various ships and rigs we had plenty of tales on this part of the passage by men who had served in them through long, hard voyages. "The average British sailing ship is a disgrace to the red ensign," was the way Hitchen put it when speaking of the ships of his native island. "She feeds poor, very little is spent to maintain her, the running gear is one mess of splices before it is picked into oakum, and very little work is done. The British Monarch was a fair sample of this class of vessel. I wouldn't say anything if we did not know how to do things better. Take Lord Brassey's ships; the old sailers of the White Star Line, in which they trained their officers for the liners; these vessels are a credit to the flag. But too many of our ships are run on the cheap. I don't say that they are hard on the crew, in fact they are easy, but it's rotten poor grub and no pride. You hate them at sea and are ashamed of them in port."

"The bounty ships are good; they carry a good crew, and do a lot of sailing. Not much laying in port. You see they must cover miles to get their subsidy from the government. Sailors is what the French people want. The pay is too little for me. Anyhow, I'm going to quit," was Frenchy's contribution.

"For hard work and hell, give me the Rickmer's ships out of Bremen. Next to the American ships, they are the worst; regular German army discipline on the water. They feed and pay better than most Dutchmen, but they don't care how many men they kill on a passage." Brenden's opinion was authoritative.

We all, however, agreed, that the Yankee sailing ship was driven as hard as any ship afloat, and that the grub, in port at least, was the best fed to sailors on any sea.

"Say, if our grub is good, what in thunder do you call bad grub?" I asked one day, after one of our learned discussions.

"My boy, bad grub," and Hitchen, to whom I had put the question, dwelt lovingly on the words, "bad grub"! "Bad grub is Act of Parliament rations of so much, or I should say, so little, meat, either salt pork or beef taken from the pickle in the harness casks and weighed on a rusty scales by the second greaser each day, and given out to the crew. So much flour, so much pease, and so much hard tack. All rationed out with the whack of water, and carried to a filthy galley where the unappetizing slops is cooked up in some tropic region, and served to the British merchant sailor with a regulation dram of lime juice, just calculated to keep the scurvy out of his knuckle joints. That is bad grub. Yes, we have about the same scale here, but you don't see them follow it so close. The American shipowner knows better, he wants to get a lot of work out of his crew, to keep his ship up and to make fast passages; he knows he must feed the gang to make them do it without chucking overboard a lot of corpses. I tell you, lad, bad grub is a rotten dish, but not a rare one. When your meat sours, and the filthy flour is full of blue mold, say, you are getting it rich then. Did you ever drink sour goat's milk? No? Well, bad grub is as bad as that."

"That sounds bad, but how about the weevils?" I asked, thinking he had forgotten our white worms.

"Weevils! Why, weevils are a sign of good grub. Grub fit to feed weevils is tip-top fodder. See how nice and fat they get. A mess of fresh weevils is simply another way of getting your game with the taste of white plump meat."

"You make me sick, Hitchen," I burst out, as I dropped over the edge of the top and down onto the futtock shrouds. I gained the deck fairly nauseated—a near seasickness, a malady that otherwise never troubled me. My stomach was as empty as the famous cupboard, and with the keen sea air and the healthy appetite of a boy of eighteen, I was famished as I went forward to supper, but Hitchen's philosophy of food values so upset me that I could eat nothing but a piece of selected tack, one free from holes that I was fortunate enough to find in the bread barge.

After that I steered clear of food discussions, and tried to forget the whole subject; it was hardly worth while talking about anyhow. We confined ourselves to talk about timenocles, catharpins, and of the best way to thoroughfoot a rope. Frenchy, who had sailed in the Mediterranean a good deal, told us of the strange craft called a ybeck, her mainsail having a large button in the belly of it, to hold in the bulge of the sail, somewhat after the manner of our midship tack.

We talked of bonnets, and of Jimmy Greens, and of the ancient curse of stunsails. These men had sailed in the East, and knew the queer rigs of the great junks and seagoing sampans of the Yellow Sea and the Inland Sea of Japan, places I was later on to visit, and to verify the stories told me on the Fuller. There were tales of paper flareups, and on the part of Frenchy, who had chased them in a frigate, of Chinese pirate junks armed with stink-pots, and smooth-bore carronades.

Of our own rigging, and of what went before it, we were of course amply reminded by our work. In the older ships, when tophamper was not as refined as on the Fuller, the royal yards, and higher, if crossed, would be sent down on the approach of heavy weather. In some ships, men-o'-war especially, the sending down of royal yards at night was a regular custom. In some of the old Dutch East Indiamen, it was also the custom to shorten down for the night, and make all snug; a comfortable way of doing things in keeping with large well-fed crews, Edam cheese, and waistlines of ample proportions.

On the later ships, the Yankee sailors of the day whereof we write, nothing was ever sent down. Yards might blow down, but they never came down by the free will of the master. The extensive use of wire in rigging, and the more secure type of metal fittings, bands, etc., made the old precautions unnecessary. Besides, time had to be considered as an important element in the profits of the voyage. As freight rates became lower, the rate of driving increased, and speed was more and more necessary to success.

CHAPTER XXXII

THROUGH THE TRADES

While still in the S.E. trades we started our last long drill of all hands on deck in the afternoon; the final clean-up for port was to be a thorough one. Paintwork was scrubbed and, when clean as new ivory, it was given a coat of fresh white paint, stroked on with the greatest care. This done, the decks were again holystoned fore and aft; a most thorough job. We then knocked about in the doldrums for a week or ten days, and on Sunday, August 21st, we crossed the line for the last time on that voyage.

Ordinarily one might suppose that this last leg of the long passage home would be the most pleasant of all and that as port loomed ahead we would once more feel the genial glow of good fellowship that blossomed so warm upon our approach to Honolulu. But we were apparently nearing a bleak coast; a hard material country where the sailor-man was on a strictly commercial basis of so little per month, and more men than billets; the crew would go, of course, and no one cared how much they cursed the ship, for they would do that anyway. The grub was worse because it was older; weevils were more in evidence than before, not to mention other pests such as rats and cockroaches, and we were feeling the effect of too close associations, a period of discontent, soon to change, but at that time most trying. Also, it was hot, as hot as it ever gets on the sea; our irritation became worse with every delay of head wind or of calm.

Mr. Zerk, for reasons unknown to us, became exceedingly brash; he went about looking for trouble, and always found it, working us without mercy in the heat of the day, and horsing us about at night. His relations with the second mate were strained more than ever, and some of the men of the starboard watch came forward with a tale of a big row between the skipper and the mate, the sounds having come up from the after companion; of course, anything like that would never take place upon those well-disciplined decks.

This succession of troubles had its climax one morning when the mate set upon Chips, that most gloomy and industrious of all carpenters. The lanky one, in returning from the poop with the running lights, had through some carelessness allowed several drops of oil to smirch the spotless planks.

"You dirty low-down bum! What do you mean by spilling that grease all over the deck?"

"Ay spill nothing!" shouted Chips, his slow soul riled to the point of protest at this latest insult.

"You didn't, hey? Well, I'll spill something!" The mate jumped down the ladder from the poop and made after Chips, who was in the waist. Chips saw him coming, and as he had a heavy brass side light in each hand, he was helpless. Realizing this, he started to run and reached the door of the lamp locker as the mate came up to him. Chips turned, dropping the lights, and as he faced the furious first officer, that gentleman let drive a terrific crack with his right, fetching Chips just below the ear, and lifting him clean over the sill into the lamp locker. The mate went in after Chips and for a few minutes the place was in an uproar. The mate stepped out, his hands covered with blood.

We were taking down the gear from the pins, after the washdown, and a number of us stood horrified in the waist, a feeling of deep repulsion coming over us. A big splotch of blood on the shirt front of the mate must have come from Chips' nose.

The mate looked at us. He opened his mouth as if to bawl some order, or hurl some epithet at the men of his watch who had witnessed the brutal assault. Suddenly he turned round, and looked into the door of the lamp locker, a small room in the after end of the forward house.

"Get a bucket of water and clean up this mess. It's a lucky thing you didn't bust them lights when you dropped them." He was addressing Chips, who came out of the door a moment later, hobbling to his room. The mate went aft, washing off his hands in a bucket of water that stood on the main hatch.

No one said anything, even in a whisper, but when we went below at eight bells and were assembled around the kids, one of the boys spoke up.

"Chips is cleaning up the lamp locker."

"I hope he reports Mr. Zerk to the Shipping Commissioner," I said. "If he does enter a complaint he has plenty of witnesses. It will mean jail for that bully, and he deserves it."

"Sure, he deserves to be hung," said Brenden. "But Chips will keep his mouth shut."

"Why?" I asked.

"If he makes a squeal, this will be his last ship. Chips has seen worse than he got, and should have kept his mouth shut. He gets forty dollars a month, ten more than the second mate. The Squarehead's no fool."

"Well, I call it a dirty piece of work."

"Righto!" agreed Australia. "That rotten bull ought to be hung by his thumbs."

While little was said about this particularly raw piece of brutality, it made a great difference to us in so far as we seemed to realize, of a sudden, that the fo'c'sle was apart from things aft, and that it was just as well that we felt a little more agreeable toward each other.

The constant rubbing noses over the stinking grub, and the continued driving, with no rest in the afternoons, made life anything but pleasant while we lingered in the tropics. But the blood spilled by the mate, as I have said, clarified our atmosphere forward.

Talk of the days to come again waxed plenty, and plans were gone over and over in the night watches. In calm, we fretted and fumed, watching and whistling for a breeze as though our very lives depended upon the blowing of a gale. Hitchen, one calm Sunday afternoon, cut a cross in the mainmast in order to bring on a wind; as this piece of vandalism was done in the second mate's watch, and in a place where it could not be seen without a search, no evil consequences ensued.

As on Sunday we got our watch below in the afternoon, word was passed to us of the port watch, about the cross on the main mast, and in the first dog watch I went aft and inspected it, pretending to hitch up a coil of rope that hung inside of the fife rail. We lay with our head yards sharp up to starboard, and the after yards back against the starboard rigging, on the other tack, the courses were guyed out by slap lines, and as the ship yielded to the gentle roll of the swell, the reef points would ripple against the canvas in a way that sounds different from anything else in the world.

We were speculating upon the efficacy of the cross.

"We will have a wind before midnight," declared Frenchy with positive conviction, and during the dog watches we talked of nothing else.

Charlie Horse came out on deck in the second dog watch carrying his Bible, with a quotation about the wind. "Thou hearest the sound, but canst not tell whence it cometh," he read, "for the wind bloweth where it listeth." Charlie Horse placed a deep significance upon the cutting of the cross in the mast. The faithful became more and more perturbed as the sun set and no sign of wind rewarded their belief in the cross.

We came on deck for the first night watch, and it was still dead calm, the sky clear and the stars shining with extraordinary brilliancy. A slight dew began to settle as the watch wore on and presently a sound aloft of the flapping of a skysail started us to attention. Wind! But where from?

Aft the mate and Captain Nichols were holding up wetted fingers trying to feel the direction of the airs, that were undoubtedly stirring from somewhere.

Frenchy used a different method, one I prefer to the wetted finger, as it gives a more accurate sense of direction. He held his hand, palm down, and with fingers slightly spread. By pointing the fingers around the horizon, the slightest breeze will make itself felt against the sensitive skin between the bases of the fingers.

"There!" cried Frenchy, his hand pointing broad abeam to starboard. I tried it, and sure enough, I felt the slightest coolness between my fingers. Indeed our paws were none too sensitive, being calloused and hardened by many moons of hauling at gear, and from much anointing in slush and tar pots. Presently things were moving aft.

"Port main; starboard crojik braces!" sung out the mate, and we walked the yards around lively. The canvas began to belly out, and in a few minutes our hot faces were fanned by a refreshing breeze. This was the first touch of the N.E. trades, and by midnight we had our yards trimmed with the wind close hauled on the starboard tack and the Fuller heading well on her course toward home.

When the starboard watch came on deck, Hitchen was all smiles, and the wise prognosticators of both watches were well pleased with themselves. They had got away with it by a narrow margin.

"I predicts that it's colder tomorrow," chipped in Australia.

"We got bean soup tomorrow, I bets," Scouse ventured, for in spite of the vindication of Frenchy, Hitchen and the others, we let it be known that luck was given the credit—luck and the cross. Most sailors of those days believed certain things, and a cross in the mainmast was as sure to bring wind, as a ring around the moon was a sign of rain.

During our last spell in the tropics, with our clear nights of calm, Australia astonished us by his remarkable familiarity with the names and constellations of the brightest stars. As I had a fair knowledge of these from my studies on the schoolship, and also had my Lecky, with the wonderfully simple star charts prepared by that master mariner, we passed some profitable and interesting hours. Even today I never miss a chance to glance at the clear sky at night and renew acquaintance with the great stars of the heavens.

Australia had picked up his knowledge from a sheepherder in that far country and knew the southern constellations better than I did. We all know the Southern Cross, or at least have heard of it, and by the way it is not much of a cross, though one of the two large stars pointing toward it, Alpha Centauri, is said to be the nearest to the earth of all the fixed stars. This is also a double star, but a powerful telescope is needed to distinguish the separate bodies.

Canopus, another whopper of the southern heavens, ranks next to the Dog Star, Sirius, and we never tired looking at these magnificent gems of the night as they shone with living fire in the clear deep blue of the tropic heavens. As I gaze from time to time at the constellations, at Cassiopeia's Chair, the Great and Little Bear, the Swan, and the giant Vega, at Orion, Leo, or the Sickle, and The Cutters' Mainsail, I think of those days on the Fuller when we conned them in mute wonder, as sailors have in countless ages gone before, and listened to the names by one more learned than the rest. Altair! Regulus! Aldebaran! Arcturus! Capella! Procyon! Sirius! Spica! Antares! Fomalhaut! Achernar and Adara! what do these names mean to the modern human calling himself educated? Since those days I have spent four years at a university, and have drilled through the technical course in astronomy, given to civil engineers, but I don't recall what was taught about the great stars of the heavens that we learned to know by their first names on that far off voyage. Of the present rank and file, who discuss anything and everything smart folk busy themselves about, how many can identify this company of noble names of the great blazing suns that swing across the heavens?

And black nothingness is also to be found in the heavens, in the Coal Sack, a blank space of the night sky, near the Southern Cross, in the black depth of which no telescope has yet revealed a star.

CHAPTER XXXIII

APPROACHING HOME

Once well in the trades we sailed along with great regularity, running up our latitude with the precision of a steamer. While still within the belt of thunder showers I had an experience that cured me of a habit of long standing. I would, whenever possible, if on lookout, strip on the approach of a shower while in mild weather, and enjoy a fresh water bath. I usually pulled off my shirt and trousers, and balling them in a knot would tuck them around the clapper of the great bell on the foremast, this kept them dry, and left me to enjoy the refreshing rain. Of course lookouts were only stood at night. This last time, a beautiful black cloud came down with the wind, we were close hauled under all plain sail, and it did not look like a job that would need me down from my station. Accordingly, I stripped and going to the bowsprit, caught hold of the fore stay and started some gymnastics in anticipation of a real douse from aloft. It was not long in coming, and with the coldness of it, and the look of the white caps lashed up under the cloud as it bore down on the ship, I felt that I had made a mistake. It was hail and not rain that came and while I was dragging my clothes out from under the bell and getting into them, I underwent a pummelling that left me sore from head to foot.

Of course we always went barefoot, except in real cold weather, and on the clean decks of a ship, this has much to recommend it. On the St. Mary's the order to go barefoot was always given when at sea during warm weather, and on the Fuller I found that all hands forward did this as a rule. How beautifully simple it makes things cannot be imagined, except by those who are lucky enough to be able to look back at barefoot boyhood days.

While working up in the trades, we again shifted to better canvas, and also got our cables up and shackled to the anchors, these being sent off the fo'c'sle head and hung under the catheads, the flukes, of course, gripped into the bill boards.

We had a lot of rain at this stage of the voyage, and as the wind was strong the rigging would dry out rapidly after each wetting. Manila rope shrinks very much when wet, and this sort of weather always kept us on the go "checking" ropes to prevent damage to gear aloft, and then as the stuff dried out we would have to take in the slack all round. The remarkable strength of this shrinking process is shown in the grip of lashings put on dry, and then wet just before taking up their work. Rafts put together on deck and hove overboard are a good example of this sort of thing.

September 10th, found us one hundred days out from Honolulu. This was on a Saturday, and that afternoon we were permitted to have a last field day. Also we sighted a steamer, a welcome indication of approaching shore lines.

"Here, Felix, take this." Australia handed me a sheath knife that I had always admired. "Remember me by it," he said. We were digging among our personal belongings, and as Australia passed around a number of things among the watch, the crowd all looked over their gear and there was a general exchange of remembrances. Scouse gave me a tintype he had taken in Honolulu, and Frenchy gave me a handsome pair of beckets with turks heads, that he had worked for my sea chest. Pipes, and even tobacco, changed hands.

The weather was much cooler, though far from uncomfortable, and as we neared port, talk about the future again came to the fore, there having been a lapse of several weeks, almost a month, following the great revival of interest when we had put the Horn safely behind us. Work kept up incessantly, and as a final splurge, we scrubbed the ship over the side down to her copper composition, and painted her fore and aft, finishing off with a white stripe in the line of her sheer. As the scroll work forward, under the bowsprit, that did duty in place of a figurehead, and the scroll work aft, had been gilded only the voyage before, the Fuller presented a very neat appearance.

The brass work lining the pin rails, and aft on the poop, was polished to perfection, and every last turn and corner was done to the final satisfaction of the mate. Aloft we were as trim as a ship ever got. No loose ends, all mats and chafing gear neatly stopped in position, masts scraped clean and rubbed with just enough grease to keep the parrals from sticking, yards scrubbed and painted, and the tops and doublings bright as a new pin. We were to go into port with the old girl reflecting a well spent voyage, for the critical eye of Captain Burnham would appraise her, and rate his captain and mate acccordingly, for he was a most knowing old ship manager.

A week of rains and blows with fair wind was followed by a day of calm, a heavy fog settling down. We had been sighting vessels constantly, schooners and steamers, and knew we were close to our port. The old mechanical fog horn, an ancient device worked by hand, was set croaking on the fo'c'sle head, a job as bad as the bilge pumps, and we lay flapping our idle wings in the mist. Several casts were taken with the deep sea lead; we were in soundings.

The following day, Sunday, it cleared a bit, with a warm sun on the waters, but the wind was still up and down and a rim of mist shut us in, for our horizon was very dim.

"Keep that horn barking!" shouted the mate after the washdown. I was on the fo'c'sle head breaking my back over the ancient contraption, when an echo seemed to come in over the bow. The fog had shut down again.

"Steamer off port bow!" I shouted, for I recognized the deep tones of a whistle.

"Aye, aye! Give her the horn!"

I pumped down hard, and a moment later a tug shoved her nose through the mist, a stumpy craft with the typical high pilot house of the American tug boat; we were home at last!

"Where bound, Captain?" came the hail.

"Delaware Breakwater!"

"Want a tow?"

"How far are we?"

"About three miles!"

"All right, give us your line!"

As the tug ranged ahead and took our heaving line, we read her name; she was the Atkins Hughes, of Philadelphia.

Droughing slowly through the heavy fog, we furled sail and toward noon were at anchor behind the Delaware Breakwater. A launch came out and we found the war with Spain was over, the date of our landfall being September 18th, 1898.

We heard of the great battle off Santiago, and that the Hawaiian Islands had been annexed. Peter and I got the surviving Kanakas, Kahemuku and Joe, up on the fo'c'sle head and made them give three cheers for their new country. After several starts they did this very well, much to our amusement.

"Where is Pilladelpia?" Kahemuku wanted to know.

"Right up there, Kahee," said Peter, pointing up the Delaware. "Now that you are an American citizen you will have a fine time when you get there."

That Sunday afternoon we sat about yarning; anchor watches were chosen, and a full night in was before us. We were tired and sea worn and a trifle sad. Back of us the hard days of the voyage, ahead of us, what? We were soon to part and no one mentioned this important fact. We were glad, of course, happy to so soon collect that long looked forward to payday, and to carry out the great plans so long in the making. I felt a hollow homesickness that had to be suppressed with a firm hold and, as we rested, smoking and yarning, I have no doubt many wondered if they were really to act upon the good resolutions so bravely determined.

Axel and Frenchy joined me on the fo'c'sle head and we talked of many things. I was going home, but they wanted me to surely write them. Both were to ship as soon as possible for their native shores. Old Smith was as quiet as it is possible for a sailor of the old school to be. He sat on the forehatch smoking. "What are you going to do?" I asked Smith.

"Well, if what I have done before is any criterion," he said grandly, "I guess I am going to sea again as soon as my pay is spent and I get a ship. China for me next, I am through with the Horn."

**WATCHING SHORE AT DELAWARE BREAKWATER**

The light on Cape May, the twinkle of lights ashore, and the clear autumn night following the day of fog, came as a welcome relief. We needed sleep; we were tired and we were on the eve of parting. I remember during my anchor watch, from two to four in the mid watch, I stumped the deck in a highly reminiscent mood. Several times I went to the fo'c'sle doors and looked in; bad as the drill had been, I hated to leave it.

On Monday, Captain Nichols went ashore and sent out fresh provisions, but there was no mail for us forward. Orders were to come soon and we spent the time polishing and cleaning as if our salvation depended upon the brilliance of the ship. The day passed without word, and we kept at our brass and paintwork until Wednesday, when orders were received for New York. The Hughes was notified, and on Thursday noon, a break in her engine having delayed her, the tug took us in tow for Sandy Hook. We found the wind favorable off the Five Fathom Bank lightship and set all plain sail to top-gallant-sails. At midnight it started to rain, and the wind freshening, we were startled by a commotion under our bows and found we were bearing down on the Atkins Hughes, her smoke pipe sheering off to one side of our flying jibboom, and her steam whistle protesting in strident blasts.

We at once shortened down to lower tops'ls and topmast stays'ls, and as we gathered in her wings the old ship lay back on the hawser; for the last time that voyage she had felt the independent urge of her canvas.

CHAPTER XXXIV

THE END OF THE VOYAGE

A gray dawn broke to seaward, and as the flash of the Navesink Light dimmed, and the bulk of the land defined itself in the lifting haze to the west, we picked up our pilot. In past the low spit of the Hook, up through the main ship channel and past the Narrows, we labored aloft, furling sail, giving it a harbor stow, while Mr. Zerk watched us with critical eyes.

The day was fine, warm sunshine welcoming us, and a strange unnatural brightness seeming to radiate from every nook and corner of the Fuller—she was groomed, polished, and triple polished for this very day. We brought up near Bedloe's Island, under the lee of the great statue, anchoring shortly after noon. The glitter of the tall buildings on Manhattan, and the busy harbor scenes, constantly called to our sea weary eyes. All hands went forward to a dinner of cracker hash, and a pale looking duff to which Chow had added an extra ration of molasses, black like tar, and a huge can of coffee; all of the tack in the bread barge was broken and mealy as if it had been searched for weevils before coming forward.

"To hell with this grub," growled Old Smith, as he filled his pannikin with coffee and lit his pipe. "I'm eating white man's tucker tonight. To hell with this, I can wait."

However, most of us were too hungry to wait; but the near approach of human victuals made our mouths water. All about the fo'c'sle bags and chests were hauled out from under bunks and benches and were being stowed.

"That looks like them!" Australia at the starboard fore channels was scanning several small boats coming out toward the ship. "I bet old pedlar O'Brien is coming out to make me a present of a watch," he said, at which we all laughed.

"Where are they?" a half dozen got up to watch the boats coming out from the Battery with interest.

"Are you going to stay by?" asked Frenchy. "If you've got any place to go to, don't leave, but stay by."

"Guess I'll stick," I said, "as I am going to my uncle's house. Why don't you stay by?"

"They make it tough for you if you do," said Frenchy, nodding at the boats which were now coming alongside with a spurt, the runners, for it was they, racing to see who would get over the side first.

At that time there was a gentlemen's agreement—if we may call it such—between the boarding house keepers, in the business of fleecing sailors in the port of New York, whereby all victims were parcelled out according to an impartial schedule, so many sailors to each house. When a rich deep waterman came in, the boarding houses in the combine would each get two or three men, stripping them of the greater part of their payday. When a crew was wanted for a vessel outward bound, they would supply the men in the same manner, taking the advance notes in payment for board, clothes, and what not. Sometimes a sailor beat a boarding master but not often, for Jack generally came in fat and went out under bare poles, with nothing but a kit of second hand slops, as the sole increment from his previous voyage.

As the runners bumped alongside, with a great show of rivalry and cheery greetings, for they all knew just who was on board, we were treated to an exhibition of rapid fire generosity and open-handed welcome, by gentlemen of the waterfront, men wearing derby hats and stiff shiny collars, watch chains, and flashy pins stuck into bright neckties. These worthies scrambled up the fore channels like monkeys and onto the deck. The game was to get a sailor to accept a card. As soon as one of the boarding house cards was in the horny fist, that man was marked and belonged to that particular house. This rushing at first consisted in a scramble for the most desirable victims, that is the weakest and most easily fleeced.

An evil-looking, pimply-faced runner backed me against the forward house and thrust a card into my hand. He insisted, and I protested. He had a breath that was strong, and told me how well his house could take care of me. Good grub, a good crowd there, and he even mentioned other advantages. He tried to put a five dollar bill into my hands. He was most insistent; finally he saw that he was wasting precious time, and darted after an easier victim. The runners swarmed about the decks, two and three men from each house. In the two sides of the fo'c'sle the crimps were assisting the men in the final roping of their dunnage, bottles of whisky were being sampled. Some of the men proudly handled showy watches, Australia surely got his watch, a big gilt turnip which he showed me with pride.

"See, I got it."

"How much?" I asked.

"Only ten dollars—take it off my pay day. This watch is worth half of that," and Australia winked at me. He had a bottle of whisky in his jacket pocket.

All hands were becoming hilarious. The runners seemed uneasy, for the Fuller was known as a bit of a rough ship, and it was strictly against the law for them to be on board. But a pay-off of close to three thousand dollars forward was too tempting to allow around loose in the harbor.

"No more of this work wagon for me," shouted Australia. Snatches of song were interrupted by an order of unmistakable force.

"Lay aft, all hands!" It was Mr. Zerk who came forward and bellowed at the gang about the fore fife rail.

We mustered aft, the shore harpies watching us from the sides of the forward house.

"All here?"

"All aft, sir," Old Smith answered.

Captain Nichols stepped out on the break of the poop.

"Men," he began, "the voyage is over, but we will lay in the bay and strike t'gallant masts before we go under the bridge. You can do this if you want to, or you can go ashore now. I have found you a good crew, ready, and sober. Those who want to go ashore step over to port." All hands did, including Second Mate Tom, who now stood with his old messmates, after a brief four months as an officer aft.

"Peter, come back, and you, Felix. You two stay aboard till we dock. The rest of you can go. I want to say 'good-bye' and wish you good luck. Be careful where you go and what you do."

As the skipper finished the longest speech we had ever heard him make, he turned sharply and walked aft to the companion. We felt like giving a cheer, but the cold eye of the mate was on us. There was a shuffle and hesitation as to what was next.

"Lay forward and get your dunnage, mind that paintwork when you go over the side." Mr. Zerk had given his last order to our crowd.

With discipline a thing of the past, with the hasty donning of wrinkled shore clothes, and the ever present tempters, plying them with whisky, the crew became a strange, wild-eyed crowd. Old Smith, Hitchen, and Axel seemed to know what they were about. Scouse was belligerent, half tipsy, and wild with the knowledge that he was at last to step from those hated decks. Frenchy, of all the gang, showed the most sense. "I am saving all I can out of this," he said. "I will ship across to England or France, as soon as possible."

"Come on, stay aboard," I urged.

"If I do, I'll never get a ship out of New York," and he knew what he was talking about.

Brenden was frankly drunk, soused was his condition, and as fine a sailor-man as there was. I had a lump in my throat when the boats pulled away. There was much hand shaking and waving. Peter and I stood on the fo'c'sle head watching them row ashore. Scouse got up in his boat time and again and shook his fist at the ship.

Among the departed ones, Kahemuku and Black Joe were in tow of a colored mission that had sent a boat for them. These poor Kanakas had very little coming to them, and they offered no temptation to the greedy runners. On the other hand, Tommy, for a brief term second mate, at thirty dollars per month, presented the juiciest picking, and strangely enough fell to the lot of the most inexperienced of the crimps who picked him up by accident after the struggle was supposed to be over as he emerged from his exalted cabin under the poop. Tom also departed from the immaculate decks with a feeling of genuine relief.

"Well, they're gone," said Peter.

"I wish they were back," I said.

"Me too," was his reply.

When the last boat had vanished beyond the South Ferry slip, we entered the deserted fo'c'sle. The disorder incident to such hurried departure was everywhere evident. Small personal belongings of no intrinsic value, but speaking eloquently of their owners on the long voyage past, were scattered about, Brenden's calendar over his bunk attracted my eye, and I saw that he had carried it along to the last day and had evidently made a calculation of his payday on the beam over his bunk. Names were scratched over most of the bunks. Frenchy, always neat, had left behind a small canvas pouch in which he kept his tobacco and pipe, this was empty, however; a few old burnt pipes, easily identified, were abandoned in favor of the more effluvious five cent cigars so liberally passed around by the runners. In the starboard fo'c'sle, Charlie Horse and Tony had cleaned up their bunks before leaving, but Old Smith left his a sight. Odd playing cards were scattered about, and the smell of whisky, from recent spillings, gave this austere den the air of a blind pig. Old oilskins that had been cast off, by the advice of some of the crimps, were all missing. Peter remembered seeing one of the shore gang bundle these up and take them, no doubt to help outfit the poor fellows again in exchange for their advance; not an item seemed to have escaped the plundering crowd from the beach. The fo'c'sle on my side was populated with ghosts; I was glad when the mate called us aft and ordered the decks swept down.

"Cabin grub for supper tonight," announced Peter, coming from the galley. Sure enough, we were given two plates of corned beef hash, made with real potatoes, while some letters that had come aboard were sent forward. I was happy to learn that my folks were well and knew of our arrival, having received the report from Delaware Breakwater. We were particularly happy in all this, but in spite of good news, of good food, and our approaching liberty, we were sad. The Fuller was peopled with the spirits of those so recently departed. Somewhere on shore among the twinkling lights that began to flicker as the dusk crept over the bay, our shipmates were carousing in the wicked city, laying the foundation for another voyage of endless hardship and privation.

Peter and I, with Chips, who remained on board, were told off as anchor watch during the night, each taking a three-hour shift; three hours that to me passed very quickly as I tramped the decks of memory on that haunted ship, and thought of that first night watch when Frenchy and I paired off to stump from the pin rail to the forward house, and spin our yarns, and lay the foundation for a friendship that I have never forgotten.

In the morning the shore riggers came on board, taking complete charge. Mr. Zerk walked the deck but never gave an order, and those rough and ready men struck the topgallant masts in jig time, lowering the skysail masts so the tall trucks of the Fuller would clear the span of the Brooklyn Bridge. How they went rough-shod over the decks with their spiked boots, while we had to submit all of our shoes to the mate for inspection before wearing them so he could satisfy himself that no nails remained in the soles.

By two that afternoon, the topgallant masts were lowered and a tug came alongside, making fast to our quarter; we slowly headed up the East River, past the South Ferry, and our starting berth at the foot of Maiden Lane, then under the Brooklyn Bridge. The rattle of the trains, the near approach of the life and hum of the great city filled me with a strange wonder. As we came alongside at Williamsburgh, Mr. Zerk said we might pack up and go when we pleased. Captain Nichols called Peter and me aft and handed us each a letter; mine was to serve me two years later—when I was twenty-one—as part of the required service testimonials for admission to the examination for second mate in sail and steam vessels. The letter read:

NEW YORK, Sept. 24th, 1898.

This is to certify that Felix Riesenberg has made the voyage in the Ship A. J. Fuller from New York to Honolulu and back to New York, and I have found him to be a smart, steady, and faithful young man.

C. M. NICHOLS, Master, Ship A. J. Fuller.

I am as proud of this letter now as I was on the day it was given me, and with this precious paper in pocket, our chests trundling along behind on an express wagon, Peter and I walked up the wharf, two sea-tanned, hard-fisted youngsters in a land of strange activity, noise, cobblestones, and freedom. We parted at the Brooklyn Bridge, he going to friends in Brooklyn, and I to the home of my uncle in Manhattan. Behind us lay one of life's great experiences—a voyage around Cape Horn in an American three skysail yarder, a last proud example of the fine sailing ships that once carried the starry ensign to the four quarters of the globe.


CHAPTER XXXV

THE LONG-LOOKED-FOR PAYDAY

On Monday, Sept. 26th, 1898, three days after our arrival in the bay, we were paid off before the United States Shipping Commissioner, the short interval having worked a deplorable change in the crew. Whoever was responsible for a condition so well calculated to cause the downfall of the returning deepwaterman, has a great weight of iniquity resting against his eternal soul; no doubt this responsibility was so well divided that each and every one of those guilty felt that his individual part in the great scheme of debauchery would go unnoticed.

I like to believe that all of them, boarding masters, crimps, runners, politicians, shipping officials, owners, managers, and masters who were parties to the fate that befell the men of the Fuller, have long since received their due reward in full consciousness of its meaning. Nowadays things are managed better, thanks to the greater influence of such noble establishments as the American Seamen's Friend Society, the Seamen's Christian Association in West Street, and the Seamen's Church Institute, on South Street, clubs where sailors are given room and board, are outfitted, and are able to bank their payday. Healthful amusements and recreation are provided, without that sanctimonious atmosphere that seems to curdle many well-meaning attempts of this sort and most of the shipping companies secure their crews through the Institute.

But in 1898, the deepwater sailor was at the mercy of the hungry sharks who had full sway in the vile business of ruining the souls and health of sailors in order to rob them of the few dollars earned during a year or more of cruel labor on the sea.

I have forgotten just where the shipping office was located, but it was somewhere near Beaver Street and the waterfront. I was on hand bright and early, anxious to see the crowd. The three days of rest and good food, and wholesome amusement, those happy days at the home of my uncle, had put me in fine condition; I never felt better in my life, and I was looking forward to a visit with the old gang. I wanted to take a trip around the waterfront with Frenchy and Australia, as we had often planned, and have a good dinner ashore, such as Frenchy and Tommy and I enjoyed in Honolulu.

The shipping office, as I remember it, had a dingy outer room in which the crew to be paid off awaited the pleasure of the haughty officials. One must be a sailor about to receive the scant reward for a year of toil, to fully appreciate the high and mighty character of such minor public officers as waited upon us on that bluest of all blue Mondays.

A gruff understrapper told me where to wait, and in the course of a half hour the crew, in tow of the crimps, appeared on the scene; I would like to draw a veil over this part of the story and leave the reader the simple picture of the men rowing toward the Battery, with Scouse shaking his fist at the ship, but realism, which in itself constitutes the highest romance, bids me tell things as I saw them, and the final tragedy is a part of the old days under sail that none of us wish to see return.

I looked for Frenchy, but hardly knew him. His beard was trimmed close to his chin, he wore his old cap but had on a cheap new suit of clothes, wrinkled as though he had slept in them, and his eyes were bloodshot. He seemed to avoid me, as he hung in the rear of the crowd. For every man to be paid off, at least two crimps were on hand.

All were more or less under the weather, the smell of cheap whisky permeated the room, and the ribald jests of the crimps, the constant whooping up of an ill-sustained merriment, gave the gathering a ghastly character that drove home to me with peculiar force. No doubt the close approach to the money caused the robbers more than a passing thrill. A couple of special bouncers from the inner office appeared when the gathering became too obstreperous, and I had a chance to say "hello" to the gang. Peter was there, sober, and wide-eyed with astonishment, having come from the house of Mrs. Burdick, the good angel of the waterfront. Australia, in a new rig, derby, watch, and soiled linen, kept bursting into song; not the songs of the sea, but some cheap new airs picked up along the Bowery.

"I owe them half of what's coming to me," he whispered, as if this was something to be proud of; a crimp slid up, and he at once ceased his confidences; all hands acted as though they were in charge of jailers, which in fact they were.

Brenden, Charlie Horse, and Tommy sat in a corner, sullen, and I judge partly sober.

Their attendants were anything but friendly. Martin, Fred, Tony, and Old Smith had given themselves over body and soul. Smith was already promised a ship, to sail in a week, so he had seven more days of hilarious living to look forward to, and then another drill, around the Horn or the Cape of Good Hope; another such voyage as we had just passed through.

Axel and Hitchen were in their old clothes; they had seen the sights, but seemed far steadier than the rest.

I cornered Frenchy. "What are you going to do when you get your pay?" I asked.

"I will pay up what I owe and ship for England or France."

"Better buy a steerage passage for Havre," I reminded him, when the crimp who owned him closed in, and a bull voice from the back room ordered us to line up for our pay.

My name was one of the last to be called, and as I got my pay, something over one hundred and twenty-five dollars, with slops and allowance given in Honolulu deducted, I returned to the outer room and found most of the men gone. As fast as they had got their money, the crimps had hurried them off to their respective boarding houses. The Kanakas came in, still in charge of the colored mission, or whatever it was, that had them in tow, apparently the only honest people there, and I bid those simple fellows good-bye; whether Kahemuku ever got to "Pilladelpia," I don't know; I hope he did.

Presently I was on the street. The crew of the Fuller had vanished. I looked for Peter; he was gone. I stood alone and strangers passed, bumping into me, no doubt thinking me a sunburned country yokel, stranded in those busy, narrow streets.

That afternoon I saw Captain Shackford, of the American Line, and was promised a billet as cadet on the St. Louis, just returned to the passenger service after her brief career as an auxiliary cruiser during the war with Spain. My service in sail was completed, and I was to experience eighteen months, as quartermaster, for I was soon promoted, on the St. Louis, during her golden age, when for a brief period it looked as though the Stars and Stripes were again to come into their own upon the Western Ocean.

www.ingramcontent.com/pod-product-compliance
Lightning Source LLC
Chambersburg PA
CBHW071659040426
42446CB00011B/1841